Making Magick

About the Author

Edain McCoy became a self-initiated Witch in 1981, and has been an active part of the Pagan community since her formal initiation into a large San Antonio coven in 1983. She has been researching alternative spiritualities since her teens when she was first introduced to Kaballah (Jewish mysticism). Today she is a part of the Wittan Irish Pagan Tradition and is a Priestess of Brighid within that tradition. An alumnus of the University of Texas (B.A. in history), she currently pursues part-time graduate and undergraduate studies at Indiana University. Edain has taught classes in guided meditation and automatic writing, and occasionally works with students who wish to study Wiccan and Celtic Witchcraft. She is an ordained minister of the Universal Life Church, a member of the Indiana Historical Society, the Authors Guild, the Wiccan/Pagan Press Alliance, and is a former woodwind player for the Lynchburg (VA) symphony. A descendant of the infamous feuding McCoy family of Kentucky, Edain also proudly claims as a forefather Sir Roger Williams, the seventeenth-century religious dissenter.

To Write to the Author

If you wish to contact the author or would like more information about this book, please write to the author in care of Llewellyn Worldwide and we will forward your request. Both the author and publisher appreciate hearing from you and learning of your enjoyment of this book and how it has helped you. Llewellyn Worldwide cannot guarantee that every letter written to the author can be answered, but all will be forwarded. Please write to:

Edain McCoy
℅ Llewellyn Worldwide
P.O. Box 64383, Dept. K670-X
St. Paul, MN 55164-0383, U.S.A.

Please enclose a self-addressed stamped envelope for reply, or $1.00 to cover costs. If outside U.S.A., enclose international postal reply coupon.

Making Magick

for Witches & Pagans

Edain McCoy

2004
Llewellyn Publications
St. Paul, Minnesota 55164-0383, U.S.A.

FIRST EDITION
Sixth printing, 2004

Cover Design by Gavin Dayton Duffy
  Girl with light photograph © Eve Morcette/Photonica
  Candle images © Photodisc
Editing and Book Design by Rebecca Zins

Permission granted to quote *Techniques of High Magic* by Francis King and Stephen Skinner, published by Destiny Books, an imprint of Inner Traditions International, Rochester, VT 05767. Copyright ©1976, 1991 Francis King and Stephen Skinner.

Library of Congress Cataloging-in-Publication Data

McCoy, Edain, 1957–
  Making Magick: what it is and how it works / Edain
McCoy.—1st ed.
      p.   cm.
  Includes bibliographical references and index.
  ISBN 1-56718-670-X (trade paper)
  1. Magic.   I. Title.
BF1611.M39   1997
133.4'3—dc21   97–20979
                                                              CIP

Llewellyn Publications
A Division of Llewellyn Worldwide, Ltd.
P.O. Box 64383, Dept. 1-56718-670-x
St. Paul, MN 55164-0383
www.llewellyn.com

Printed in the United States of America

If someone gives you a spell
you can make successful magick once.
If someone shows you how to analyze spell
structure and to construct your own spells,
you not only can make magick forever,
but you will become magick as well.

Other Books by Edain McCoy

Advanced Witchcraft

Astral Projection for Beginners

Bewitchments

Celtic Myth and Magick

Celtic Women's Spirituality

Enchantments

Entering the Summerland

How to Do Automatic Writing

Magick & Rituals of the Moon

Mountain Magick

Ostara

Past Life & Karmic Tarot

Sabbats

Spellworking for Covens

The Witch's Coven

A Witch's Guide to Faery Folk

Witta

Contents

Preface

The magickal arts continue to intrigue today's Witches as much as they did Witches of yesteryear. It is rare that a week passes when someone does not ask me questions—either in person or via the mail—about specific techniques of natural magick. Since I became involved in the Craft in 1980, I have discovered that the questions of newcomers vary little from year to year; the same information is always sought by those embarking upon this path.

Do I need tools to make magick work? Which tools do I need the most? How do I learn to visualize? How do I raise and send energy? What are words of power? How do I know if I am using the right words? Can I use a fire-ruled herb in a love spell? How about a water-ruled herb in a protection spell? What guidelines can help me decide which is which? How do I find spells, and how do I know they are constructed correctly? How do I make my own spells? Are my own spells as good as those I find in other people's spell books? What happens if I make a mistake? Why do I need to keep written magickal records? What about the moon's role in magick? How do I know if I am violating someone's free will? What is psychic self-defense and how do I achieve it? How do I astral project, and how do I work magick on the astral plane? What is the role of the elements in magick? What is sex magick all about? Is there such a thing as advanced natural magick, and how does it work?

I wrote *Making Magick* in response to these questions. By the time you finish working through it from cover to cover, I sincerely hope that you will have all the answers to your questions about basic natural magick—and about some of the advanced techniques as well. But having magickal knowledge is only a small part of being a successful Witch. The focus and the skill must also be in place, and there is no way to acquire these but through practice, practice, practice.

It is to all seekers, with their many thousands of questions, that I dedicate this book. I pray to Brighid it throws open the doors of the magickal world so that you may step inside and flourish there.

Brightest Blessings!

Acknowledgments

Several key people in the Llewellyn family either helped to make this book a reality or gave the sort of encouragement and input that made the job of creating it much easier.

First and foremost, to the patriarch of our publishing family, Carl Llewellyn Weschcke, thank you for your enthusiasm for this project and for taking the time from your busy schedule to write and tell me so. Praise and encouragement of that sort are more precious than gold. To Nancy Mostad, the calm breeze in the gale-storm of writer's angst, thank you for being there to put fears to rest and to stroke the ever-fragile egos of the artists with whom you work. To Becky Zins, my eagle-eyed editor, thanks for wanting to be a part of this project and for your good sense, balanced judgment, and many hours of hard work. To fellow author, Dr. Jonn Mumford, thank you for your kind words and encouragement. They mean more to me than you can know.

And to all of you who have written to me over the years or have pulled me aside during workshops to ask questions about magick, this book is yours. I hope I've been able to answer most of your questions and helped to illuminate the pathway to magickal success.

Bright Blessings to all!

Introduction

The Magick of the Witch

Magick!

The word conjures up images of Witches murmuring over bubbling cauldrons, fragrant herbs drying near old stone hearths, country wise women and cunning men carrying their healing brews to sick children, and covens joyously dancing under the moonlight while chanting their spells into manifestation. Modern Witches still use magick in much the same way, and for many of the same reasons, as our ancestors did. We use what nature has provided to help us cast spells for health and healing, for love and fertility, for prosperity and strength.

The ancient spiritual traditions of western Europe, sometimes collectively referred to as the religion of Wicca, is alive and well, and so are its magickal teachings. Magick is part of our religion but not a requirement. Quite a few Witches have never cast a spell. Others wait for years before studying the magickal part of our faith. But whether we choose to craft magick or not, seeing ourselves as magickal beings is part of our basic self-identity. In defining ourselves as Witches we are stating that we view ourselves as instruments, conductors, shapers, and controllers of energy.

One of the two root words for the modern word *Witch* is the Old English *wyk,* which means "to bend or shape," as in the shaping of energy. The other origin is the Anglo-Saxon *wit,* meaning "to have knowledge or wisdom." These roots imply that those who best made magick were people who studied and worked with their art, all the while gaining the wisdom to perfect it. By using this wisdom they could shape or bend the physical world to reflect their will. This skill is still vital to the successful practice of Witchcraft whether we are using it to make magick, to astral project, to meditate, to create a ritual, or simply to assist us in paying honor to our deities.

The terms *Witch* and *Wiccan* have taken a beating in some arenas, with detractors arguing that ancient Pagans never used these labels for themselves. This is true, since there was no need to name a religion in a community where simply being born into the tribe or clan automatically made one a part of its spiritual life. Those who possessed religious titles held them mostly to define their function within society (i.e., priest, priestess, bard, elder, et cetera), and not to mark the boundaries of spiritual belief. For these old Europeans, magick and religion were one, and both were an integral part of everyday life—it was what they were! They would not have identified themselves as part of a religion called Wicca, but would have said they *were* Wicca, or they *possessed* Wicca—the knowledge, wisdom, and ability to bend or shape their chosen reality.

Naturally some people were—and still are—better at this process than others, but all of us possess the inborn ability to develop magickal skills. *Making Magick* is written as a complete course in natural magick. This does not mean it is the complete book on magick; I doubt such a compendium could exist. Its goal is to teach you how magick works and to give you the confidence in yourself to craft successful magick *on your own*. This is why you will not find this book to be merely a collection of spells. If someone gives you a spell you can make successful magick once. If someone shows you how to analyze spell structure and to construct your own spells, you not only can make magick forever, but you will become magick as well.

Through exercises designed to develop basic skills, *Making Magick* lays down a firm foundation of elemental magickal wisdom. The first chapters begin with an introduction to magick and how it works. We will study Craft tools, learn to connect with the elements—the building blocks of magick—and delve into the intricacies of spell construction and timing. The last half of the book will take us into the advanced magickal arts, which rely on highly honed skills of meditation, astral projection, visualization, and the sustaining of creative energy.

Witches believe in the cyclic nature of all things—that everything in existence is part of the giant wheel of life, death, and rebirth—and this book reflects those beliefs. Because the theme of elemental energy permeates all operations of natural magick, we start our magickal journey in *Making Magick* by learning about basic skills and the role of the elements. We end by probing the elements again, this time with a more advanced approach, through the tattwa symbols, potent Indian archetypes that literally open the astral doors to the elemental world and allow us to step inside and explore it firsthand. The underlying elemental theme inherent in all natural magick should be readily apparent to the serious student by the time this book is completed.

Natural magick is a never-ending study that will take you around the circle of endings and beginnings over and over again, each time opening new worlds of wisdom to you. You should feel free to bring into this magickal journey any previous knowledge, to cross-reference my methods with those in other magick books, and always to ask yourself questions, questions, questions! There are many techniques of natural magick. No one method works best for everyone, and no single approach is the definitive. You will do yourself a disservice not to strive to learn all you can from all available resources, distilling them into what works for you.

A magickal journey is not an easy one. Magick is work, much more so than many who embark upon this path realize. Its techniques can be learned and mastered, but it requires commitment. If magick were as easy as merely reading a book, then going out and instantly getting what we wanted, we'd all be rich, famous, successful, and beautiful. We can have what we want if we really do want it badly enough *and* we make the effort to obtain it. I have lost more than a few

Craft students who tell me they have come to learn about the religion but get hung up on the magick. When they realize the immense output required of them—for both the religion and the magick—they usually drift on to another, less demanding spiritual path.

Whether you have officially dedicated yourself to the Old Religion, or are still deciding if the Craft is the spiritual path for you, you can learn to use magick to enhance the quality of your life and the lives of those you love. It is a perfectly natural practice, a gift given to you at birth, which only waits to be developed. We begin this journey into the magickal by seeking to live our lives in harmony with nature and by looking at the universe with eyes that see beyond arbitrary divisions between the worlds of form and of spirit. In doing this we become one with these universal energies and find we can shape and direct them at our will.

May all your elements be in balance and all your shapings be successful.

And so mote it be!

1

Natural Magick and How It Works

Magick is what makes things happen. When we make magick, we actually alter the landscape of our reality. Magick has always been a part of Witchcraft, a natural force drawn on for thousands of years to help shape lives for the better. Magick heals, comforts, and gives hope in the face of despair. It offers us a positive focus for our thoughts while working toward our goals, and permits us to recognize that we have control over ourselves and our realities.

Reclaiming magick as a positive, active force in our lives is likely one of the draws that has made the various paths of Paganism one of the fastest-growing religions in the world today. People are tired of feeling helpless, sick, and at the mercy of churches, governments, and big businesses. They want to take back the personal authority these power brokers have stripped away over the centuries.

Contradictory to what the church and its cohorts would have the public believe, magick is *not* evil. It does not draw on a devil or anti-God as a catalyst for its success, and it does not thwart the natural laws of the universe. These ideas were planted in people's minds in a concerted effort to take away personal power and replace it with groveling loyalty to the church and state that, at one time, were inextricably linked.

For example, the St. James version of the Christian Bible (seventeenth century) used the word *Witch* in place of *poisoner* in a key passage in Exodus in order to have church authority to carry out their Witch hunts.

Magick is wholly natural, its operations driven by the Witch's inborn willpower. A definition of magick I have always liked was coined by the infamous ceremonial magician Aleister Crowley in the late nineteenth century: "Magick is the science and art of causing change to occur in conformity to will."

The use of the word *science* in Crowley's definition is telling. The natural laws of the universe are fixed. They cannot be defied even through magick. Therefore all magickal energy has to conform to these laws. The first natural law of the universe taught to students of physics is one you probably heard in junior high school, that matter can neither be created nor destroyed, but may only change form. Through magick we attempt to reshape energies that *already exist* by feeding them new energies of our choosing in order that they might grow into that which we desire. Never can we create something from nothing. The natural laws of the universe will not allow it.

> For the old Witches, magick was not viewed as an operation of supernatural forces since, logically, nothing supernatural could exist. Whether one believed the universe was created by a sentient deity, or wished to believe that it exploded into existence of its own accord, the fact remained that certain natural laws operated from which no deviation could occur. Cats don't sprout antlers overnight, autumn does not suddenly appear to follow winter, and a maple tree doesn't become an elm at will. Everything has its place in the time/space continuum . . . including magick.[1]

At one time in the not-too-distant past, many of the marvels of modern living we take for granted would have been considered magickal, and therefore evil. Even the electric light you are now reading by would have been viewed as a

1. From my previous book, *Lady of the Night: A Handbook of Moon Magick and Ritual* (Llewellyn, 1995), 102.

manifestation of magick, which would have got you hung as a Witch even though the principles driving it are wholly natural. They were simply ones that were not understood at the time. To make an electric light today we still have to use these natural laws and scientific principles as our foundation. As much as we'd like to, we cannot snap our fingers and manifest such things from nothing.

Natural magick is generally defined as being that of the common people, a building process using the Witch's own energy and items from nature as catalysts for change. The magick is not in these catalysts themselves, but in the one who draws the magick from them. The word "magick" came into English from the Greek *magikos* meaning "power of the magi (magicians)." The Greeks took it from an even older Persian term meaning "to control the elements." Modern Witches would think more in terms of "joining with" the elements to create new realities, merging with or drawing from those powers rather than dominating them. We use these links to help boost and fuel our energy stores for use in spellcrafting.

The methods we use to make natural magick today are basically the same ones used thousands of years ago. Unlike Ceremonial magicians, we rely more on the energies of the elemental world than with inhabitants of the many unseen realms to help fuel our spellwork. Ceremonial magick seeks, in principle if not in fact, to unite the magician with the divine rather than focusing on worldly goals such as a new home or new romance. Our principal magickal goals have remained the same for many centuries as well. We still strive toward manifesting love, security, health, protection, knowledge, and fertility.

The Role of the Elements in Magick

Witches use a variety of catalysts to help boost a spell to success. Deciding which one to use and in which method it should be employed can be an overwhelming prospect for new Witches. For instance, do you use apple blossoms or orange peels to aid a love spell? Do you use the stone you have just found as a protective amulet, or is it better to use your pentacle necklace? Is candle magick appropriate for assisting a past-life regression, or should you use a water-based spell instead?

Learning about each type of magick and magickal catalyst requires a lot of time and thought, though it is an art in which you will eventually become proficient. Think of your magickal studies as being like those piano lessons you used to have to take. When you first began, you had to stop at each note and think about where your fingers needed to go in order to play them. After you'd been at it a while, traveling the keyboard became almost instinctive. It is the same with magick.

One way to speed up the learning process and get to where you land somewhat near the bull's eye each time is to pay attention to the elements: earth, water, fire, and air (all discussed at length in chapters 3 and 10). These elements were once thought to be the source materials of all things that existed. For Witches this is still a basic tenet of our belief. Everything in creation—all objects, ideas, creatures, and plants—are primarily governed by one of these elements. When we understand the elements and their associations and affinities, we can learn to relate them to our magick. For example, dream magick is in the realm of water. Think of the association of depth, mystery, and flow. Protective magick falls under the rulership of fire. Think of our ancestors lighting fires in the night to drive away predators and evil spirits.

As you start your magickal studies it is a good idea to set aside some time each day to look around your environment and make a mental list of which items you feel fall under the rulership of which element. You don't need to have any special knowledge to do this; just go with your first reaction. Later you can compare your feelings to popular wisdom and see where you stand. Keep in mind that just because you feel an item is ruled by a different element than another Witch says it is does not make one of you right and the other one wrong. There are quite a few catalysts that are not as easily pigeonholed as others. You will run across numerous articles that are either elementally ambiguous or that share a dual rulership.

Your fireplace might be said to be ruled by fire (for the fire built in it) or earth (the ruling element of the home), but that fog outside your window that made you want to light a fire in the first place is ruled by both air and water. The sooner you start making these intuitive connections between objects, events, et cetera, and their ruling element, the sooner you will be making successful magickal decisions.

The Prerequisites of Successful Magick

There are generally recognized steps Witches are taught to use to create successful spells. Most long-time Witches put their own spin on them but, underneath, the steps remain basically the same from Witch to Witch, tradition to tradition, and from past to present. This magickal link with our ancient past is one of the few things we can be reasonably sure has remained constant in our ever-changing religion.

Natural magick requires six basic components for success. This is sometimes seen as a four-part process using "To will, to dare, to know, and to keep silent" as its basis. I prefer to expand this old formula into the following six parts:

Six Steps for Successful Magick

1. Desire and need
2. Emotional involvement
3. Knowledge and realistic expectations
4. Belief
5. The ability to keep silent
6. Willingness to back up magick in the physical world

Desire and Need

Desire and need drive the Witch to construct a plausible spell. This creates links to the wished-for outcome both on the physical and otherworldly planes. It is this otherworld, or astral plane, where spells must first take shape before they can be drawn down into physical manifestation.

Sound hard? Not when you truly need and desire what you are working toward. With this in place, your thought forms are powerful enough to record themselves in the astral, making them easier for you to build on. To put it in very simple terms, they grow so "real" that they become too dense for the astral world, so they have no choice but to manifest in the physical.

Emotional Involvement

Your emotional involvement fuels your desire and need, tightening those physical/astral links. It also creates a personal investment in the outcome intense enough to allow you to see the spell through to its end. Think about it. Anything to which you have an emotional attachment is very hard to let go. Every day many people seek professional mental help to release people and situations to which they have become emotionally attached.

Knowledge and Realistic Expectations

A Witch must have enough magickal knowledge to be able to construct an appropriate spell. This includes choosing the proper words of power, having the ability to visualize correctly, and having the knowledge to select the tools and catalysts that are most compatible with the energies of the spell. For example, choosing an herb known for attracting love would not be as useful in a spell for banishment.

Magickal timing is also important. If the astrological timing is not going to work out, a Witch has to know how to adjust the spell accordingly to take advantage of the existing astrological conditions.

Knowledge means wisdom. This means we must each know when magick is really needed and when it is best to tackle a problem by conventional means. Joining the Spell-of-the-Day Club and hauling out your ritual gear for every little problem will only cause a scattering of your energies, and you will find you cannot ever focus on one problem long enough to solve it. Magick makes an excellent backup support for our problems, but is not a panacea for all our woes. Heredity Witch and author Sybil Leek thought this tendency to jump into magick without forethought meant that a Witch needed to "clean house" first,[2] meaning that the Witch needed to get other aspects of life in order before tackling something as demanding as magick. It works best with a clear head, a clear focus, and when life is—if not perfect—at least under some semblance of control.

Knowledge also means knowing when to call for outside help. In the case of a serious illness you may need a qualified doctor's help, preferably one sympathetic to the inclusion of the natural healing techniques in your regimen. Remember that magick is not a cure-all. Our spells expect us to use all our available resources to effect a successful outcome, and sometimes this might mean coupling our efforts with conventional wisdom.

A Witch must also be rational enough to know which magickal goals are realistically attainable and which are not. Any spell whose goal is in violation of the natural laws of the universe is doomed to fail from the start. No magickal spell can make you sprout wings and fly, or render your physical body invisible. However, a spell can allow you to do both things in the magickal state known as astral projection (see chapter 9).

Belief

Successful Witches must believe in the outcome of their spells and have confidence in their ability to bring it into being. Magick involves a change of consciousness; it is an operation that takes place largely in the mind. This does not make the result any less real, but it does lay a myriad of obstacles in our way, all of them generated by ourselves. Because we are dealing with a mental operation, any lingering doubts floating around in that same mind will only hinder our work.

The popular Wiccan end tag to spells and rituals, "so mote it be," is another affirmation of belief in our efforts. This obsolete English phrase means "so must it be," and has for many

---

2. *The Complete Art of Witchcraft* (Signet Books, 1971).

centuries been used at the end of spells to assert their reality in the here and now. This tag line has other incarnations as well, and the variation matters less than the intent behind it— that your magick must happen, and must now be a fact, because you will it so.

Self-confidence is built through practice. If you are a novice, start with the exercises on page 10, which will help demonstrate to you your personal power.

The Ability to Keep Silent

Keeping silent is a time-honored magickal custom that helps protect the energy we have put into our spells. There is an old occult adage that teaches "power shared is power lost." Keeping our magickal goals to ourselves allows us to focus our energy and attention on them and not on bragging about our hoped-for successes.

Talking about your magick, even casually, to the wrong person can hamper your work if that person has a vested interest in your failure. Don't automatically assume that your best friend of twenty years will be delighted to learn that you are into the fortieth day of a sixty-day spell for drawing romance into your life. Don't assume that just because that person has been your long-time trusted companion that he or she will want to see you get your heart's desire. Even if this person truly wants to be happy for you, jealousy is still an unpredictable, but ever-present, part of the human condition. Perhaps your friend feels threatened that if you find a romantic partner you will not have time for your friendship anymore. Or perhaps your friend is afraid you have your hopes pinned on the same person he or she has been trying to attract. Random negative energy can do as much harm to your spell as could an experienced Witch deliberately whammying you with a counterspell.

Willingness to Back Up Magick in the Physical World

Magick is not an instantaneous process. The language that has evolved around it over the centuries underscores that it is a step-by-step process. We speak of spinning, weaving, casting, working, crafting, and creating to describe our spellwork. Like many of our old Goddesses who are portrayed as spinning and weaving things into creation, we as Witches also craft our magick in this painstaking, piecework way.

For example, if you want a new house, don't expect to cast a spell and have it land on top of you as if you were the Wicked Witch of the East in *The Wizard of Oz*. You will have to create and work your spell and then take to the streets and begin your search, confident that your magick will point you in the right direction.

To sum it up, magick works for only one reason: because it is the will of the Witch that it should. Successful Witches:

- Have a need they are emotionally involved with
- Have the knowledge to create the spell and the belief in themselves to see it through
- Know how to visualize the spell, creating thought forms in the unseen, or astral, world that they know only they can draw into the physical world through will and the continued feeding of energy into the effort
- Back up their magickal efforts on the physical plane
- Keep quiet about their goals
- Seek outside assistance when necessary
- Keep studying their Craft and living their faith, knowing that a Witch's education is a never-ending process

Where the Elements Fit In

The elements are building blocks of manifestation. In keeping with the old occult adage "as above, so below" (meaning that the microcosm, or self, reflects the macrocosm, or universe), the elements have both a physical and an astral, or spiritual, form. The ancient people of many cultures saw the elements—earth, water, fire, and air—as being the basic ingredients composing all existing things. Though our thought forms are shaped by our will in the astral, we need the elements to help give them the substance allowing us to pull those thoughts down into reality. This is why we divide magickal operations into goals we ultimately say are ruled by a particular element, meaning that each goal is largely composed of a specific elemental essence.

As we move through our exploration of the elements in chapters 3, 4, and 10, the subtle working of the elemental forces, and their impact on our magick, should be made clear.

Testing Your Personal Power

To make any magick work, we have to know beyond any doubt that we are one with the forces of nature and that we can act as a channel for those forces when we need to.

If you are still a novice, the following three exercises are designed to show that you are indeed a reservoir of untapped energy. Hopefully, these will give you a boost of confidence as you begin your magickal studies.

The Power in Your Palms Test

The palms of your hands are natural energy centers through which you can direct power. Hold your hands up in front of you about a foot apart, palms facing together. Close your eyes to aid your concentration, and focus your attention on the space between your palms. Between them is a low energy field similar to two opposite poles of a magnet facing each other. Like magnets, they can attract or repel other energies depending on how you set them up to work.

With your eyes still closed, bring your hands slowly to-gether and begin to rub your palms vigorously against one an-other. Feel the heat they create. This is heat born of energy you are creating. Memorize the sensation.

After a minute or two, move your hands back apart. Now concentrate on the feeling passing between them as you move them slowly toward each other again. Can you feel their resis-tance to each other? You are sensing the expansion of the en-ergy field you have created projecting outward from your palms. It has created a slight, natural barrier to the energy of the other hand. Memorize the sensation so that you can be confident when you conjure it again.

Before you quit the exercise, take your hands and place them on the ground, mentally willing the excess energy you raised to be grounded away from you. You should never allow unused magickal energy to remain on you or to randomly go else-where. Leaving it will only permit it to work against you, mak-ing you feel frazzled and unfocused. In extreme cases it can cause you to feel as if you are being haunted. (This wise and ac-cepted magickal practice is discussed in detail in chapter 2.)

The Navel and Solar Plexus Test

The navel and solar plexus areas are major chakra centers, part of the seven primary centers of power that are aligned down your body. These were discovered many centuries ago in India, and have been successfully used by Witches and ma-gicians ever since to project power, balance the body, and re-ceive psychic impressions (see chapter 2 for more on the chakras).

The navel chakra, located just below the belly button, is one of the most powerful chakras on a woman's body. Men tend to do better with the solar plexus, the area halfway be-tween the bottom of the breastbone and the top of the navel. With eyes closed to aid concentration, move your hands out in front of your bare body with palms facing the appropriate chakra area. Hold your hands at least a foot away from your body and focus your mental attention to this area.

When you are ready, move your hands to the chakra area and begin massaging in small circles with both palms. Feel yourself consciously awakening this energy center. After a few minutes, pull your palms away. Take a deep breath, and then move them slowly back towards the chakra area. You should feel the pressure of the awakened energy pushing against your hands.

Because the chakras are larger energy centers than those in your palms, you can play around with the energy you raised for longer before it starts to scatter. This is a good time to practice contracting and expanding the energy by mentally sucking it back into the chakra in a tight ball, and then expanding it out in front of your body about ten to twelve inches. Try this several times, using your mind to will the process. You may use your palms to assist in pushing the energy in and out and also to help gauge your success.

As suggested in the first exercise, before you quit, place both palms flat on the ground and mentally expel the excess energy you have raised.

The Candle Flame Test

Light a taper candle and place it on a table or other sturdy surface where there is absolutely no chance of encountering a draft. Do not use a votive candle for this exercise as the glass container can hinder your ability to affect the flame. You will also need to close windows, turn off ceiling fans, air conditioners, and furnaces to avoid indoor air currents.

Stand before the flame and, with eyes open, will your own energies to merge with those of the flame. This can be visualized any way you like. You can think of your physical body as merging with that of the flame, or of the flame burning inside yourself, or as a blending of your subtle energy bodies. Whatever you choose to do, consider this fusion as a pathway to the candle that will allow you to manipulate it without physical contact.

When you feel you have made a connection, mentally will the candle flame to waver as if you had just used your palm or your lips to send a small current of air its way. Try to visualize this both as a continuous stream of energy bombarding the flame and as little bursts of energy. One method may work better for you than the other. You might also try visualizing this energy as coming from one of your chakra areas. Sometimes this will work better for you than imagining a hand or your mouth sending the air, and it can also tell you which of your chakras is most magickally developed (see page 28 for a chakra location chart).

Unless you are about to be declared the thirteenth wonder of the world, don't expect the flame to tap dance for you. With practice you will notice a slight waver of the flame in response to your will. If you have eliminated all other sources of air currents and you succeed in moving the flame at least half the times you try, consider your experiment a success.

The Importance of Keeping Records

As you work through each step of your magickal training you should record your findings, failures, successes, and feelings in your Book of Shadows so they may be examined further at a later date. The Book of Shadows goes by other names as well, including Book of Lights or Book of Lights and Shadows. It is not important what you call it, only that you use it.

By any name, it is a Witch's personal magickal diary and working guidebook. It has become a standard tool in modern Witchcraft, though its widespread usage probably only dates from the very late middle ages when literacy became more commonplace. In its pages are kept texts of rituals, records of spells and their outcomes, transcriptions of dreams and astral travels, insights on meditations, and other magickal recipes. For the student Witch it functions as a customized textbook and, when more experience is gained, it serves as a record book charting our highs and lows so that our successes can be reproduced and our failures avoided.

The name of the book is thought to have two derivations. One refers to the fact that once upon a time the book had to be hidden, just like the Witches themselves, to avoid detection by Witch hunters. It was literally a book kept in shadows. Others say the label is a metaphor; that spells and rituals left unenacted are without form, and therefore are merely shadows of themselves.

European Witch legends tell us that these books were once written in secret alphabets in case they fell into the hands of Witch hunters. This is questionable considering the low literacy rate of the common people of Europe before the late eighteenth century. Nonetheless, many of these attractive old alphabets are used in today's books, though the bulk of the writings are recorded in the first language of the individual keeping them. This is simply to make them easy to read.

Some books are very fancy and full of lovely artwork. Many occult shops sell elegant blank volumes bound in black leather or carved wood that can be very pricey. Your book doesn't have to be expensive. Mine has always been kept in a looseleaf notebook. I prefer this method so I can change the format at will, or add and delete pages as needed.

There is no rule that says you have to keep your entire Book of Shadows between one cover. Some Witches prefer to keep their magickal diary portion separate from their written rituals. Others keep a spell and magickal recipe book separately from the main book. The attractive blank books carried in most book stores can make lovely ritual binders. Most are not expensive, and some of the decorative covers speak to Pagan taste.

Tradition dictates that a Book of Shadows be kept in your own handwriting. If not merely another apocryphal anecdote, this might have been a precaution adopted during the years of Witch persecutions when no one would have wanted such a book with their condemning handwriting emblazoned in it to fall into the wrong hands. Each student of the Craft was required to keep notes, recipes, et cetera, in his or her own writing. That way, if the book was confiscated, only the one Witch would be at risk. I know of at least one present-day Craft teacher who still starts her new students out by having them copy her entire Book of Shadows word for word in their own hand.

Without the worry of a clerical inquisition hanging over our heads, there are still advantages in keeping to this old custom. Copying words in your own hand always ensures that they fully sink in, and each one can be carefully weighed in your mind as it is written down. But times change, and I very much believe it is acceptable to type your Book of Shadows. I even know a few modern Witches who keep theirs on computer databases! The important thing is that you actually do the recording of all the information yourself, whether you type or write, so that each word has meaning for you as you enter it. This means don't download someone else's database, or photocopy pages from someone else's book or from published sources and paste them in. You will do yourself more good by writing down the main points of what you find valuable in other writings, and then making your own observations and commentary alongside.

As you practice building your magickal skills, record each effort in your book along with the time, day, date, and the sign and phase of the moon. This data will help you later to pinpoint when you are at your best psychically and magickally, and will be very useful to your future work. You may also want to record other pertinent information such as temperature, weather conditions, location, and other astrological data. This information can be derived from a variety of astrological sourcebooks readily available at most bookstores and libraries. You should also jot down your feelings before, during, and after magickal exercises. Getting in the habit of recording your magickal endeavors now will make it easier to do so in the future, and will make your Book of Shadows an indispensable tool.

Magickal Ethics

People today are well aware of the consequences of the abuse of power. It is arguably the single greatest source of the injuries done to this planet and her inhabitants. When people begin to pursue power for its own sake, they become blinded to the suffering caused by their actions. Eventually the wheel of life comes full circle and that harm comes home to rest, but usually not before irreparable damage has been done.

Magick is power and, like any other form of personal power, it can be abused. The temptations are sometimes great, but those of us who call ourselves Witches adhere to a spiritual system that recognizes we are connected to all other living things and cannot allow ourselves to fall prey to the abuse of power without suffering in kind.

Within the Craft we seek to live our lives in balance with all creation. This is what makes our magick its most potent. When we are in balance, our personal energies resonate with those of the universe; being as one with it, we can more easily draw on its resources. When we break that balance by sending negative energies out along the wheel of life, we set the motion of the wheel off kilter and it begins to wobble. Eventually the vibrations set up by that wobbling work their way back to us and we pay dearly. It is an old and accepted metaphysical adage that like attracts like. Therefore, imbalance will attract imbalance.

This is hard stuff for a lot of folks to handle. Until finding Paganism, many people foundered in religions that did not teach the concept of self-responsibility. To the contrary, the mainstream religions don't want you thinking for yourself. They want you to sit in their pews, week after week, while someone else dictates to you what you should and should not do in the week to come. In many cases, the mere questioning of these edicts from on high will get you punished by earning you the public disapproval of that religion's leaders.

The Pagan religions—Witchcraft included—are religions of the individual. The ultimate decisions about what to think, how to behave, and how to live rest within each of us. There is no excommunication from this path and no ecclesiastical court sitting in judgment of us. There is no one on whom to shift the blame should something go wrong. Even if you are part of a coven, you, and only you, are still responsible for the kind of magickal energy you put out onto that wheel, since only you will bear the repercussions of your choices.

There are few rules that govern a Witch's actions, but there is one axiom almost universally recognized as our governing code of ethics. We call it the Wiccan or Pagan Rede and it states:

> *As it harms none, do what you will.*

We have the freedom to do anything we choose, magickally or personally, so long as we are sure our efforts and actions cause harm to no one. This "no one" includes other people, spirits, animals, and—some argue—ourselves. We may not take actions, even well intentioned, that infringe on anyone else's free will. We may not attempt to manipulate or seek to gain power over someone, and we may not even foist our positive magick on anyone without their express permission to do so.

Witchcraft is not alone in its adoption of this Rede as a central spiritual focus, though I believe we do spend more time thinking and talking about it than do followers of other religions. (There is even an organization called The Golden Rule Society, which has combed the earth to collect versions of our Rede.) These are found in virtually every spiritual system. In Christianity, this Rede is known as the Golden Rule. Its Christian expression is found in the New Testament in Luke 6:31: "Do unto others as you would have them do unto you." In Judaism the Rede was codified 2,000 years ago by the great Rabbinic teacher Hillel, who once told a group of potential converts, "What is hateful to you, do not do to others. All the rest is commentary. Go and learn." From the African traditional religions the Rede comes to us in the form of the popular adage "What goes around comes around."

Witches are not perfect—no more than any other religious folks are—and we occasionally break this code of ethics either accidentally or knowingly. When we do, we must be prepared to bear the consequences of our actions. In our spiritual system we have no Hell to be cast into as punishment; this is not a fitting retribution for someone on the path of self-responsibility. Instead we get our absolution in accordance with what we know as our Threefold Law. This tells us that all energies we send forth, either positive or negative, will return to us three times over. This is not a fear tactic created to keep the faithful toeing the party line. It is simply the natural result of living on the wheel of life. We cannot escape its turning. We alone must take what we give and reap what we sow when the cycle returns our way.

Contrary to mainstream views, the terms *black magick* and *white magick* are not popular among modern Witches. They imply that all actions can be easily categorized into neat columns of good and bad. If they are really that easy, then magickal ethics would not take up so much space in magickal books or in the private teachings passed from one Witch to another. Nothing in life is ever this clear cut; why should magick be any different?

Somewhere along the journey someone coined the term *gray magick* to refer to that unclear state in between good and evil. This is unsatisfactory, however, for it is generally interpreted to mean magick that is not wholly good but that someone wants to do anyway, hoping that the evil portion is so small that it will not amount to much when it returns threefold.

One often-cited example of gray magick is performing healing magick for someone who needs it but either will not give permission for it or is never even asked. The rationale is that the Witch who wants to do the spell has the best interests of the sick person at heart, and so that certainly must make it good magick.

Wrong!

Any time you violate free will you are drawing on the negative aspects of magickal power. I have heard new Witches repeatedly argue that if they are sending out good intentions, even without permission, then they will only get good intentions in return.

Wrong again!

If your magick is unwanted, even if well intentioned, what comes back to you will not be positive. Under no circumstances is it acceptable to meddle in someone else's life. This is a gross violation of free will and can be called nothing else but manipulation. What you will get back from your efforts are not good intentions but a threefold blast of manipulation and infringement on your own free will.

When applied to spells, these color labels only serve to cloud magickal thinking. There is no black, white, or gray. There is only raw magickal power. It has no moral character and we may draw from it as we will. This is the same way the Pagan deities differ from the mainstream Gods. For instance, Christianity has a good God, Jehovah, and a bad God, Satan—two completely opposing entities who each embody a pure essence of either good or bad. The Pagan deities are simply beings who possess power. Sometimes they use it wisely and sometimes they do not. A large portion of extant mythic stories tell us the consequences of their misuse of power.

This concept is at the root of the often misunderstood aphorism "The Witch who cannot kill cannot cure." By saying this, no one is advocating that you rush out and prove your destructive talents in order for your constructive ones to be acknowledged. It is but another affirmation that the power from which we draw our magick is neither good nor bad—it is just power, and a fully knowledgeable Witch knows how to draw on it no matter what outcome is desired. If the path of the Craft is right for you, you will find this knowledge of infinite power humbling, not ego inflating. Egotistical Witches usually find their powers turned against them in the end. To know that such power is accessible to you, and to choose to honor it by handling it responsibly, is the most truly empowering mystery in the Craft. True and lasting power is not brandished about like a weapon, to be pulled out only when one wants to show off; it is simply a part of who the magician is, and is worn with the ease of a second skin.

It can be all too easy to be lured into a false sense of security where magickal ethics are concerned. In your early efforts you may step over the line of "harm none" and, though braced for the backlash, you find none comes. So you step over the line again and wait. Still nothing. After that you get smug and think those old Witches who tried to teach you didn't know what they were talking about—maybe they just wanted to keep all the power plays to themselves. First of all, negative retribution is not meted out like a tennis ball being bounced against a brick wall. There is no instant bounce back. There seems to be nothing the wheel of life likes more than smacking the face of complacency at its zenith. As my teacher once phrased it, trust that eventually someone will come knocking on your door to tell you it's payback time. Secondly, you may not even notice the little down turns indicating that payback time has come when you are just starting out. You simply will not have developed the magickal skills to create enough stress on the elastic of the wheel to cause it to snap back at you with noticeable strength. As you build your skills and are able to send greater energies onto the wheel, greater energies will be returned to you. Whether they are positive or negative is up to you.

One last word and then I will stop preaching! Those of you who have decided to heed the warnings of the Rede will do so, and those who choose not to will probably just have to learn the hard way. But please, if you still doubt the power of the Threefold Law, seek out someone who has been practicing the Craft for a while. Any old-timer should have at least one or two stories to relate about how they, or someone they once knew, abused their inner gifts and how they paid for the transgression.

▼

2

Developing Magickal Skills

All arts have their prerequisite basic skills, the ones that must be mastered at the beginning level of study if the student wishes to become adept at the craft. The same is true of the art of magick, perhaps even more so since ours is an ongoing discipline in which there is always something new to learn. In order to advance to these higher levels, we must first command the elementary skills so thoroughly that we can slip into them as easily as we can into a silken robe.

Basic Magickal Skills

- Visualization
- Centering and balancing
- Raising and sending magickal power
- Charging, enchanting, and empowering
- Altering consciousness
- Grounding excess energy

In theory all of these are simple skills, so much so that we might be given to wonder why everyone is not using them to work magickal miracles in their lives every day. The truth is that, though they are easy in concept, they can be hard to master if students refuse to practice or choose to fool themselves about their abilities. When you are just starting out on a magickal path, and if you wish to remain always a beginner, you may get away with fooling yourself. But these six abilities are literally the foundation upon which all other future magickal skills will be built. If you cannot do all of them with reasonable proficiency, not only will your spellcraft suffer, but likely other aspects of your Craft spirituality will as well.

I frequently get letters from readers who have questions about one or more of these skills. These fall into one of two categories: those who ask for tips on improvement, and those who want to know how they can be sure when they have been successful.

Improving is simply a matter of practicing and of finding the precise method and mental imagery that triggers success for you. Compare these skills to the simple matter of falling asleep. We all know the basics of how this is done, but everyone has their own twist on which works best for them. For instance, some people have to lie on their backs to sleep while others have to have windows open or be wearing a favorite pair of pajamas. Eventually we all get to the same place. And so it is with magick. The exercises and methods given in this chapter are not the only ones that can help you learn these six skills, but hopefully they will give those of you who are novices a place to start exploring.

Knowing when you are successful is another very customized experience. The physical sensations and inner-world events we encounter as we gain wisdom speak to us with different voices, telling one of us one thing, and another of us something else. Sorting it all out can be confusing. At first you may feel as if you are making up everything you see and perceive, and in some ways this is true. All things that manifest must first be born as an idea in someone's mind. If you want to master the basic skills of natural magick you must first *see* yourself doing so in your mind. With time and practice, those mental images and the physical sensations they cause will take on a character all their own, and you will know that you are successful.

Visualization

Visualization is the art of being able to see with your mind. Applied to magick, it refers to the creation of mental images sustained and energized by intensely concentrating our focus on our desired goal. The concept is simple: what your mind sees and is truly made to believe becomes your reality. This belief has origins in the old acceptance that each mind is a universe unto itself and that the person who inhabits it is the God and Goddess who create all that lives there, and also in the belief that thought form, once given life on the unseen or astral plane, are real and can then be brought into the physical world.

Visualization is probably the single most important magickal skill to perfect. Not only does it fuel the goals of your magickal infancy but, when you mature, this skill will allow you to do amazing things with your mind, such as divide your consciousness in half, allowing each part to be focused and fully absorbed on two different issues or tasks. When done right it can literally be like being in two places at once. But before you can fly you have to put some feathers on your magickal wings by learning to master this basic skill.

Many beginners make much too much of the visualization process. I do not mean this in terms of its importance to magick. It is *very* important! I refer here to what they expect the experience to be like. We all visualize all the time. Visualization is as simple as daydreaming, as easy as thinking. When was the last time someone waved a hand in front of your unblinking eyes because you had drifted off into your inner self? Unless you are a total recluse, it was probably not too long ago. What was it you were thinking about? A potential lover? Your dream home? Money? Personal success? Revenge (ah, those thoughts occur to the best of us)? Consciously harness those mental images and you will know how to visualize.

As you continue to develop this skill, you will notice that as you end visualization sessions, you feel as if you have truly been elsewhere . . . and so you have. You have visited your inner-world which has the power to create for you anything you can envision.

Several years ago I received a series of letters from a reader who insisted she could not visualize. I sent back whatever suggestions I could think of that might help, and still she said she was having no luck. She wanted to know "the secret," and was absolutely sure that I knew it and was holding back.

There is no secret to visualization. Some people are better at it than others, usually because they have always had a rich inner life, but everyone can learn to do it effectively. You are probably better at it than you think but, simply because it is so automatic and natural, you just have not as yet recognized the process for what it is.

Start to practice visualization now with these simple exercises that should show you just how easy the mental images come when you let them.

Mental Pictures from Random Thoughts Visualization Exercise

What happens when I ask you to think about your best friend? What mental images come to mind? Do you see his or her face? Mentally hear his or her laugh? Do you picture the fun you've had together or a problem of his or hers you are privy to?

When I ask you to think of your boss, what comes to mind? What feelings are aroused, and how do they color your mental imagery?

Think about your bedroom. Can you see it? Smell it? What color is it? How does it look when the sun streams through the window, or when the breeze filters in on a warm day?

Think of your first-grade classroom. Can you see your classmates? Your teacher? Yourself?

Who did you look up to as a child? Who did you run to for comfort? See that person's face. See the smile. Hear the voice and words of encouragement. Feel the loving touch as if it were happening now. How do you see yourself responding to this contact?

All these scenarios should trigger images in your mind. Stop now and allow a clear mental picture of each of these places and people. It is impossible to have even the most random thought about anything without some vision of it popping into your head, especially when your emotions become entailed. Hone in on the first mental picture that springs to mind. Hold it there and see it in living color. When you can see it, fill in the details so that it is as real a mental image as you can create. This is visualization, a thinking process you already use all the time.

See, no trick.

To refine this process for magickal use, you need only to be able to sustain the mental pictures to the exclusion of all other thoughts. Keeping your emotions involved in the imagery will help your maintain your focus, which is why I asked you to think about people and places that would likely trigger an emotional response as well as a mental one. This emotional connection should be cultivated as it is necessary for turning your mental images into magickal reality. If you are one of those people who regularly indulges in healthy mental fantasies you will find this comes easily. Even if you have never tried to control your inner world, you can learn to hold the images in your mind and invest them with magickal power. Some people do better holding a series of still pictures in their heads, like a sequence of slides projected onto an inner screen in the mind. Others do better with entire movies playing through their minds in which they star and direct the action.

I prefer the movie version of visualization because it allows room to play and adds a richness of sensations that fill it out and make it real. An inner-world movie can include sounds and background music, touch, gestures, and even scents. The more of your senses you bring into your visualization, the magickally stronger the images will be. When you are doing spell-work later on you will be investing the images with the power you raise, and the clearer and more real they are to your mind, the easier they will be to empower.

The Daily Routine Visualization Exercise

To show you how easy it is to focus on an inner-world movie, select a sequence of events you deal with nearly every day and work through it in your mind. Most of us have an outside job or other place we are required to be several days a week, and our method of getting there is usually the same. Take time now to visualize yourself going through the beginning of an average day.

See yourself in bed sound asleep just before your dreaded alarm goes off. Hear the alarm in your head. Recall the horrible feeling its intrusion into your rest causes. See yourself hitting the snooze button and rolling over for another ten minutes of shuteye.

Hear it going off again. Feel yourself shutting it off, hear the plastic click it makes, and hear your groan as you slide out of bed. Feel your room with all your senses. Is your room chilly or warm? Does it raise goose flesh or make you want to jump in a cool shower? Head for the bathroom and feel the shock of the cool bathroom floor under your bare feet. Hear and smell the water being turned on in your sink. Do you shiver as you wait for it to warm up?

What does your hairbrush feel like in your hands? What does your toothpaste smell like? Taste the toothpaste in your mouth. Step into the shower. Feel the warmth of the water in your shower. Smell your soap and feel it slide over your awakening skin.

Take a deep breath of the morning air as you mentally step outside your home. What does your neighborhood smell like? Does it take your car a long time to warm up? Do you have a long wait at the bus or train stop? Is traffic heavy or light? How does it feel to be driving your car? Riding the bus? Taking the train? Mentally experience it all using every sense you possess.

See yourself walking into your place of employment. Notice the morning smells: the brewing coffee, the co-worker who always wears too much scent. Who greets you first? How do you feel about that person? What do you hear: a ringing telephone, a copy machine?

Continue visualizing your daily routine until you feel you have a solid sense of how easy it is to create mental imagery.

Centering and Balancing

Centering and balancing are terms often used synonymously in magick, but they are slightly different. Centering means to draw your consciousness or center of power into one place in yourself. Balancing means to have all your power centers open and fully functioning so that you are a perfect conduit for magickal energy. The basic procedure for doing these operations is the same, only the end result is different.

You must balance before you can center. To balance yourself means to be in harmony with the energies of the universe. It also means to have all those energies equally distributed within yourself. One very common exercise for achieving this state is to imagine yourself as a huge tree. This tree meditation is one I have seen used in virtually every Wiccan/Pagan group situation in which I have participated. It is an excellent way to balance yourself and start to feel the extent of your personal power. Stand with your arms above your head and visualize them as the branches reaching high into the sky. Your feet should become your roots connecting you with Mother Earth deep beneath you. Your torso will be the trunk, bridging the gap between the manifest and unseen worlds where you stand as the conduit between them.

Another way to balance is to cleanse, energize, and open your chakra centers. *Chakra* is a Hindustani word referring to the seven major energy centers that are aligned down the human body from the top of the head to tailbone (see chart). They are visualized as fist-sized spheres centered down the inside of the spine. These energy centers were discovered in India hundred of years ago, and have been used by Witches and magicians ever since to provide balance and to raise and project power.

Each chakra has a spectral color that is traditionally associated with it:

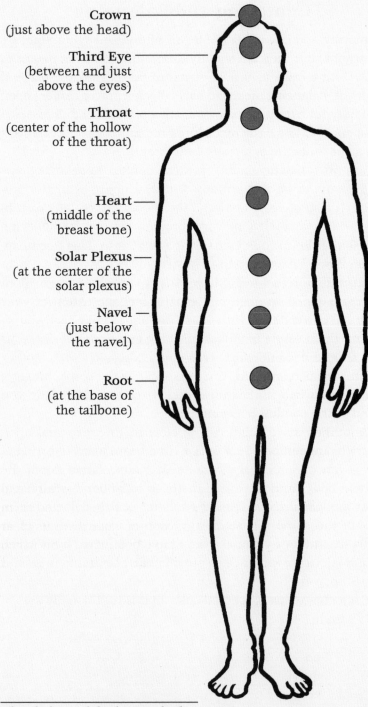

Crown ———
(just above the head)

Third Eye ———
(between and just
above the eyes)

Throat ———
(center of the hollow
of the throat)

Heart ———
(middle of the
breast bone)

Solar Plexus ———
(at the center of the
solar plexus)

Navel ———
(just below
the navel)

Root ———
(at the base of
the tailbone)

The chakras of the human body

Chakra Name	Location	Color
Crown chakra	On top of the head	Violet
Third Eye chakra	Between and just above the eyes	Indigo
Throat chakra	At the level of the larynx	Blue
Heart chakra	At the center of the breastbone	Green
Solar plexus	Just beneath the breastbone above the stomach	Yellow
Navel chakra	Just below the navel	Orange
Root chakra	At the base of the tailbone	Red

To work with the chakras you need to keep your back as straight as possible while still remaining relaxed and comfortable. I recommend either sitting on the edge of a chair or standing in what is known as the Star or Goddess Position—legs apart and arms apart over the head. Mentally draw down a ball of white light from high above you and allow it to enter your crown chakra. Then draw up a similar light from the Mother Earth below you and allow it to enter your root chakra.

Send the balls of light up and down your spine, awakening the sleeping chakra centers and connecting them to the universal life energy you have called on. Starting at either the root or crown chakra, visualize this center opening fully, and all dark patches, which indicate blockages, being burned clean by the pure light. See the chakra point pulsating in its clear true color. Move up or down your spine, depending on which place you started this process, and take the time to do the same with each chakra until you have worked your way through all seven.

When this is done, allow a bright white light to engulf your body and give a final balancing through the chakras. White is usually used at the end of color therapy sessions to balance any overstimulation that might have been given to any chakra and helps keep the energies of the whole system in balance.

To center yourself, you should mentally direct all your balanced energy to one point in your body and allow it to go there. You should choose the one chakra area you feel is your personal power center, the spot from which you are most likely to send out raised magickal energy.

Raising and Sending Magickal Power

Magickal power is the energy the Witch raises and shapes before directing it out toward its goal. Being able to call on these energies quickly and efficiently is essential to being a properly trained Witch. Remember our discussion of the meaning of the word *Witch* from the Introduction? We got our name from being benders and shapers of energy.

Some newcomers to this path are reluctant, even afraid, to raise energy at all. They say they fear they will somehow drain their personal reserves of life-supporting energy and harm them in some way. Some say they fear opening themselves to illness or mental disorders by expending magickal energy. These worries always make me think of a scene from the movie *Cocoon II* in which one of the elderly men, who has returned to Earth after visiting another planet populated with beings who excel at energy manipulation, expels his own life-giving energy to save the life of his wife, who has been struck by a car. Doing this allows an old cancer to revive and thrive, and it soon kills him. When I saw that scene I thought how pointless it was to be trained in energy projection but still not have any idea how to keep from draining yourself in the process.

Done properly, magickal energy will not hurt you or drain your vital energy reserves. It will take effort on your part, and requires some expulsion of personal will, but it will not open you to sickness. As I described when writing *Inside a Witches' Coven*,[1] a good power-raising and sending session is like enduring an intense aerobic workout. You will feel spent, but you will also find yourself invigorated and recharged. This is because it is not your energy being used for the effort. You

---

1. Llewellyn, 1997.

draw magickal energy from other sources, such as the earth or the divine, or you raise new energy within yourself. Your own energies will naturally merge and blend with these new ones, making it possible for you to direct their flow.

Energy is simply molecules in motion. All objects, people, and plants—everything—have a molecular structure that is always in motion, no matter how solid they appear to be. This vibrational rate determines two things. On the physical level, it determines the solidity of a thing and the amount of kinetic energy that can be stored in it. On the non-physical, or spiritual level, higher vibratory rates are associated with higher consciousness and higher spiritual beings. When we talk about raising this energy, we are referring to the process of setting the molecules in greater motion, agitating them so that they store more potential energy for us and thus increase our compatibility with higher spiritual and magickal goals.

Earlier I discussed the art of balancing the chakras. Part of this process included the drawing up and down of energy from sources outside yourself. This is what you should always do before expelling magickal energy. Mother Earth below us, and the divine beings we visualize as being in the otherworld above us, have limitless stores of power that we can draw on.

Practice pulling this energy into yourself until you can feel it happening easily at your will. Close your eyes and send your consciousness far down into the womb of Mother Earth, or take it high into the otherworld. Then will it to be pulled up or down into you. Once inside you, feel it charging every cell and atom of your being with magickal potential.

You can also raise new energy inside yourself to use for magick. Dancing, drumming, chanting, singing, walking, and meditating are all good ways to raise power around you. Simply engage in any of these activities while continuously focusing on increasing the energy flow in your body. Sexual energy is also a good source of power, but controlling and expelling it are usually considered advanced magickal arts and will be discussed in greater detail in chapter 8.

The best magickal energy comes from a blending of pulled-in energy and new energies you have raised within yourself.

This forces the power you draw in to conform itself to your personal energy patterns and makes it a true extension of yourself.

When you feel this energy within you has reached a peak, you are ready to send it out toward its goal. If you are merely practicing these arts and currently have no magickal goal, simply send the energy into Mother Earth to heal her many wounds.

To send out the raised energy, center the power you have raised within yourself by directing it to a single location within yourself. The third eye, heart, or solar plexus chakra centers are the ones usually selected, but any place from which you feel you can easily project out the energy will do. Then, through visualization and will, send that energy out in the direction you want it to go. This might be directed toward a place, a person (remember that permission is required to work spells on behalf of someone else!), a thought form (a result of intense visualization), or into a clear piece of mental imagery you have been working on building.

You should mentally reinforce the power of your energy sending by using a physical gesture to back up your effort. Pointing, exhaling, spinning, collapsing, or any other physical act that makes you think of power spent will work. Keep your mind on your goal until you feel the raised power has been completely expelled.

Charging, Enchanting, and Empowering

These three words are virtually synonymous in magick. They refer to sending personal energy into an object that will act as a catalyst for magick. Most often this is an herb, a stone, or other magickal talisman known to possess energies compatible to our goal so that it can help attract that goal to us.

Take the object you wish to empower and hold it firmly in your power, or projective, hand. This term denotes the hand that is dominant for you. In other words, if you say you are right-handed, then your right hand is your power hand. The other hand would be referred to as your non-dominant, or receptive, hand. Spend as much time as you can holding the object, allowing your own energies to merge with those in it. If you have nothing else you wish to empower at this point, go outside and find a small stone that appeals to you to charge as a talisman of good luck.

You can also send empowerment into an object by sending energy into it through your hands, or you can employ any one of the chakra points to similarly aid you. For instance, if you feel your navel chakra is especially strong, hold the object against your navel area as you expel the empowering energy.

Raise energy in any manner you like, all the while keeping your desired result clearly in your mind and, when you feel the energy you are raising has peaked, sending it into the object all the while still focusing on your will. If you are empowering the stone for luck, you would do this by focusing your energy into the stone while holding the visualization of your goal in your mind.

Altering Consciousness

Altering consciousness is a complete study unto itself, one on which entire books have been written.[2] In this receptive state of awakened mind and slowed body, you can access almost any sentience that ever was, is, or will be. You can gain spiritual insights, do excellent divinations, meet with deities and other spirits, experience past lives, astral project (see chapter 9), work with dreams, and enhance virtually every magickal and ritual task you undertake. In the lower altered levels, such as deep alpha and theta, the mind becomes very receptive to any imagery you program into it, and the conscious and subconscious minds are able to better communicate and work in tandem toward your goal. In this altered state all visualization has magickal potential.

---

2. One of my favorite guides to the meditative arts is Adelaide Gardner's *Meditation: A Practical Study* (Wheaton, IL: Quest Books, 1968). Though it is written from a Christian perspective, the exercises are non-denominational.

Brain Wave Levels in Various
States of Consciousness

State	Cycles per Second	Condition
Beta	5-18	normal wakefulness, alertness, study, conversational level (Person is aware of all physical sensations and bodily needs)
Alpha	8-12	light to medium meditation, day-dreaming, focused concentration, drowsiness, cat napping, some astral projection, easy guided meditations, very light sleep (Person finds waking from this level not difficult)
Theta	4-6	deep meditation, medium to deep sleep, complex astral projection, complex guided meditation, light un-consciousness (Person finds waking from this level moderately to very difficult)
Delta	O.5-2.5	very deep sleep, coma or deep unconsciousness (Person has little or no consciousness of physical sensations or bodily needs)

Acquiring an altered state of consciousness has taken on an aura of mystery in our modern world, one that some even fear as a sinister force. There is nothing unusual or sinister about altering one's consciousness. It is perfectly natural, even un-avoidable, and we all do it all the time. The term "altered state" refers to changing the cycles per second on which our brain waves operate from normal alertness to a more dream-like sta-tus. These fluctuations go on all the time; the only difference is that in magick we seek to gain conscious control of the process. There is nothing any more sinister about controlling this bodily function than there is about potty training. You change your state of consciousness every night when you go to sleep, or when you daydream, or when you watch television. If you were attached to an EEG (brain scanner) machine as you sit reading this page, the cycles per second reading would show that you are in a high alpha state—a light hypnotic trance just below the level of normal waking consciousness.

A few years ago I read about a school district somewhere in the United States in which a group of Christian fundamentalist parents were protesting the rhythm music classes in the public kindergarten for fear that all the rhythmic pounding would put their kids in an altered state of consciousness. While this is probably true that it did, it was also happening during story hour and nap time. We cannot avoid altered states. They are as essential to our mental health as sleeping.

What the parents feared was brainwashing, a state of mind in which thought control is relinquished to an outside force. Inducing receptive states of consciousness is part of the classical brainwashing technique, but for these to be fully effective they have to be coupled with other control devices such as peer pressure, transfer of dependency, controlled positive reinforcement, and deprivation of food and sleep. The parents were wasting their time trying to keep them from slipping into altered states. If they really wanted to protect their children's minds, they would be better off teaching their children to know and understand how their minds work so that they can better protect themselves if invasive brainwashing techniques were ever used on them.

All the famous mystic schools of virtually every culture on the planet have sought to teach its students to discipline their minds to alter their consciousness at will. The methods vary. Some schools, such as Zen, teach altered states that attempt to stop all conscious thought. Others focus solely on a deity or a specific spiritual quest. Some use counting back methods to slow the mind, and others focus on symbols. All these variations still qualify as meditations whose end goal is to alter the consciousness to allow us to shape our reality at will and to connect with the divine—which is, after all, the principal pursuit of all religions, Witchcraft included. With practice in meditation and sustained concentration, your altered states will become longer and deeper. The key is learning to concentrate on one item or issue for increasingly longer periods of time.

There are almost as many methods of inducing an altered state of consciousness as there are Witches, and eventually you will settle on one you like. The two exercises in this chapter will help get you started understanding and practicing meditative techniques. If during any of these, or any other altered-state exercises, you notice your mind starting to wander, don't get frustrated and stop. This will happen when you are learning. It even happens occasionally when you are experienced at the process. Just bring your attention gently back to the exercise and keep going.

Be sure to get comfortable before you start. Find a position, seated or lying down, in which your arms and legs are not crossed in any way. Crossing them puts stress on the joints and impedes circulation. While this might not bother you at first, after thirty minutes of holding one position you will begin to feel very uncomfortable and this will not be conducive to good meditation. You will also need a quiet place to meditate where you can be sure of being undisturbed for at least a half hour (longer is better).

Altered State Exercise 1

Relax your body and take a few deep breaths. Mentally and physically try to release all the tension points in your body. Then look around you and select an object to study for the next half hour or so. Allow your eyes to settle on it in a relaxed, half-opened manner. Do not stare. This is another stress builder and is not compatible with your goal. Focus all your concentration on the object to the exclusion of all else. Contemplate the object's texture, recall what it feels like to touch it, try to imagine all the hands that have held it over time. Focus on its shape, its size, its color, and what it means to you. Why is it here in the first place?

Keep practicing until you can do this for at least five minutes without your mind seeking other recreation.

Altered State Exercise 2

Close your eyes and take a few deep breaths. Allow your body to relax fully. You may want to employ a classic meditative inductive technique like mentally counting backwards, falling through space, or sailing over a rainbow to help you achieve the slowed brain activity you need.

When you are ready, focus your mind on the same object you used in Exercise 1. Contemplate it from all the angles you did when your eyes were open, only this time use your powers of visualization to do the work.

Keep practicing until you can do this for at least five minutes without your mind wandering.

Practice both of these exercises with other objects. Start with very simple items, and then try more complex ones with more curves, colors, parts, et cetera. The more complex they are, the better your visualization skills will have to be. Practice mentally placing the item in different settings, places, and times until you feel you can hold a mental picture of anything you choose for at least five minutes.

Other methods of helping take you down into an alpha or lower state include:

- Counting backwards from one hundred
- Visualizing yourself falling through endless space
- Counting your breath each time you exhale
- Focusing your consciousness on the center of your mind
- Reciting a mantra, or phrase which has meaning to you (a single word or short sentence is sufficient)
- Gazing into a candle flame or dark water until your eyes become heavy and your mind slowed
- Taking deep rhythmic breaths
- Visualizing a blank screen in your mind; attempting to think of nothing
- Sitting completely still and focusing on the rhythm of your heartbeats

After you find a method of altered state induction that you like and that works for you, it is best to stick with it. Once your deep mind (sometimes referred to as the Higher Self) has been conditioned to the process, it will quickly understand what you want of it each time you begin to meditate and you will find achieving an altered state of consciousness to be incredibly swift.

You can increase the speed at which you reach an alpha or lower state by combining your chosen induction method with a physical trigger. This can be a gesture, word, or position. In Tibet, the Zen masters liked to adopt what they referred to as a *mudra* position, a way of holding the fingers together while they meditated. The most popular of these was holding the pads of the thumb and forefinger together as they began their quest for an altered state. With long-term practice, using such a gesture in tandem with your regular induction method can produce an almost instantaneous descent into the theta levels.

Don't get discouraged if you feel you are not progressing with altered state work as quickly as you would like. I would be willing to bet that you are doing much better than you think. Acquiring an altered state is a subtle shift in reality, not one that stands up and screams at you demanding to be noticed. If you do feel you need some extra help, Witches have many tricks in their magickal repertoire that can help put the mind into these receptive states without resorting to harsh chemicals that work very well on paper but do not allow the Witch to remain in control of the process.

Taking a purifying bath prior to altered state, or meditation, work is a time-honored Pagan practice, and is in itself a ritual. In a cheese cloth or soap bag, place dried herbs known for their purifying effects on the body and spirit (see below). Leaving the herbs loose in the bath is a sure way to clog your drain, and they can be a real challenge to comb out of your hair. Trust me on this—I made these mistakes once and have no wish to repeat them, especially paying another large plumbing bill! You may also want to add a large handful of oatmeal to the bag to help keep the water soft and less irritating to the skin. Becoming itchy during a meditation is a guaranteed way to spoil it.

Herbs generally thought to have strong purifying powers include basil, bay, camphor, heather, hyssop, lemon, parsley, pepper, peppermint, rosemary, sage, and turmeric.[3] You may use just one or any combination of these in your bath. As you run your bath water, place the bag in the tub near the faucet so the force of the running water can release the energies of the herbs. Visualize the cleansing power of the herbs filling the water. As you step into the tub, begin to imagine all the impurities of body, mind, and spirit being pulled away from you and trapped in the water, leaving behind a balanced, vibrant you.

As you continue to soak, focus on the goal of your upcoming meditation—even if that goal is merely learning the basics! Don't strain to do this. Simply lie back and daydream, allowing yourself to become relaxed, contemplative, and centered on your purpose. When you can no longer maintain your thoughts in the right direction, it is time to stop. Before getting out, pull the plug from the drain, allowing the water to exit while you are still sitting in the tub. You will feel gravity begin to pull on you more strongly as the water drains—an excellent sensation for helping to focus on a new, purer self. Visualize all those impurities being taken down the drain into Mother Earth, where they are grounded harmlessly away from you.

If you do not have a bathtub, or prefer not to bathe prior to meditation, you can substitute an herbal tea made from ingredients that have purifying affinities. You can also add to this herbs that help open the psychic channels, or those ruled by the element with which you hope to work to help you attune to its energies.

---

3. Four good texts to consult on the magickal/ritual associations of herbs and oils are Scott Cunningham's *Cunningham's Encyclopedia of Magical Herbs* (Llewellyn, 1985), or his *The Complete Book of Incense, Oils and Brews* (Llewellyn, 1989); Richard Alan Miller's *The Magical and Ritual Use of Herbs* (Destiny Books, 1983), or Paul Beyerl's *The Master Book of Herbalism* (Phoenix, 1984).

In a tea ball, place a total of one total teaspoon of herbs, mixed or singly, for each cup of tea you wish to brew. Choose from one or any combination of the following to get started. Some of them do not smell particularly pleasant, and others do not taste very good. Remember that in magickal herbalism (also known as "wort cunning") it is the final outcome that is important, and many herbal preparations leave a lot to be desired in the aesthetics department. Herbs that make excellent teas to help open those psychic centers are anise, catnip, eyebright, jasmine, rose hips, mugwort, or valerian.

I love to use valerian, and consider it to be one of the best psychic enhancers there is. It is not addictive or harmful in small, infrequent doses, and its energies seem to aid us in keeping an inner focus. But valerian has two serious drawbacks. First of all, it is a strong sedative, which can make some people too sleepy to focus. Secondly, it smells pretty awful. I have found that adding peppermint to it cuts the smell and improves the taste significantly. If you find you simply cannot work with valerian try my second favorite psychic herb—catnip.

Before ingesting any herb, it is wise to take a few preliminary precautions. First of all, make absolutely sure you know exactly what herb you are taking. Many herbs resemble one another, and sometimes only an expert can tell them apart. More than a few herbs are deadly poison, and some nontoxic herbs can still cause serious physical damage to the body if used over a prolonged period. Otherwise benign herbs can sometimes cause severe allergic reactions in sensitive people. Unless you are a highly skilled botanist, it is best to get your herbs from a mail order supplier or local garden shop, which can sell you the whole plant or seeds. It is also wise never to take large or protracted doses of any herb without consulting a qualified botanist or doctor.

Grounding Excess Energy

I briefly mentioned at the end of chapter 1 that after any magickal operation all excess energy should be grounded into Mother Earth. There is *always* excess energy! No matter how well you think you have sent out the energy you have raised, you can never get rid of it all. Think of your energy sending as being similar to cooking. No matter how nonstick your pots are, there is always something left to clean up.

Magickal energy, left to its own devices, will eventually die for lack of being fed fresh energy reserves, but in the meantime it can be a grand nuisance. Take it from someone who has been there that these are situations you do not want to court. Uncontrolled magickal energy can make you feel jittery and restless and it can knock about your house, giving you a feeling of being haunted. It can also turn against you if it falls into a place in your home where the energy patterns are negative, such as where there has been an argument, and then it will become negatively charged and roaming free throughout your home, looking for a place to land.

Fortunately the solution is simple. Just ground the energy!

The easiest and most popular way to ground energy is to place the palms of your hands flat on the ground or floor while visualizing the excess draining away from you. This only takes about thirty seconds of your time and can save you lots of hassles in the long run. I always take a deep, relaxing breath and exhale as I ground. This allows me to relax so I can sense if any "unrelaxed" residual energy is still in me. I describe these as psychic stress points, spots that feel irritated when I focus on them. Try this and in a short while you will instantly know when you are through grounding and when you are not.

You can also ground through the soles of your feet whether or not you are wearing shoes. Simply follow the same procedure you would use for your hands. I often use the soles of the feet for grounding when I am at work and feeling jittery, or when I am collecting too much of the negative energy that inevitably invades the workplace. As with your hands, simply place your feet flat on the floor and exhale as you visualize the excess energy sinking to your feet and passing out of you.

Remember that magickal operations ultimately take place in the mind and that you can successfully ground even if you are in a plane six miles above the Earth! From your sitting position, draw all the excess energy into your chakras. Mentally draw down a beam of cleansing energy from high above you and allow it to enter your crown chakra and filter down through it to your root center. As it travels downward see it taking away all the excess energy, leaving each chakra clean, open, and calm. Allow the beam to continue out through the root chakra and down into the ground far below you. Keep up the visualization until you are sure all the excess has been expelled.

Practice Schedule for Magickal Novices

Practice is vital when you start learning any new craft. Until you become proficient at these basic magickal skills, you should set up a weekly routine that includes all of them in varying degrees. You do not have to do all of these skills every day—there just wouldn't be time, and Witchcraft, though a discipline, is meant to enhance your life, not hinder it.

For the first few months I recommend beginners follow a schedule that includes a daily meditation and visualization practice, a balancing and centering practice three times a week, and a power raising/sending practice twice weekly. Each practice session should end with a formal grounding of all excess energies.

After the first three months you can cut your meditations down to three times a week without harming your progress. Practice your visualization, balancing, and power raising/sending as needed. All sessions must still end with proper grounding.

If this schedule sounds too rigorous to you, you may want to rethink your commitment to Witchcraft. Ask anyone who has had some experience in teaching the Craft and they will tell you that a great many students are lost when they realize just how much work is involved in mastering the basic Craft skills. Those of you who persevere will eventually discover that all this "Witch stuff" has become a natural part of your life and that you can call on these skills as easily as a concert pianist practices playing scales.

Times When Magickal Skills Should not Be Practiced

Even though I have tried to emphasize the fact that, properly done, magick will not deplete your own energy stores to a serious level, it does require effort and that in itself can sometimes be tiring. Just as you wouldn't go out and run a marathon if you were under extreme stress or feeling ill, you shouldn't overtax an already overexerted system with magickal effort either.

It is wise to avoid strenuous magickal work when you are ill, tired, angry, or under the influence of other negative emotions such as fear, jealousy, hatred, or extreme stress. When you are ill or tired you simply will not be able to think and focus properly, and the energy centers of your body will be out of balance as they work to heal you. You don't need to strain them unnecessarily with magickal practice. When you are angry you will not be drawing on positive energy, but on negative, and you do not want to get into the habit of working with negative energies. They can feel very powerful, and they can be addictive, but in the end they are counterproductive to your goals.

The magickal arts should always be approached holistically, with a balanced body and mind, and with a positive "harm none" attitude. Only then will the rewards be worth the output.

▼

3

Connecting with
the Elements

Since before recorded history, humans have cherished their magickal beliefs. One of the most prevalent of these beliefs is that certain basic components, called elements, rest at the core of all creation, and that all things contain the properties of one or more of these elements. Each thing in creation is believed to have one principal element that rules or governs both its internal and external characteristics above all the others.

These elemental teachings are among the first lessons taught to newcomers to Witchcraft. This system of correspondences that give our elements their characteristics can at first be confusing. The late Wiccan Scott Cunningham wrote that "it is unwise to view the four elements in purely physical terms;"[1] yet when we we begin to look at the tools traditionally associated with them, we are faced with items that are physical and appear to be representative of the most physical aspects of each element. Unfortunately, when we discuss the metaphysical, we have no choice but to talk in concrete, material metaphors. We humans are corporeal beings, and these physical descriptions are easy for us to relate to. Sometimes they are all we can relate to. Unfortunately, this semantic problem has caused a great deal of difficulties for students of the occult, and for many new Pagans as well.

By learning about each object's elemental properties and rulers, our ancestors found they could connect with all creation on an intimate level, using this connection to gain knowledge, advance spiritually, and manipulate articles to work at their will. In other words, they could use the elements to make *magick*. This belief was well summarized in the sixteenth century by occultist Cornelius Agrippa:

> There are four elements . . . of which all elemented
> inferior bodies are compounded; not by way of
> heaping them together, but by transmutation and
> union; and when they are destroyed, they are
> resolved into elements. For there is none of the
> sensible elements that is pure, but they are more
> or less mixed, and apt to be changed one into the
> other. . . .And this is the root and foundation of all
> bodies, natures, virtues, and wonderful works; and
> he which shall know these qualities of the elements,
> and their mixations, shall easily bring to pass such
> things that are wonderful and astonishing, and shall
> be perfect in magick.[2]

The elements are earth, water, fire, and air.[3] As Migene González-Wippler states, "These elements and their different compositions are at the root of all matter and extend beyond into the realm of spirit."[4] Because they are part of all creation, they exist in both the seen and the unseen worlds, all coalescing in a fifth "element" we know as spirit, which is in and of all elements. This unity of the elements in spirit enables us to use them to draw down the powers of the unseen worlds into our physical world—a definition of magick at its most basic! Experienced Witches know that magick ultimately takes place in the mind, but we also know that it somehow has to translate itself into the physical for it to be called successful. Whether we are consciously aware of it or not, it is the elements themselves we harness to weave the tapestry of reality from the depths of our imagination.

Not only can we pull down universal, or divine, energy through the elements, using their powers to create manifest reality from the thought forms we project into the unseen world (see chapter 9), we can also travel up them to reach the spiritual realm through the world of the divine, an ancient art we call mysticism. Traveling up through increasingly less dense aspects of the elements, we can eventually reach the Godhead, a metaphor for that state of unity with the creator that has been sought diligently by mystics since humanity first recognized a creative force greater than ourselves.

The great appeal of the elements is simply knowing they are a part of all that is, which reduces everything into manageable pieces that can be easily analyzed in order to help us understand and use them magickally. We humans are not exempt from this pattern of creation. The elements are part of us as well; by studying how each one manifests its characteristics in our personalities, health, and thinking, we can learn to better understand ourselves. When we understand the elements we lack, or that are too prominent, we can work to correct these imbalances to improve all aspects of both our inner and outer lives.

In the rituals and magick of modern Witches, the elements are honored by being called to witness our circles, used as catalysts for spells when the need or goal is governed by a particular element, and can be contacted to help fill holes and gaps in our inner selves. Tools that symbolize each element are placed on Wiccan altars to symbolize balance and harmony and to help us attune with the powers and attributes of the elements (see chapter 6).

1. *Earth Power* (Llewellyn, 1983), 21.

2. Donald Tyson, ed. *Three Books of Occult Philosophy by Cornelius Agrippa* (Llewellyn, 1995), 8 (originally published 1531).

3. Though many magickal writers, both ceremonial magicians and Pagans, refer to this quartet as being a universal absolute, there is at least one noted exception. In the Chinese magickal traditions there are five elements: earth, metal, wood, fire, and water.

4. *The Complete Book of Spells, Ceremonies and Magic* (Llewellyn, 1988), 79.

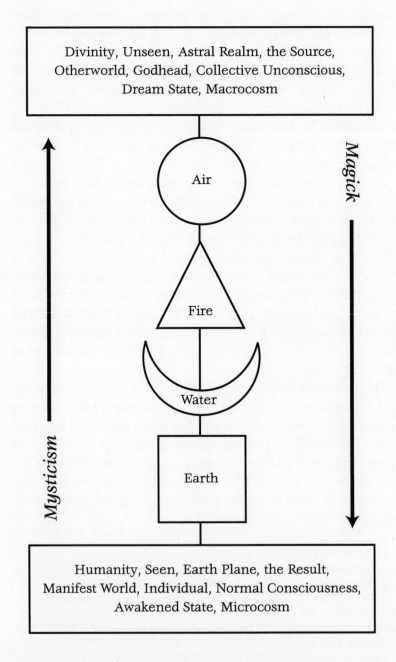

The Difference Between Magick and Mysticism

Writings about the elements and their mystical and magickal aspects can be found in the mythological collections of
most every culture. From these stories, many based on the observations and spiritual practices of ancient peoples, magicians and mystics of today have literally centuries of elemental knowledge to draw upon to help us understand and work
with them. But having a reading knowledge is not enough if
we wish to reach the full magick potential they offer. We have
to delve deeper, lifting the veil of mystery separating our
physical consciousness from the universal, and literally step
into the world where the elements live and rule.

Some Witches make the mistake of thinking that the elements are merely essences of something spiritual rather than
being sentient, spiritual entities in their own right. The very
fact that when we cast our circles of containment and protection we call upon the elemental beings of each directional
quarter should awaken us to the fact that these are real entities, and not figments of the magickal imagination (see circle
casting information in chapter 6). Agrippa refers to this sentience as the soul of the elements, the inner spirit required of
all beings who wish to create and who wish to connect their
spiritual selves with all other living things.[5] Like all sentient
beings, the elements can decide to like, love, or hate us, and
they can grant or withhold their favors, depending on their
opinion of our worthiness to possess their gifts.

There is a popular Pagan writer who insists that the elements have no sentience, only energies we can draw on. I
find that point of view sad and completely contradictory to
standard Pagan practice. Anyone who has been in the Craft
for a while can tell you that pools of water, blazing fires, or
even stones can find ways to communicate their feelings and
intent to us if we let them. In fact, there are quite a few books
on the market that teach just how to do this. This sentience is
due largely to the presence of elemental nature spirits who
live in the physical manifestations of the elements and animate them the same way our souls, or life forces, animate us.

5. Tyson, p. 419.

In Europe these spirits are called *numina,* and the Native Americans know them as the *manitou.* When we call out to a stone it is the numina who answers, just as when someone talks to you, or asks you to throw your energy behind a task, it is ultimately your soul who responds and moves your physical body to action. If that soul were to leave your body, it would drop into a lifeless heap. As long as you are alive your soul and body are wedded together, allowing your physical form to manifest energy to meet your desires or the needs of others. The same is true with the elements.

Our Pagan ancestors knew that arrogance in the face of the elements was counterproductive but that a willingness to seek them out, as one would any worthy teacher, would yield valuable results. They knew that learning to understand the elements at their deepest levels brought great rewards, including the complete mastery of that element in magick. To do this they had to be receptive to the teachings of the elements, to respect their power, and then accept their challenge to grow by entering the elemental realm itself, facing its terrors and splendors and emerging to put that hard-won knowledge to work in the physical world.

Being granted mastery of the elements makes all our own attempts at creation easier. Whether we seek spiritual knowledge, magickal goals, or if we are merely trying to live in harmony with nature, being granted access to the basic building blocks of creation is more necessary than incidental. In his *The 21 Lessons of Merlin,*[6] a book about the Druidic magickal arts, author Douglas Monroe includes a compelling look at an elemental adventure he terms "The Wild Hunt." In Celtic mythology the hunt is a metaphor for the nightly ventures of the Gods of the otherworld who roam the earth seeking souls to teach, challenge, or take back. Translated from macrocosmic terms into a microcosmic concept, the hunt becomes a high-stakes game between the magician and the elemental forces he or she hopes to master. Monroe describes the deliberate unleashing of these elemental forces, the all-night challenge to keep one step ahead of them while racing through an elemental obstacle course over a predetermined territory, the winner retaining mastery of the elemental forces of the area where the battle of wills has been fought.

Certainly these venerable magicians of the past would not have undertaken so arduous an event for mere sport, nor would they have taken the challenge so seriously had they felt they were dealing with unthinking essences rather than sentient beings, or with the trivial rather than the consequential. They entered the contest knowing full well who and what they were up against, and knew any hazards were worth the risks because the wager was well worth winning.

As skilled magickal folks have shown us through the centuries, the only way to know and work successfully with the elements is to *experience* them for yourself. Magickal textbooks—this one included—can only explain what you ought to know about the elements; only you can take those fragments of learning and turn them into true wisdom. With wisdom comes power. The elements are part of all that is—a key to understanding both the self and the divine, to making magick, to traveling the inner planes with ease, and for linking the modern working Pagan to the primal powers of nature, of which the divine are a part. All together the elements make the full *circle* of magick, symbolic of our place in the ever-turning wheel of eternity and completeness. Learn to know the elements, and you will inherit their power. They will become a part of you on all levels of your being, and will yield unto you their greatest gifts.[7]

Elemental Attributes

Each of the elements has activities, objects, and ideas with which it shares an affinity. In magickal terms we often say that everything is ruled or governed by a particular element, meaning that its dominant characteristics share those of either earth, water, fire, or air. Many activities and objects

---

6. Llewellyn, 1992, pp. 297–310.

7. Advanced Craft practitioners may wish to look ahead to chapter 10, which discusses the art of astrally entering the elemental world through the Indian tattwa symbols.

have secondary elemental rulers as well, and a careful study of the magick you hope to achieve should reveal to you what these are. It is for this reason that some activities and objects are listed below as being under the rulership of two different elements.

The elements are also said to be either feminine or masculine in character. These ancient labels sometimes seem out of place in our modern world, and their use has caused some squabbles among various Pagan traditions. Just as the elements are not really physical in nature, but only described that way, they also do not have a specific gender. The feminine and masculine qualities we speak about are metaphysical, representing receptive and fertile qualities versus projective and barren ones. Where the feminine elements encourage magickal change through growth and construction, the masculine elements cause change by restraint and destruction. Again, construction and destruction are magickal terms, and neither are inherently good or evil, and both can lead to positive ends. For example, fire burns and destroys, but it can be destroying something we don't need in our lives. On the other hand, earth encourages growth and manifestation, but not all magickal manifestations are positive, even when our best intentions try to make them so.

Earth

Earth is the densest of all elements, the one most closely linked to our physical world, a place often referred to as the earth plane. This feminine element is the realm of stability, growth, and the Mother Goddess, a place to sink our roots as we stretch out our arms and reach toward new experiences.

Activities and objects governed by the earth element include fertility, pregnancy, prosperity, grounding, stabilization, children, money, planting, growth, the home, harvesting, pets, cattle, serpents, burrowing animals, buried objects, dancing, many stones, tubers, image magick, and drumming.

All plants, trees, and grasses have earth as either a primary or secondary ruler, though they may be chiefly governed by another. An example are the "fiery" or hot spicy plants from which we get cayenne or cinnamon, which are principally under the rulership of fire.

The following chart outlines some, but not all, of the items, herbs, beings, et cetera, that are governed by or are associated with the earth element. Those who are sincerely interested in magick have been known to chronicle pages and pages of such information, some taken from other sources, and some gleaned through personal experimentation.

When working with elemental magick, and until your elemental insights start to come instinctively, it is wise to refer to a chart such as this for helping you decide what herb is best in an earth-elemented spell, what direction to face, which non-physical entities might be most sympathetic to your need, which stone shares an affinity for your goal, et cetera. For instance, if you were wanting to create a spell for fertility—a goal governed by earth—you might look to this chart and see that you would probably want to orient yourself facing north, perhaps work the spell at midnight, use a drum or some clay as a tool to direct the elemental power, use the herb bistort as a catalyst to your need (see chapter 4 for more on catalysts), and call upon the name of the Goddess Eriu.

Even if you just want to understand earth better, the chart can give you suggestions for surrounding yourself with the essence of earth, a big boon prior to the elemental exploration meditations found on page 69. For example, clutching a bowl of salt or feeling the presence of friendly Brownies can make your earth elemental connections easier and more insightful.

The precise uses of a few of the correspondences mentioned below are used mostly in magickal systems outside of Paganism/Wicca (such as the archangels) while others belong to the realm of very advanced practice (such as working with some of the elementals or the kerubs) and are not covered in this book. They are presented here so that you have a fairly complete idea of what types of things make up a standard elemental correspondences list.

Earth Correspondences Chart

Gender: Feminine

Season(s): Autumn or winter

Wiccan Directional Attribute: North

Other Directional Attribute: Any, depending on
  Pagan tradition followed

Days: None

Celtic Time of Day: Midnight

Astrological Signs: Taurus, Virgo, Capricorn

Planet: Earth

Colors: Brown, green, blue, yellow

Chakra: Root (at base of tailbone)

Archangel: Uriel

Kerub: Bull

Tools: Disk, carved wood block (the pentacle), hammer,
  stones, clay, bowl of earth, salt, double-headed axe,
  shield, wheel, necklace, club, roots, drum, bronze, bow,
  animal fur/pelts, sand, mallet

Irish Name: Talamh

Sanskrit Name: Prithivi

Qualities: Stabilizing, grounding

Sense: Smell

Properties: Cold and dryness

Alchemical Symbol: Inverted triangle bisected by
  a horizontal line

Tattwa Symbol: Yellow square

Magickal Associations: Fertility, magick for the home
  and animals, eco-magick, prosperity/wealth, healing,
  centering/grounding

Stones: Amazonite, cat's eye, emerald, geodes, jade,
  jet, malachite, olivine, peridot, turquoise

Metals: Lead, mercury

Elemental King: Gnome

Other Elementals: Attorcroppes, Brownies, Bwbachs, Clurichauns, Elves, Fireesins, Gruagachs, Huldrafolk, Knockers, Kolbalds, Korreds, Leprechauns, Menehunas, Skogrsas, Sylvans, Trolls, Zips

Tarot Suit: Pentacles or Stones

Tarot Card: The Empress

Runes: Fehu, wunjo, jera, berkano, mannaz, othala

Animals: Snakes, burrowing animals, and many spiders

Celtic Sacred Trees: Ash, Dwarf Elm, Hawthorn

Herbs and Plants: Alfalfa, barley, bistort, cotton, horse-tail, mugwort, vetivert, patchouly, pine

Kaballistic Sephira (from Hebrew Tree of Life): Malkuth (Kingdom)

Gods: Dagon (Phoenician), Ishuara (Hindi), Aker (Egyptian), Ashi Nadzuchi (Japanese) Mullas (Mayan), Consus (Roman), Hapi (Egyptian), Nai-No-Kami (Japanese), Natigai (Mongolian), Onamuji (African), Tekeitsertok (Inuit)

Goddesses: Odudud (West African), Eriu (Irish), Tellus Mater (Roman), Habondia (Celto-Germanic), Aeracura (Celtic), Erce (Slavic), Zemyna (Lithuanian), Yak (Malaysian), Waramurungundji (Aboriginal), Taillte (Irish), Mati (Slavic), Gaia (Greek), Hybla (Italian), Beruth (Phoenician), Apia-Fellus (Scythian), Coatlicue (Aztec), Ma-Emma (Baltic), Isong (West African), Hertha (Teutonic)

Water

Water is the other feminine element, one linked to the mysteries and magick of the moon. It is dense in nature but still possesses fluidity, which is why it is linked to profound change and inner transformations. In many cultures the Land of the Dead is perceived as being below or across a body of water to which the soul must return before it can be rebirthed. Water is also the home of our psychic selves, which governs our intuition and dreams.

Activities and objects governed by water are childbirth, pregnancy, cleansing, inner transformation, psychic endeavors, divination, purification, the emotions, romantic love, spirit manifestations, death, rebirth, past life explorations, and fish and many other sea creatures.

All liquids have water as a primary ruler, but some raw materials that go into the making of certain drinks are ruled by other elements. For example, coffee beans are generally thought to be ruled by air, but when made into a beverage, they fall into the realm of water.

The following chart outlines some, but not all, of the items, herbs, beings, et cetera, which are governed by or are associated with the water element. If you wanted to create a spell for self-purification, you would see that purification is one of the known qualities of water. You would see that you might want to choose a chalice for your tool to direct the water energy, face west as you do the spell, or choose the stone beryl as a catalyst.

Even if you just want to understand the water element better, the chart can give you suggestions for surrounding yourself with water's essence, a big boon prior to the elemental exploration meditations found on page 72. Clutching a sickle or feeling the presence of friendly water sprites can make your elemental connections easier and more insightful.

Water Correspondences Chart

Gender: Feminine

Season(s): Autumn or winter

Wiccan Directional Attribute: West

Other Directional Attribute: Any, depending on Pagan tradition followed

Days: Monday, Friday

Celtic Time of Day: Dusk

Astrological Signs: Cancer, Scorpio, Pisces

Planet: Moon

Colors: Silver, purple, white, blue, indigo

Chakra: Navel (just below the belly button)

Archangel: Gabriel

Kerub: Eagle

Tools: Cup, chalice, cauldron, hollow horn, bowl, pitcher, goblet, ring, wine cask, barrel, silver items, any cool liquid, tea kettle, shells, paint brushes, sickle

Irish Name: Uisce

Sanskrit Name: Apas

Qualities: Purifying, contracting

Sense: Taste

Properties: Cold and dampness

Alchemical Symbol: An inverted triangle

Tattwa Symbol: Silver crescent with horns pointing upward

Magickal Associations: Love and romance, psychic power, astral travel, dream work, meditation/pathworking, healing, spiritual pursuits, childbirth, death/rebirth, spirit contact

Stones: Amethyst, aquamarine, beryl, chalcedony, coral, lapis lazuli, marble, moonstone, pearl, sapphire, selenite, sodalite

Metals: Copper, silver

Elemental King: Undine

Other Elementals: Alvens, Ashrays, Banshees, Nixies, Merpeople, Glaistigs, Kelpies, Shoneys, the Leanansidhe, the Lorelei, Ly Ergs, Mal-de-Mers, Rusalkis, Selkies, Shelleycoats, Snow Faeries

Tarot Suit: Cups

Tarot Cards: Death, The Moon

Runes: Uruz, gebo, hagalaz, isa, pethro, ehwaz, laguz, dagaz

Animals: Fish and other aquatic creatures

Celtic Sacred Trees: Alder, Hazel, Linden, Reed, Rowan, White Poplar, Willow, Yew

Continued

Herbs and Plants: Belladonna, blackberry, jasmine,
vanilla, lotus, valerian, yarrow, lilac, mesquite,
comfrey, burdock, camphor, myrrh, orris

Kaballistic Sephirot: Hod (Splendor), Chesed (Mercy),
Binah (Understanding)

Gods: Poseidon (Greek), Neptune (Roman), Lir (Welsh),
Mannanan (Irish), Achelous (Greek), Indra (Hindi),
Aegir (Norse), Alphaeus (Greek), Apo (Persian),
Apsu (Babylonian), Chiaga (Central American),
Ea (Chaldaean), Dylan (Welsh), Imset (Egyptian),
Inachus (Greek), Bn-ym (Phoenician), Tamesis
(English), Melqart (Phoenician), Nakki (Finnish)
Ngurvillu (South American), Nun (Egyptian),
Oluksak (Inuit), Proteus (Greek), Untunktahe
(Native North American), Yamm (Babylonian)

Goddesses: Sequana (Celtic), Boann (Irish), Amphitrite
(Greek), Cleone (Greek), Doris (Greek), Fand (Irish),
Anuket (Greek), Liban (Irish), Ganga (Hindi), Nammu
(Sumerian), Jurate (Baltic), Sarasvati (Hindi), Ran
(Norse), Rosmerta (Celtic), Huixtocihuatl (Aztec), Juras
Mate (Lithuanian), Venus (Greek), Cacce-Jienne
(Lapp), Ceibhfhionn (Irish)

Fire

Fire is a vibrant, masculine element whose principal attribute
is action. Often symbolized by the sun, it is the realm of transformation, passion, and abruptness.

Activities and objects governed by fire include transformation, protection, employment, legal matters, destruction/con-
struction, acting, sex, sex magick, strength, lust, cleansing,
candles, hearths, exorcism, banishing, and lizards and many
other reptiles.

The following chart outlines some, but not all, of the items,
herbs, beings, et cetera, which are governed by or are associated with the fire element. If you were preparing a spell to
create passion, you would look on the chart and find that this

is an area governed by fire. You would also see that you might want to choose a red candle for your tool to direct the fire energy, face south at noon as you do the spell, or choose the golden stone known as pyrite as a catalyst.

Even if your goal for the time being is just to better understand the fire element, the chart can give you suggestions for surrounding yourself with fire's essence and give a boost to the elemental exploration meditations found on page 75. Clutching a symbol of fire, gazing into the fire alchemical symbol, or feeling the presence of friendly fire faeries can make your elemental connections deeper and more insightful.

Fire Correspondences Chart

Gender: Masculine

Season: Summer

Wiccan Directional Attribute: South

Other Directional Attribute: Any, depending on Pagan tradition followed

Day: Sunday

Celtic Time of Day: Noon

Astrological Signs: Aries, Leo, Sagittarius

Planets: Sun, Mars

Colors: Red, gold, yellow, orange

Chakra: Solar plexus (center of stomach)

Archangel: Michael

Kerub: Lion

Tools: Candle, all blades forged in fire, wand, red or orange stones, pike, claymore, matches, flint, ashes, wheel, torch, bracelet, solar disk (equilateral cross in circle), besom, gold, spear, lariat, scourge/whip, ram's horn, fan, pen/pencil, letter opener, shepherd's crook

Irish Name: Tine

Sanskrit Name: Tejas

Qualities: Transformative, expansive

Sense: Sight

Properties: Heat and dryness

Alchemical Symbol: An upright triangle

Tattwa Symbol: Upright red triangle

Magickal Associations: Banishing/exorcism, strength, passion/lust, employment, protection, change, sex magick, legal matters, courage, anger, curse breaking, fidelity

Stones: Amber, Apache tear, bloodstone, carnelian, citrine, diamond, flint, garnet, obsidian, onyx, rhodocrosite, ruby, tiger's eyes, topaz, zircon

Metals: Brass, gold, steel

Elemental King: Salamander

Other Elementals: Brown Men, Drakes, Gwyllions, Oakmen, the Red Cap, Will o' the Wisps

Tarot Suit: Wands

Tarot Cards: The Emperor, Strength, The Sun

Runes: Thurisaz, kenaz, naudhiz, sowilo, ingwaz

Animals: Reptiles dwelling above ground, like tree lizards; animals symbolizing strength, like the bear and lion

Celtic Sacred Trees: Blackthorn, Holly, Ivy, Oak, Silver Fir

Herbs and Plants: Allspice, basil, bay cinnamon, dill, fennel, garlic, ginseng, ginger, gorse, hyssop, rosemary, thistle, wormwood, tobacco

Kaballistic Sephirot: Netzach (Victory), Geburah (Judgment), Chokmah (Wisdom)

Gods: Prometheus (Greek), Lugh (Irish), Agni (Hindi), Atar (Persian), Auahi Turoa (Aboriginal), Da-Bog (Slavic), Futsunushi (Japanese), Gibil (Babylonian), Kago-Zuchi (Japanese), Duamutef (Egyptian), Govannon (Celtic), Katcochila (Native North American), Matarisuan (Hindi), Ogun (West African),

Svarozhich (Slavic), Tohil (Central American),
Ueueteotl (Aztec), Vulcan (Roman), Wekwek
(Native North American), Xiuhtectli (Aztec)

Goddesses: Yamaya (West African), Brighid (Irish), Aine
(Irish), Maia (Greek), Vesta (Roman), Yolkaiestsan (Native North American), Loo-Wit (Native North American), Davata (Hindi), Feronia (Italian), Pele (Polyne-
sian), Fuji (Japanese), Holika (Indian),
Chuginadak (Inuit), Aetna (Italian), Hestia (Greek),
Grian (Irish), Lucina (Italian)

Air

Air is the least dense of the elements and the one living closest to the world of spirit. This masculine element governs the
unpredictable realm of the human mind, where all things we
wish to manifest must first be conceived.

Activities and objects governed by the air element are intellect, study, writing, the elderly, astral travel, communication,
music, sound, weather magick, birds, and power raising.

The following chart outlines some, but not all, of the items,
herbs, beings, et cetera, which are governed by or are associated with the air element. If you were working out a spell for
increasing your intellectual powers—an arena governed by
air—you might choose to use lots of blue or yellow in the spell
(in your clothing, altar cloths, candles, et cetera), face east as
you do it, or perhaps use a consecrated blade of some sort as a
tool to direct the air energy.

Even if your goal at this point is just to better understand the
air element, the chart can give you suggestions for surrounding yourself with items that capture air's essence, something
that can help boost your appreciation and enjoyment of the elemental exploration meditations found on page 77. Having a
gentle incense of lavender burning nearby, gazing into the air
tattwa symbol (for more on tattwas, see chapter 10), or facing
east as you meditate may make your elemental connections
easier and more insightful.

Air Correspondences Chart

Gender: Masculine

Season: Spring

Wiccan Directional Attribute: East

Other Directional Attribute: Any, depending on
   Pagan tradition followed

Day: Wednesday

Celtic Time of Day: Dawn

Astrological Signs: Gemini, Libra, Aquarius

Planet: Neptune

Colors: Yellow, pale blue

Chakra: Heart Center (area of breastbone)

Archangel: Rafael

Kerub: Human being

Tools: Staff, trident, stang, athame, wand, sword,
   feather, incense, sling, claymore, pike, axe, dagger,
   spear, javelin, earrings, club, besom, wind instruments,
   smoking pipe, copper, arrow, scourge/whip, lariat

Irish Name: Aer

Sanskrit Name: Vayu

Quality: Mobilization, swiftness

Sense: Touch

Properties: Heat and dampness

Alchemical Symbol: An upright triangle bisected by
   a horizontal line

Tattwa Symbol: Blue circle

Magickal Associations: Travel, astral travel, intellectual
   matters, communication, musical spells, fidelity

Stones: Adventurine, mica, pumice, sphene, meteorites

Metals: Aluminum, tin

Elemental King: Sylph

Other Elementals: Bocans, Chi Spirits, Djinn, Dryads, the
   Fachan, Foletti, Flygiars, Gryphons, Gremlins, Leshess,
   Lobs, Orculli, Phookas, Pixies, Pillywiggins, Spriggans

Tarot Suit: Swords or Blades

Tarot Cards: The Hermit, Wheel of Fortune

Runes: Ansuz, raidho, eihwaz, tiwaz

Animals: Birds and flying insects

Celtic Sacred Trees: Alder, Birch

Herbs and Plants: Agrimony, dandelion, hops, lavender, marjoram, mistletoe, holly, parsley

Kaballistic Sepherot: Yesod (Foundation), Tipharet (Beauty)

Gods: Ioskeha (Native North American), Aleion (Phoenician), Aquillo (Roman), Boreas (Greek), Auster (Roman), Awhiowhio (Aboriginal), Ecalchot (Central American), Ehecatl (Aztec), Enlil (Sumerian), Esaugetuh (Native North American), Zephyrus (Greek), Shu (Egyptian), Favonius (Roman), Hino (Native North American), Qebesenuf (Egyptian), Ilma (Finnish), Meuler (Incan), Tatsuta Hiko (Japanese), Ukko (Finnish), Vaya (Hindi)

Goddesses: Oya (West African), Feng Pho-Pho (Chinese), Guabancez (Central American), Mardeq Avalon (Russian), Ninlil (Babylonian), Shina-to-be (Japanese), Yondung Halmoni (Korean), Iphigenia (Greek)

Spirit

The fifth element is spirit, which has no gender association and is accorded no one single place inside the ritual circle (see chapter 6). Directionally it is seen above and below, inside and out, in the center and all about us; it is in and of all the other elements, and it both transcends and interpenetrates them. Spirit is the unifying force uniting and animating the other elements, giving them life and enabling them to communicate and work together. Because spirit exists in all worlds, it is the road by which magick travels from the otherworld to our world.

There are no standard tools used to represent spirit, but it is sometimes associated with magick using cords, cloaks, or any item that ties, binds, unifies, or connects other elements.

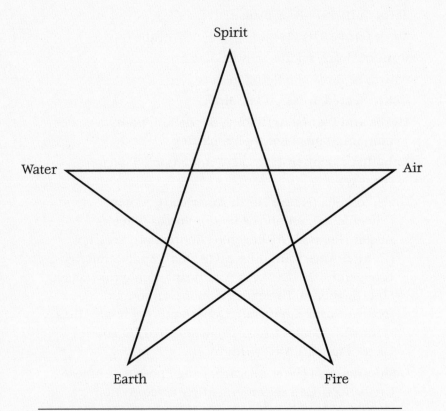

One of the interpretations of the pentagram, the five-pointed
star that has come to symbolize much of western Paganism,
is one of elemental unity.

The relationship between spirit and the other elements can
be conceptualized on the pentagram, the five-pointed star that
has come to represent much of western Paganism. Spirit rules
the top of the star, the apex, under which all the other elements take their place. I have heard this five-point system crit-
icized as being a practice of ceremonial magick. While this is
true, it does not make it their sole property. The pentagram is
an ancient symbol, one used in natural Pagan magick long before the Kaballistic teachings on which ceremonial magick is
based were codified. If one wishes to shun the pentagram because someone else has used it to suit their purposes, then we

would have to extend that logic to our working tools, many of which came to us from ceremonial magick as well.

Unlike the other elements, spirit cannot readily be captured by an herb, stone, or tool. Occultists have long chronicled certain correspondences to spirit, but this has been more to help us fully understand the elusive, yet omnipresent, nature of spirit rather than to encourage us to try and harness its power for magickal purposes. Certainly spirit can be honored within the boundaries of magickal practice; after all, it is the glue that binds the other elements in place. Using any of the following attributes, spirit can be given a place of honor in your magick, and its cohesive abilities assist you in garnering the forces of the other elements for obtaining your goal.

Spirit Correspondences Chart

Directional Attributes: Center and/or above

Colors: White and/or black

Chakra: Crown (at top of the head)

Tools: Cords, cloaks, medicine bags, et cetera; anything that symbolizes the binding or unification of the other elements

Sanskrit Name: Akasha

Latin Name: Aether

Other Names: Quintessence, Nyv

Qualities: Pervasive, omnipresent

Sense: Hearing

Alchemical Symbol: Sometimes the Star of David, also known as Solomon's Seal; two interlaced triangles, one pointing up and the other pointing down

Stone: Quartz crystal

Tattwa Symbol: Black oval

Tarot Card: The World

Celtic Sacred Tree: Apple

Kaballistic Sephira: Kether (Crown)

Deities: All

Getting Personally Acquainted with the Elements

Getting to know each element leisurely and thoroughly, the way you would get to know a good friend, is essential for anyone who hopes to master the magickal arts. Even Craft oldtimers can find their magick greatly enhanced by taking the time to get reacquainted with these powers on a regular basis. To do this, we must immerse ourselves in that part of nature that is linked to the element with whom we wish to connect—listening to its stories, learning its lessons, and meeting its inhabitant spirits.

Directed meditation is the quickest, surest way to open ourselves to the elements. Before you begin any ritual or meditative exercise, it is wise to spend some time preparing for it both mentally and physically. This is a good habit to get into regardless of what type of rituals you want to do, as the very act of preparation triggers your deep mind that a profound change is about to take place in your consciousness. In essence, the preparation becomes the start of your ritual (refer to chapter 2 for suggested preparations).

If you use ritual baths prior to altered state work, you might want to consider adding herbs sharing an affinity with whichever element you are going to be working with:

Element-Ruled Herbs

Earth Ruled

- barley
- bistort
- honeysuckle
- onion
- potato
- rice
- vervain

Air Ruled

- anise
- benzoin
- chicory
- clover
- dandelion
- lemon grass
- marjoram
- mint

Fire Ruled

- allspice
- angelica
- bay leaves
- cloves
- cinnamon
- cumin
- dill
- fennel
- ginger
- mullein
- orange
- rue
- woodruff

Water Ruled

- apple blossom
- boneset
- cattail
- chamomile
- comfrey
- orris
- sea weed
- vanilla
- violet
- willow
- yarrow

Another way to connect with a specific element prior to meditating on it is to use an oil made from essences sharing its attributes. A ritual oil constructed with a single element in mind can be worn on the skin or used in the bath, providing it contains no known irritants. It can be used to anoint candles, burn as an incense, or inhale as a perfume to help strengthen our links to that particular element.

The following recipes are not the only blends possible from the hundreds of oils available. Feel free to use only one ingredient in each recipe, or to add and subtract other scents to create your own unique elemental blends. Mix the oils you will be using in small glass bottles, preferably dark glass containers meant to be used with an eyedropper (you can purchase these inexpensively at most pharmacies). Place the essential oils drop by drop into a $1/2$-ounce base of a low-scent oil such as olive, saffron, or almond.

Earth Oil

1 drop patchouly

8 drops honeysuckle

3 drops pine

13 drops magnolia

Water Oil

12 drops sweet pea

4 drops jasmine

2 drops ylang-ylang

7 drops camellia

4 drops lotus

Fire Oil

3 drops cinnamon

12 drops orange

4 drops clove

7 drops nutmeg

2 drops lemon

Air Oil

6 drops sandalwood

3 drops benzoin

12 drops lavender

9 lemongrass

You may wish to experiment with herbal baths, teas, and oils to see which one, or combinations of them, work best in helping you attune to the magick of the element you want to work with. This can be useful information to have later on when you are trying to connect with elemental powers for spellwork or ritual.

Connecting with Earth

> . . . I began to feel myself sinking, as if I was being
> sucked into the ground. It should have been a
> disturbing sensation, but instead I only felt very
> relaxed. All the sand burrs and other prickles I felt
> when I first stretched out [in my backyard] were gone,
> and I no longer feared the approach of rattlesnakes
> or fire ants. I felt as if I was being hugged by a gentle
> parent who soothes a beloved child after a nightmare,
> and the child knows that she is protected. . . .Every-
> thing seemed so "firm." That's the only word I know
> to use! And I felt as if I had just been given some
> new and infallible foundation upon which to
> continue building my inner temple.
>
> Edain McCoy's Book of Shadows
> Full Moon, Saturday, April 10, 1982

The best place to get to know earth is on the land itself, our Great Mother, which is the element's primary physical world manifestation. You only need a small bit of ground you can sit

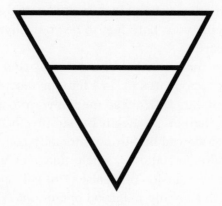

The alchemical symbol for Earth

or lie down on, allowing as much of your body as possible to be in contact with her. This can be done in a backyard, in a woods or park, or anywhere else that the element is manifest. Just make sure prior to your exercise that you will be safe and undisturbed. Having to keep one ear constantly attuned for intruders is not conducive to successful meditation.

Before you begin, prepare with either a ritual bath, a tea, or any other method that helps you relax and open to other worlds. Then spend a few moments gazing into the alchemical symbol for earth: an inverted, equilateral triangle bisected by a horizontal line. You may also wish to do this the night before your meditation. Gaze into the symbol for several minutes just before you fall asleep, allowing it to imprint itself on your mind. The image will implant itself in your subconscious, forging a magickal connection that will begin to work immediately to attune you with the energies of earth. You may even find you dream of earthy things, and these should all be recorded in your Book of Shadows upon awakening. You will also find that your meditations to get to know earth will run much more smoothly and be more powerful after having engaged your subconscious in this manner.

Begin your connective meditation with the earth element by settling yourself on the ground. You may sit or lie down, whichever is more comfortable to you. You might also choose to stand, allowing your bare feet to be your physical connection with the earth.

Spend a few moments breathing deeply and relaxing, allowing your consciousness to slow into the receptive levels (if you are not familiar with these meditative processes, please refer back to chapter 2). Begin by simply focusing on the rhythm of your slowed breathing, mentally count backwards from one hundred, or allow a single image or word to enter your mind to the exclusion of all else. This will take practice to master, but with so many magickal operations relying on this skill, it is one you should pursue with vigor.

Allow at least ten minutes for the relaxation and mind slowing part of the exercise, longer if you are still a novice. When you feel sufficiently relaxed, close your eyes and continue breathing deeply. Become very aware of any sensations you are experiencing at all points where you make contact with the earth. Feel the sentience of the elemental nature of the ground. Allow yourself to breathe it in through your entire body, visualizing the element of earth being inhaled and exhaled through every pore. Let yourself melt into the earth, becoming one with its own energies. If you start to find that you are having trouble recognizing where earth stops and you begin . . . excellent!

At this point you may begin to sense the presence of gnomes or other earth-related faery life around you. This is a natural side effect of this type of meditation and should not worry you. In fact, you may view the phenomenon as an indication that you are doing everything correctly. Only if you feel threatened or apprehensive in the presence of these elemental beings should you stop what you are doing and come out of the meditation. Not all the denizens of the elemental realms are friendly to human explorers, and while the chances of your meeting up with any of them at this point in your studies is unlikely, you need to be aware of the possibility.

As you continue to connect with the physical earth, allow yourself to open to the element of earth that dwells therein. Mentally call out a greeting to the element and ask it to teach you about itself. We all experience these teachings in our own way, so be open to the guidance you receive. Some people are swept away on involved inner-journeys with the element, others are taken in hand by the gnomes and shown the way, and still others will have to wait for dreams or for a friendly tree or stone to teach the lessons needed.

If during this meditation you have mentally traveled to another place, it is wise to come back to your starting point before coming out of the meditation: "Same way in, same way out." This is another of those old tidbits of occult wisdom that help our conscious and subconscious minds work together in harmony as we develop our magickal skills.

You may come out of the meditation when you feel you are ready, knowing that you may return any time you choose. Finish by recording your experiences in your Book of Shadows.

Connecting with Water

> I had to wait forever until the kids all went home,
> presumably for dinner, before I could have the spot
> near the falls to myself. I felt really self-conscious
> about sitting there with my eyes closed, and I thought
> I was going to have to give up and try this somewhere
> else. I could hear the occasional car going over the
> crossing, probably not paying me any more attention
> than I ever paid to anyone I saw in the water when I
> was driving past. Candy [my dog] was on the watch, so
> I felt little concern about someone sneaking up on me,
> but she was fidgety, and I could tell she could not
> understand why we were sitting in the water rather
> than playing in it. This was very distracting until she
> finally settled down. . . . I began to feel a sinking, a
> drop in personal gravity, as if I was dissolving and
> being spread out all over the water. I kept sensing
> playful water sprites tweaking my legs, as if daring
> my spirit to jump out of my body and follow them
> downstream. The mental image I had of the creatures
> was ever-changing, as fluid as the water itself. I even
> thought they were deliberately altering their forms
> just to gauge my reaction.
>
> Edain McCoy's Book of Shadows
> Full Moon, Saturday, May 8, 1982

The next element we will explore is water; less dense than
earth, but still something we can see, hold, and work with in a
physical form. Water conforms to whatever vessel contains it,
and because of this fluidity it has become linked to regenera-
tion of life, transformation, and change.

The best places to connect with the water element are in
watery places. Natural pools, lakes, beaches, and streams are
ideal if you can find one that is safe, private, and unpolluted.
You may also use your bathtub, shower, kitchen sink, or even
a bucket of water you can place your feet in. When I was first
exploring the elements I decided to do each connective meditation three times. The first time I worked with water I went

to a shallow place in the Guadalupe River near Kerrville, Texas, which was a popular local spot because of the small waterfall that ran through a low water crossing. The second time I was in my bathtub, and the third time I was out in the pouring rain. Each session yielded its own unique images and snippets of water knowledge.

Prepare yourself for meditation in the manner you deem most appropriate, and spend a few minutes gazing at water's alchemical symbol: an inverted equilateral triangle. As was mentioned before, you may want to do this the night before so that your subconscious has a chance to hash over the symbol and its meaning, and perhaps send you dream insights.

Whatever environment you choose to work in, begin your connective meditation with the water element by settling yourself into it as much as possible within the constraints of the method you are using. For example, you may be lying down in a tub, standing out in the rain, sitting under a waterfall, or sponging yourself off at your own kitchen sink, but you should spend lots of time moving the water over as much of your body as you can. If you can submerge yourself totally, that is great. If not, you will not be losing out. It is the essence

The alchemical symbol for Water

of water that is of concern here, much less so than the water itself. As you do this allow yourself to center on the feeling of the water. Notice how it beads on your skin, how it runs through your fingers, how it pools in your palms. Note how the temperature and texture of your skin is changed by this contact. When you have immersed yourself in the essence of the water element as much as you can, get in a comfortable position, one in which you can meditate while still maintaining your physical contact with the water. Then spend a few moments breathing deeply and relaxing, allowing your consciousness to slow into the receptive levels. Allow at least twenty minutes for this part of the exercise.

When you feel you are sufficiently relaxed, close your eyes and continue breathing deeply. Become very aware of the sensations at all points where you make contact with the water. Note its temperature, its composition, and its weight. Allow yourself to breathe it through your entire body, visualizing the element of water being inhaled and exhaled through every pore of your body as if you were a fish taking on life through your gills. Let yourself melt into the water, molding yourself to it and becoming one with its own energies. Feel the sentience of the element of water.

At this point you may begin to sense the presence of undines or other water-related faery life around you. Make mental note of their appearance, words, gestures, or any message they seem to be trying to communicate to you.

As you continue to connect with water, allow yourself to open fully to the element. Mentally call out a greeting and ask it to teach you about itself. We all experience these teachings in our own way, so be open to the guidance you receive.

Come out of the meditation when you are ready, knowing that you may return any time you choose. Record your experiences in your Book of Shadows.

Connecting with Fire

I would like to have used a fireplace for my first foray
into the fire element, but the heat today made it impossible. Dry July is our fire season [in Texas], and grass
fires are always a concern, so even an outdoor bonfire
was out of the question. Instead, I used a simple candle
flame. . . . As I continued to gaze I clearly saw the
undulating patterns of the salamanders dancing around
the flame. I was so excited that I almost brought myself
right out of trance. But I kept my composure and, as I
watched, I saw them shape-changing into forms I could
not identify. I closed my eyes, the afterglow of the
flame imprinted on the back of my eyelids. I began to
feel a warmth flood through me starting from the solar
plexus and radiating outward. With that sensation came
another—one of primal power, and for the first time I
began to understand how I could use an element to
transform energy to my will.

Edain McCoy's Book of Shadows
Full Moon, Monday, July 5, 1982

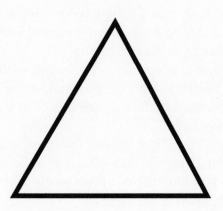

The alchemical symbol for Fire

The next element on our journey is fire, the realm of passion and intensity. Its most basic physical form is the flame, something we can see and touch, but which we cannot hold. Unlike water, fire does not mold itself to that which contains it, but burns and transforms those vessels.

The best fires to work elemental meditations with are sacred fires, such as those of a balefire on a sabbat or an esbat. Fireplaces are also excellent, as are open blazes contained in a camping area or a grill, providing you have someone else with you who can keep an eye on the blaze while you are meditating. If you have no one to assist you, then it might be best to use a candle in a sturdy, fireproof base. The essence of fire is all you need for a successful connection, and a bigger fire is not necessarily a better one. Another reason a smaller fire may be a better choice is for your own safety. Remember that you will be in a meditative state of consciousness during this exercise, with your eyes closed for a large part of it, so you must make sure that the fire is absolutely contained and not likely to spread. A candle is usually easier to control than an open blaze.

Again, prepare yourself for meditation in the manner you deem most appropriate, and then spend a few minutes gazing at fire's alchemical symbol: an upright equilateral triangle. You may want to do this the night before so that your subconscious has a chance to hash over the symbol and its meaning, and perhaps send you dream insights.

Whatever medium you choose to work with, begin your connective meditation with the fire element by gazing into it as if seeking its center. Allow yourself time to feel fully a part of its vibrant energies.

Get comfortable in front of your fire, then spend a few moments breathing deeply and relaxing, allowing your consciousness to slow into the receptive levels. Allow at least ten minutes for this part of the exercise.

When you feel you are sufficiently relaxed, close your eyes and continue breathing deeply. Become very aware of the sensations coming from the flame. Note its temperature, light, energy, and intensity. Feel the sentience of the elemental nature of fire. Allow yourself to breathe it through your entire body, visualizing the element of fire being inhaled and exhaled through every pore of your body. Let yourself merge with the essence of fire, molding yourself to it and becoming one with its own energies.

At this point you may begin to sense the presence of salamanders or other fire-related faery life around you. Make mental note of their appearance, words, gestures, or any message they seem to be trying to communicate to you. Keep in mind that though fire can destroy, nature is ultimately renewed by fire. The possession of fire was humankind's first step toward mastery of the environment, and deities who brought or stole fire for humans were greatly revered, though often reviled by their fellow deities; these include Prometheus, Yolkaiestsan, Loo-Wit, Auahi Turoa, and Tuleone. Any of these deities, or other fire Gods and Goddesses, may enter your meditation.

As you continue to connect with fire, allow yourself to open fully to the element. Mentally call out a greeting and ask it to teach you about itself. We all experience these teachings in our own way, so be open to the guidance you receive.

Come out of the meditation when you are ready, knowing that you may return any time you choose. Record your experiences in your Book of Shadows.

Connecting with Air

> . . . Finally the wind stirred sufficiently for me to be able to connect with it. I placed some sandalwood incense on the back patio and sat on the concrete floor facing the oncoming wind. It was hot and sticky, coming from the southeast off the Gulf, and I was afraid I would be completely overcome by its water energies, but as I focused on the wind itself I began to feel my spirit being nudged out of my body by the air spirits, as if they wished to carry me away on some great adventure. For a moment I was scared, wondering what would happen if I followed them, and then the capricious wind changed direction. . .

> Edain McCoy's Book of Shadows
> New Moon, Saturday, August 20, 1982

The last of the elements we shall explore is air, the one most removed from our physical world. Air is intangible. We can neither hold nor see nor capture it, yet we know it is always with us.

A windy spot outdoors or in front of an open wind can be a good place for starting to explore the air element. The type of wind and its direction of origin will undoubtedly color your perception of it. For example, a damp wind will carry with it some water characteristics, and a wind from the south may stir up some fiery images. Air is the most changeable of the elements, and the balmy south wind in which you start your meditation may be a gale force west wind before you finish.

If you cannot or do not want to work with the wind you can always use your own breath. Indian metaphysics has long taught the concept of *prana,* or the sacred breath. The word comes from two Hindustani words meaning "first unit."[8] By controlling the length and rhythm of the breath, it was discovered that specific changes in consciousness would occur. This concept and its techniques have been taught to students of ceremonial magick to help them learn to discipline their mind-body connection.

To work with your own breath as a representative of the air element, simply meditate while counting your breaths in and out, or by adapting some type of rhythmic breath such as in for six counts, out for two, et cetera. Experiment to find what works best for you without causing strain or shortness of breath.

Another alternative for connecting with air through physical means is with a fan. You can use a hand-held one that you have to move yourself but this will become tedious and perhaps even painful over the course of a lengthy meditation and is not conducive to success. A good old-fashioned box fan, the kind you might have sat singing into as a child just to enjoy the sound of your voice being chopped to bits and echoed back to you, is your best choice.

---

8. Anodea Judith. *Wheels of Life: A User's Guide to the Chakra System* (Llewellyn, 1987), 218.

Prepare yourself for this meditation in the manner you deem most appropriate, then spend a few minutes gazing at air's alchemical symbol: an upright equilateral triangle bisected by a horizontal line. As mentioned before, you may want to do this the night before so that your subconscious has a chance to hash over the symbol and its meaning, and perhaps send you dream insights.

Begin your connective meditation with the air element by sensing its presence around you and within you. Get comfortable, then spend a few moments breathing deeply and relaxing, allowing your consciousness to slow into the receptive levels. Focus on how the air element is the primary medium for this slowing of your consciousness. Allow at least ten minutes for this part of the exercise.

When you feel you are sufficiently relaxed, close your eyes and continue to breathe deeply. Become very aware of the energy in your breath, the sensation of the wind, or the breeze from the fan. Note its temperature, direction, quality, and intensity. Feel the sentience of the elemental nature of air. Allow yourself to breathe it through your entire body, visualizing the element of air being inhaled and exhaled

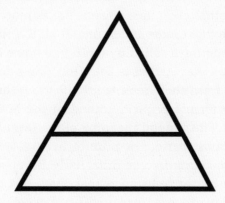

The alchemical symbol for Air

through every pore of your body. Let yourself merge with the essence of air; feel your physical self dissipating to join its free-flowing movement.

At this point you may begin to sense the presence of sylphs or other air-related faery life around you. Make mental note of their appearance, words, gestures, or any message they seem to want to communicate to you.

As you continue to connect with fire, allow yourself to open fully to the element. Mentally call out a greeting and ask it to teach you about itself. We all experience these teachings in our own way, so be open to the guidance you receive.

Come out of the meditation when you are ready, knowing that you may return any time you choose. Record your experiences in your Book of Shadows.

Connecting with Spirit

Learning about the subtleties of the "element" of spirit is somewhat more difficult than delving into the four primary elements. Spirit is completely intangible; it does not have a place or a location in any occult system that is fixed, and therefore is not tied up in a neat little package for us to take out and examine. It has no recognizable place in the physical world where we can see its manifest physical version as we can with the other elements. Spirit is not as much an element as a force, one that unites and animates all the others.

Spirit is sometimes called by its Indian name *akasha* or by its Latin term *aether.* Aether is Latin for "purer air" and is perhaps derived from the Greek word *aithein,* meaning "to kindle." Another term for spirit, coined in the Middle Ages, is quintessence. The general meaning of the term is something that is in its most perfect or pure form. It also contains the prefix *quint* meaning five or fifth. Early European occultists viewed spirit as the substance that made up the heavens, filled the void in space, or was present anywhere that other elements appeared to be mixed or nonexistent.

We all experience spirit in our own way, and it reveals its nature to us only when we are ready to understand. To help the process along, we can use oils to help us attune to its elusive nature and then meditate on symbols that embody its unifying properties. The recipe for Spirit Oil that follows is constructed from oils having affinities with the goals of spiritual growth or that have been used to help connect humanity with the divine.

Spirit Oil

10 drops sandalwood oil

8 drops violet oil

4 drops gardenia oil

Mix in a base of $^1/_2$ ounce olive, saffron, or almond oil. You may also choose to add one single drop of an oil that represents each of the other elements. For instance, you might add to this blend some patchouly for earth, lotus for water, clove for fire, and hibiscus for air. Allow the oil blend to "marry" for a few days before using.

The best symbol to meditate on before attempting to connect with spirit is the six-pointed star we refer to as the Star of David or Solomon's Seal. Within its six points and two triangles are the images of the other four elemental alchemical symbols. I discovered this early in my Craft career while meditating on the image, only to watch it break apart and reveal its inner components to me. By the time I began working with spirit, I had already developed very good meditation skills and was adept at holding a single image before my mind's eye without it wavering or changing. When the Star of David began to come apart, I was at first annoyed, thinking my control over my mediation was being tested. Then I was fascinated as I saw the Star reform itself into the four alchemical symbols. The mental picture remained that way long enough for me to grasp the idea, then reformed into the original Star. I immediately woke myself up and got up to write these insights down, thinking as many do that I was somehow the first to be given this standard occult knowledge. Whether this was information I already knew and had merely forgotten was not the point. The experience showed me that I was indeed forging a connection with spirit and that it was actively trying to teach me about itself.

Begin working with the Star of David to explore this fifth element. Gaze on it before you fall asleep each night, asking the element to teach you its secrets. Be open to what it may tell you and the way in which this information might come.

As I already mentioned, everyone's experience with spirit is somehow unique. As you start working with it, keep your mind and eyes open for objects and situations in which you perceive the other elements being contained or blended. All these things are part of spirit and will help you further understand its elusive qualities. Be sure to record all your insights in your Book of Shadows for later examination.

The Star of David, also known as Solomon's Seal, is one of the oldest symbols of the Creator. The alchemical symbols were extracted from it.

Balancing Personal
Elemental Deficiencies

Our natal charts, or horoscopes, provide us with insights into all aspects of ourselves, including where we lack a certain element in our makeup. I once thought it silly to think that one could have an inherent elemental imbalance until I began critically looking at the charts of people I knew well. It didn't take me long to realize that the plodding and reliable (but wholly unimaginative) person has an overabundance of earth and virtually no water, and that the "airhead" had no earth to ground her. After that discovery I was hooked, and have been using the elements to counteract imbalances both in my own astrological makeup, and whenever I feel I need an extra boost of a particular element. For example, when I have been too long in the inner-worlds and need a good dose of grounding, I turn to earth; and when I have spent too much time in analytical study, I use water to bring back the emotional side of my thinking.

The easiest way find out if and where you lack an element in your makeup is to take out your birth chart,[9] and, with pencil and paper at hand, begin listing the ruling element of the sign in which you find all nine planets, as well as your ascendant, descendant, and midheaven. This will give you a fairly accurate picture of your elemental makeup.

The following is a list of the twelve zodiac signs and their ruling elements:

Earth Signs	Water Signs
Taurus	Cancer
Virgo	Scorpio
Capricorn	Pisces
Fire Signs	**Air Signs**
Aries	Gemini
Leo	Libra
Sagittarius	Aquarius

If you feel any other aspects of your chart are important enough to include in this breakdown, such as one of the asteroids like Chiron or Vesta, you may want work these into your equation also. Since the jury is still out on just how important these are in interpreting horoscopes, you will have to decide for yourself how much they relate to you. Don't use one just to give yourself an edge in a certain element. For instance, my chart shows a weakness in air. My Chiron is in Aquarius, an air sign, and if I added this asteroid into my equation I would appear better balanced for it. Tempting to do, yes, but I feel that too little is yet known about Chiron's precise influences to use it when breaking down my elemental profile.

My natal chart—minus Chiron—breaks down like this:

Sun	Leo (fire)
Moon	Pisces (water)
Mercury	Virgo (earth)
Venus	Virgo (earth)
Mars	Virgo (earth)
Jupiter	Libra (air)
Saturn	Sagittarius (fire)
Uranus	Leo (fire)
Neptune	Scorpio (water)
Pluto	Leo (fire)
Ascendant	Pisces (water)
Descendant	Virgo (earth)
Midheaven	Sagittarius (fire)

---

9. For figuring your own chart closely enough to see these imbalances I recommend either Joanna Martine Woolfolk's *The Only Astrology Book You'll Ever Need* (Stein and Day, 1982), or the latest edition of Llewellyn George's classic *The A to Z Horoscope Maker and Delineator* (Llewellyn). There are also commercial astrological services available that will figure a simple natal chart for you. Look for these in many New Age and alternative spirituality periodicals.

Looking at the elemental picture, I have four parts earth, three parts water, five parts fire, but only one part air. Clearly the air element is where I could be lacking. But the astrological chart alone does not give a complete picture of an elemental deficiency. The best way to tell if you have a deficiency in a particular element is to look at your chart in tandem with other aspects of yourself. Conditions that on their own might indicate a physical or emotion illness or a chakra imbalance can, when coupled with weak or missing components in a chart, show if there is truly a lack of an element or not. These conditions can come and go, fluctuating with astrological or health changes, or they can be chronic in nature.

Symptoms of a Lack of Earth Element

Feelings of being spaced-out, being looked upon by others as an airhead, insecurity, scattered energies, sensations of being haunted, feeling a lack of connection to others or to a special place.

Symptoms of a Lack of Water Element

Always being at an emotional distance from others, lack of compassion, chronic relationship problems, bursts of temper, no intuitive skills, loss or lack of rudimentary psychic skills.

Symptoms of a Lack of Fire Element

Loss or lack of sex drive, inability to feel excited about anything, willful betrayal of others' trust, chronically low energy levels, inability to see projects through to completion.

Symptoms of a Lack of Air Element

Inability to focus or concentrate, poor grades in school, repeated nuisance problems with health, loss or lack of communication skills, inability to start projects.

No matter which element you feel you are lacking, even if you feel only a temporary loss of the element due to special astrological conditions or health problems, you can begin to restore that component of yourself by referring back to the connective meditations to begin linking yourself back with the essence of that element.

We can further rebuild our missing element by engaging in activities known to be under the rulership of a specific element, and/or to add foods to our diet that are governed by that element.

Balancing an Earth Deficiency

Two simple activities governed by earth are dancing and drumming; luckily, the two seem to go together, at least where Pagans are concerned. You don't have to be a great dancer to enjoy moving your body around, allowing it to express the rhythms and heartbeat of the earth. If you have a drum, tambourine, or other percussion instrument, use it as you dance to keep your beat. If you don't have a drum, invest in one of the many drumming tapes currently on the market. They can be found with a variety of tempos and with all sorts of interesting background sounds mixed in.

Other tasks that can help rebalance your missing earth component are taking care of pets or gardening. Even a window box full of failing seedlings will get you back in touch with elemental earth.

Engaging in grounding exercises each day can also help. To do this you must mentally or physically touch the earth. This can be done by placing your feet or palms flat on the ground, or by just sitting still and mentally connecting with the earth below you even if you are in an office on the top floor of a highrise office building. Visualize all your anxieties, lack of focus, etc., being sent into the ground and, in return, having her stabilizing and comforting influence coming up to you. Take a few deep breaths and pull yourself into a state of inner peace.

Conclude all earth activities, meditations, et cetera, with a meal of earth-related foods.[10]

---

10. To learn more about magickal cooking I heartily recommend both Scott Cunningham's *The Magic of Food* (Llewellyn, 1995) and Patricia Telesco's *A Kitchen Witch's Cookbook* (Llewellyn, 1994).

Foods Ruled by Earth

- potatoes
- carrots
- turnips
- corn
- red meats
- pumpkins
- seeds
- breads
- whole grain products
- pasta
- salt
- pomegranates

Balancing a Water Deficiency

No, I am not going to suggest taking a swim to build up your lacking water components. That sort of vigorous exercise is under the rulership of fire. Elemental water is the world of the emotions, the hidden self. The best activities for connecting with it are ones that engage the deepest part of our psyches. Divination exercises, meditation, guided meditation, and psychic development exercises are the best places to start, and are easy and inexpensive to maintain. Contrary to popular belief, you don't need lots of tools or props for divination. You can divine your future in the movements of the clouds or in the movement of the treetops; you can meditate without tools or develop your psychic skills with a set of homemade flashcards, which you turn away from yourself and then try to divine the symbol on the other side.

Begin a dream diary and allow your sleeping self to consciously communicate with you. These messages from your subconscious have much to teach and are deeply a part of the water element.

Engaging in simple activities with children or pregnant women, or indulging your romantic nature, strengthen your water characteristics as well.

Finish any water exercises with water-related foods and try increasing them in your general diet to keep your water element strong.

Foods Ruled by Water

- milk
- yogurt
- cheeses
- all dairy products
- eggs
- apples
- blackberries
- most non-citrus juices
- kelp
- many melons
- fish and seafood
- vinegar

Balancing a Fire Deficiency

Vigorous activity is under the rulership of fire, and the best place to start is with your own exercise regimen. Naturally you should not jump into an exercise routine if you have any physical problem that could be aggravated by an aerobic work-out. To quote an often-heard phrase, "Check with your doctor before starting any exercise program."

Sex is another fire activity, and lots of good—and safe—sex with a loving partner will bring out all of fire's passions and energies and keep them burning bright.

A daily dose of fire gazing, even if it is only into a candle flame, will forge your links with this element. As you practice this art, a type of scrying, you will find it has the side benefit of acting as a conduit for messages from your inner self. Don't be surprised to find you are seeing symbols, scenes, or other imagery in the dancing flames.

Fire is about passion. Allow yourself to feel deeply and strongly about issues or problems that arise. A little controlled, constructive anger can work wonders for your fire-self.

Fire is also about transformation, and what could be more instantly transforming than acting? Virtually all aspects of the theater are ruled by fire. Try out for a play or volunteer to work backstage at your local community playhouse. If this doesn't appeal to you, just pick up a script from your local library and, in the privacy of your own room, read through the parts with all the melodramatic bravado you can muster.

Follow up all these exercises with fire-related foods as well. Fire attributes can be added to many non-fire-ruled foods by grilling them over an open flame.

Foods Ruled by Fire

- citrus fruits
- tea
- curry
- cinnamon
- allspice
- pepper (seasoning)
- peppers of all types
- chili
- reptile meats

Balancing an Air Deficiency

Balancing missing air is easily done with solitary activities such as reading or studying. You don't have to be a formal student to learn about a new subject. Browse the library shelves at least once a week and find something new that interests you. This is how I have always balanced my lack of air with the other elements that are stronger in my chart, even before I knew what this side benefit of private study could be.

Communication arts also strengthen air. Write letters, poems, rituals, or anything else that intrigues you. Or enjoy a long, engaging conversation with a good friend.

Speech exercises that improve diction or boost your vocabulary also increase the air element in your makeup.

Air rules travel. If you have the time and money, take a leisurely trip, making sure to include lots of intellectually stimulating sites on your agenda. If long voyages are not in your budget, just getting away for a day trip once every few weeks can achieve the same purpose.

Follow up your experiments with air-related foods.

Foods Ruled by Air

- whipped foods
- souffles
- fowl and game birds
- honey
- coffee
- olives
- most oils
- many edible flowers

▼

4

Spell Construction, Casting, and Timing

Before embarking on any spell, make sure you already have the six magickal prerequisites mentioned in chapter 1— desire and need, emotional involvement, knowledge (which can be gleaned from this chapter) and realistic expectations, belief, the ability to keep silent, and the willingness to back up magick in the physical world. With these six factors in place, you can begin to construct your spells with confidence.

Naturally, not every spell will be completely successful, but you should feel that all do you some good, even if that good is just in showing you where you made your mistakes. When Witches' spells fail, they do not turn against the deities and rant and rave at the fates but, as befits those on the path of self-responsibility, they go back to the beginning and reexamine all the facets in the spell, from the initial desire to its final construction, looking for clues as to what went wrong. Perhaps your need wasn't as great as you had at first imagined. Maybe your goal was not clearly defined, or perhaps your spell would have caused harm to someone else. If a spell fails, and you find you still have the desire to pursue the goal, simply restructure it in a fresh format and try again.

There are sixteen basic steps for successful spellcrafting. These are listed below, and each point is followed by a detailed discussion so you can follow along step by step as you design your own spells.

Sixteen Steps for Successful Spellcrafting

1. Clearly understand and define your magickal goal
2. Plan your visualization and other wording
3. Choose your catalysts and begin to empower them
4. Decide when you want and need to do the spell
5. Be sure of the ethics of your goal
6. Gather all equipment and go to your magickal place at the appropriate time
7. Prepare your magickal space
8. Ground, center, and begin clearly visualizing your goal
9. Raise magickal energy
10. Do whatever physical actions your spell requires
11. Release the magickal energy toward its goal
12. End the spell and close your sacred space
13. Ground excess energy into the earth
14. Record your effort in your Book of Shadows
15. Back up your magick on the physical plane
16. Rework the spell as needed
17. Break the spell when necessary

Clearly Understand and Define Your Magickal Goal

While it may seem obvious to clearly define a goal before starting any sort of project, I am ever amazed at the number of Witches—many of whom should know better—who jump into the mechanics before they have fully conceptualized the dream.

You must know precisely what it is you want to obtain before you can begin spellwork. Think of yourself and your magickal goal as points on a map. If you have no idea where you want to go, you have no idea what road to take to get there. You should be able to state in a single, clear, coherent sentence just what your goal is, exactly as you would be able to name a place on the map to which you wanted to travel.

If you are having trouble honing in on your exact goal, begin by trying to give it a broad definition. Peruse the following list of common magickal desires and see if you can find one under which your need falls. At first some of these may strike you as negative, but remember that it is the ultimate intent of the spell that dictates if it is negative or not. For example, "creating discord" sounds like something bad, but it may be a necessary step to help yourself through an impasse and get you moving in the right direction again.

Magickal Goals

- Love, romance
- Blessings and purification
- Peace
- Abundance, prosperity
- Employment
- Health, healing
- Fertility (human, plant, or animal)
- Psychic protection and self-defense (see chapter 7)
- Physical protection
- Strengthening spirituality
- Connecting with the divine
- Weather Witching
- Binding
- Psychic enhancement
- Mental prowess

Continued

- Creating discord
- Banishing a bad habit
- Banishing a baneful spirit
- Banishing negative energy
- Banishing someone from your life
- Obtaining a personal physical need
  (home, car, et cetera)
- Aiding in astral projection attempts (see chapter 9)
- Inducing prophetic dreams
- Lust (increasing or decreasing)
- Luck
- Erasing memory
- Enhancing memory
- Stopping a present event
- Changing a past event
- Altering a future potential
- Viewing a past life
- Divining the future

Once you can pinpoint a general category under which your goal falls, use the key words within that category to help you create one succinct sentence by which you will define your goal. If your desire is romantic love, you might state your goal as "I want to draw a romantic situation into my life, with the right person for me at this time, which will lead to a long-term loving relationship."

Magickal wording can be tricky, and many new Witches end up learning how to play the semantics game through trial and error. The old adage "Be careful what you wish or you just might get it" was never truer than in magick. Notice in the example above that the goal states a "person" is wanted. It has been taught by many, many Witches and magicians throughout the centuries that magick takes the path of least resistance, and will attempt to bring you your desire in the easiest, most readily available form. As obvious as it might seem on the surface that you are seeking a human companion, if all you asked for was "love because I am lonely," you are just as likely to end up with an adoring pet as an adoring human being. I have also heard tales of Witches who asked for new cars and got toy models, or asked for money only to win big at Monopoly™. This is why precise wording and clear visualization are so important, and why they are deeply linked to each other in your magickal efforts.

When you are sure that your goal is worded in the most succinct and precise form possible, state the goal out loud several times as you go about preparing the spell. Write it down in your Book of Shadows as well. Making the statement concrete in this way helps form it solidly in your mind, and by doing this you will have already begun to invest the spell with your emotions and energy, thus triggering your subconscious to go to work on the problem.

If you have more than one need, you may wish to spread them out over a period of several weeks' time. You can work more than one spell at a time, but doing so will dissipate and scatter your energies, leaving less for each individual goal. I always recommend that if you feel you absolutely must do multiple spells, limit them to three and try and relate them in some way so that the energy you raise remains as focused as possible. An example of this type of trio is a spell for prosperity, one for employment, and another for a physical item you need or want. All of these are ultimately related to a need for money, so the energy focus remains similar and so likely will be the catalysts that you employ to assist you.

Plan Your Visualization and Other Wording

Plan how you will visualize your goal and believe in what you see. Start now. The moment you begin visualizing the resolution of a magickal need is the moment you begin to create the changes in your deep mind necessary for the magick to manifest.

At first many Witches feel they cannot visualize. I have had one or two Craft students who seem to have a real mental block with this process, and I have gotten a few letters from readers who have reported the same difficulties. There is no secret to visualization. Yes, some people are better at it than others, but everyone can learn to do it effectively. I have included a lengthy section on visualization in chapter 2. If you find you are having difficulties with this skill, please refer back to that chapter and work through the exercises on pages 24-26 again.

When employing visualization with a magickal goal in mind you must be sure of two things: one, that you are not dictating to the universe how the magick should manifest, and two, that you are not harming others in the process of obtaining your desire. The first point means that you visualize only your end goal and not the method by which you expect it to manifest. If you are in need of money, don't randomly decide to visualize yourself winning big in the stock market. The universe may have a different and, perhaps, better way of bringing you extra cash, and your insistence on bringing it in by a different route may either cause it to take much longer or negate your efforts altogether. The second point should be self-explanatory by this time. You don't visualize someone else losing out so that you can gain. That is the greatest magickal no-no there is, and it will only rebound on you in the end. Rest assured that there is enough abundance in the universe to go around, and you don't have to rob others to enrich yourself.

You will also need to decide on other wording that will be used when actually working your spell. These are usually referred to as your "words of power," the sentences or chants you will use to help you focus on your end goal and raise energy. You may write them out or simply remember the key phrases you wish to use as you improvise. Some Witches like to create these as simple poems so that they will be easier to remember (see the following chapter for spell examples).

Words of power are not absolutely necessary if your visualization is keen and highly perfected. Most Witches find using them very helpful. An old Witches' Rune, or saying, which may have come from the Middle Ages, states that "a charm in rhyme cuts the time," meaning of course that spellwork becomes more efficacious with the help of these little chants.

If you cannot speak, either because of a current illness or some permanent condition, you have two other choices for solidifying the words in your mind and imprinting them on the unseen world. You can think them through one word at a time, giving great mental emphasis to each, or you can write them out during the places in the spell where you would normally speak out loud.

Words of power should be as carefully thought out as the wording you used when naming your initial goal. Make absolutely sure all the imagery is correct, precise, harms none, and is compatible with your visualized goal. For example, if you want to visualize a new home for yourself, you do not want to visualize someone else's specific home, but visualize instead the qualities you want in an ideal residence.

You must also make sure all your wording is in the **present tense.** We always speak about and visualize magick as a *fait accompli,* a done deal, in which the goal is a here and now fact of existence. This is common sense. If you state your goal in the future tense, your magick will remain in the future, always a day away out of your reach. If you state it in the present tense, it naturally draws the goal toward you because you are convincing yourself that it is in fact already a part of your life . . . the path of least resistance!

Choose Your Catalysts and Begin to Empower Them

Once you know your goal and have planned your visualization and wording, it is time to select catalysts that will help you focus on the desire and assist you in drawing the energies of your goal to you.

Strictly speaking, a catalyst is defined as something that contributes to a goal but has no influence over an outcome on its own. In magick, no catalyst has power in and of itself. The power of a catalyst to influence a spell is nil until the Witch recognizes its potential to do so and uses his or her knowledge to draw it out. Only then does it have influence and become a working partner.

Ultimately the power source that drives magick is internal, though we often use many external sources to fuel and boost that power. Catalysts share elemental governors and affinities—a common vibrational rate or astral pattern—with our goals, which is why they work for us. Therefore it is important that we know enough about magickal energies to choose wisely. For instance, a form of candle magick might be selected when the desired outcome concerns profound change, passion, or other fiery issues, while cord magick might be chosen for a binding spell.

All catalysts fit into broad categories of general spell technique. Many of these are very popular methods for making magick, and entire books have been devoted to some of them. A listing of general magickal categories follows.

Magickal Categories

Candle and fire magick: Using candles, hearths, and flames

Color magick: Employing color as related to your magickal goal

Cords/string/knot magick: Using cords and knots to hold and release magickal energy

Divination tools magick: Using divination tools, such as tarot cards or rune stones, to help focus and send magickal energy

Divine/Spirit magick: Asking the assistance of deities, faeries, or other friendly spirits in your quest

Image magick: Using an image, such as a doll (called a poppet) to forge a magickal link with your goal

Incense and air magick: Using scent or the winds as a focus

Kitchen Witchery: Using the chemistry inherent in cooking to "bake" magick

Magickal herbalism: Harnessing the power inherent in herbs, flowers, plants, trees, and leaves as a catalyst for magick

Oils and essences magick: Using oils, tinctures, teas, or other blends from plants

Planetary magick: Harnessing the powers of the planets through ceremony or astrology to boost a spell's power

Stone and earth magick: Using stones, sticks, clay, salt, or other earth-related items

Sympathetic magick: The idea that like attracts like; for instance, using money in a spell to gain money

Water magick: Using water or water plants and images to raise and release magickal energy

Weather Witching: The art of causing certain types of weather to happen or not to happen; also, the art of using current weather conditions as catalysts for magick

Most of these types of magick can, and often times do, work together in the typical spell. For example, if you are working a fertility spell, you might choose to create an incense from the herb bistort, known to have affinities with this goal. You might also use clay, an earth substance that has fertile affinities as well; make a poppet of yourself or your mate clearly pregnant; employ the color red to represent the fertility of the mother Goddess; and work your spell when the moon is in a fertile sign such as Cancer. Please note that this example makes use of six of the above categories. They all have aspects sharing an affinity with the goal, and each one adds its own energy to that of the Witch working the spell. He or she carefully blends his or her energies with the catalyst (see chapter 2 on energy raising and directing), then pulls them together with his or her will and projects the need into the unseen world.

To discover the best catalyst or type of magick to use for any given spell will require some study on your part if you are not already familiar with common affinities of stones, colors, herbs, et cetera. Fortunately there are numerous books that discuss these in detail (to get you started, Appendix A lists common catalysts you can begin to work with and recaps some of the information given in this chapter). For now you can choose a catalyst simply by falling back on your elemental exercises and going with your instincts. For instance, if you have an earth-related goal, such as fertility, it is best to stick with earth-related catalysts. Choosing mud, soil, or clay to assist you is always a good bet for earth magick. You can also use herbs and plants that are earthy, such as those that grow underground, like carrots and turnips. If you are making fire-related magick, such as trying to stir up passions, think of fiery herbs and plants, spicy ones like cinnamon or thyme. For the time being, trust yourself and the rest will fall in place as you continue to work and learn.

Decide When You Want and Need to Do the Spell

Magickal timing can be a dull study, but it is a necessary skill for successful spellcrafting. Ideally magick should be done when it is needed because that is when your emotional connections are greatest. It is even better if you can time your efforts so one or more astrological aspects are at their peak. These aspects are:

- The moon's phase
- The moon's sign
- Moon void of course

- The day of the week
- The planetary hour

The Moon's Phase

The phase the moon is in during your spell is probably the single most important astrological aspect a Witch considers when planning a spell. The concept of working with the phase of the moon is ancient, dating to a time when people did not know that the moon was not actually growing full or wasting away as it waxed and waned. The moon, as the first time-keeper of humanity, was an object our ancestors centered their lives on. It dated their festivals, measured their weeks, marked the fertility cycle of females, and became a deity. In our collective genetic memory that association is still alive, which is why the symbolism of the moon's tides still triggers our minds to go in certain directions and why it is an excellent enhancement for our magickal actions.

The moon's phase can be divided into two basic parts: waxing (from new to full) and waning (from full to dark) [Llewellyn's *Moon Sign Book* and *Astrological Calendar* are good sources for this information]. Magick associated with gain, increase, or construction is traditionally done on the waxing moon. Magick for loss, decrease, or destruction is left to the waning moon. Again, the waning phase is not negative. Negativity is in the mind of the magician. Many things you may wish to decrease or destruct can have positive results, such as trying to lose a bad habit or a bad debt.

I have known many Witches who adhere much too rigidly to this formula, and cheat themselves out of needed magick in the meantime. In my previous book, *Lady of the Night: A Handbook of Moon Magick and Ritual*, I attempted to show how a spell's working and focus could be altered as needed to take advantage of this important lunar influence, no matter what phase the moon is currently in. The feedback I got was terrific! So many people had no idea they could make subtle alterations in their goal's focus to start getting what they need immediately. When the moon is in a phase seemingly incompatible with your intent, simply rethink the goal into its opposite form. For example, if your problem is money, focus your spell on its *gain* during the waxing phase and on the *loss* of debts during the waning phase. Virtually any spell can be reworked in these terms without the end result suffering one bit.

The Moon's Sign

The zodiac sign the moon is traversing through is another fact to consider, though it is of less importance than the moon's phase. Some signs are more conducive to magick in general, or certain types of magic in particular, than others. Remember that none of these transits will harm your spell in any way, but they do have their own spheres of influence that can color or boost them.

Moon in Aries

Aries is a masculine fire sign not known for being conducive to psychic work such as divination, dream work, or astral projection, though it is an excellent time to work magick for new ventures, particularly if they are financial, medical, or related to construction or conflict. It is also a good time for spells related to strength, stamina, courage, and lust.

Moon in Taurus

Taurus is a feminine earth sign and a good time for magick where issues of trust and loyalty are at stake. Astrologers say that the moon is "exalted" in Taurus, meaning that it stabilizes and refines the emotional influences of the moon. This makes this transit conducive to spellwork for the arts, love, and inner conflicts.

Moon in Gemini

Gemini is the most eclectic of all the signs, but also the most mercurial and fickle. It is a masculine air sign, an excellent time to work spells concerning communication, healing, writing, mass media, or for exposing hidden enemies.

Moon in Cancer

Cancer, a feminine water sign, is the home of the moon and the most fertile sign in the zodiac. Cancer is the best transit for working spells concerning fertility, pregnancy, children, the emotions, the home, eco-magick (magick that benefits the earth), or divination.

Moon in Leo

Leo is the most barren sign in the zodiac and not a good time for spells related to anything that fertile Cancer claims as her own. A masculine fire sign, the Leo transit is governed by the vibrant sun and makes spells regarding prosperity, employment, leadership, and celebrity work their best.

Moon in Virgo

Virgo is a feminine earth sign. This transit is best for spells whose goals are intellectual, detailed, or concerning education, volunteerism, health, or stability.

Moon in Libra

Libra is a masculine air sign as well as a sign of balance, therefore this transit is a good time for couple's magick or for spells for peace, wholeness of being, fairness, justice, partnership, and romance.

Moon in Scorpio

Scorpio rules the sexual organs and this transit is perfect for sex and fertility magick of all types. It is a feminine water sign, and the perfect transit for helping one unlock occult wisdom through divination and ritual.

Moon in Sagittarius

Sagittarius is the non-conformist of the zodiac, and a good lunar transit for experimenting with a new spell or ritual form. A masculine fire sign, it is not conducive to psychic work, but is a good time to focus on health and material concerns.

Moon in Capricorn

Capricorn, a feminine earth sign, is the best transit for spells concerning stability, peace of mind, or material items of necessity—such as that new car to get you to work and back.

Moon in Aquarius

Aquarius is probably the most misunderstood of all the transits. Magick worked in this masculine air sign can tend toward selfishness and promote thought without action. By contrast, it is also a transit that helps us reach a higher consciousness. Spells done for others work best during this transit.

Moon in Pisces

The transit through this feminine water sign brings out our psychic powers, triggers prophetic dreams, and promotes vivid astral experiences. This is a good time for spells dealing with the emotions and the inner self, past life exploration, spirit communication, and for divinations of all types.

Regardless of what transit the moon is taking when I work a spell, I faithfully record this information in my Book of Shadows. It has become valued information. I can look back on years of spell records and pinpoint which transit worked best for me for which types of spells.

Moon Void of Course

The last of the lunar influences to consider when timing a spell is whether or not the moon has moved fully into its next transit or not. When it has moved out of its last major aspect, a calculated directional relationship with another planet, before moving into another transit it is said to be *void of course.* This is usually marked on astrological data books as V/C or VoC, and they can last from a few minutes to the better part of a day.

All ventures begun during the void of course hours, spells included, tend to be difficult if not impossible to conclude, and if they do conclude they rarely pan out as expected. If the moon is void of course, put off all magick until the moon has moved safely into its next transit. Any good ephemeris or astrological calendar will have these hours clearly marked for you.

The Day of the Week

The other planets also exert an influence over our magick. Each of the seven major planets governs one day of the week when its influence is most strongly felt.

Sunday	Sun
Monday	Moon
Tuesday	Mars
Wednesday	Mercury
Thursday	Jupiter
Friday	Venus
Saturday	Saturn

Planetary Correspondences

Each planet governs its own magickal affinities and arenas:

Moon

Goddess mysteries, the home, children, childbirth, fertility, divination, motherhood, psychic powers, women, life cycles, dreams, growth, astral projection, the subconscious, water, sleep, reincarnation, private matters, the night, the home, animals, peace, tranquility, nursing

Sun

God mysteries, employment, the law, leadership, prosperity, money, protection, strength, men, royalty, theater, charity, entertainment/performing arts, heat, volunteering, law, government, self-confidence, movement/dance, fire, public matters, personal power, physical self-defense, purification, exorcism

Mercury

Communication, the intellect, fickleness, healing,
herbalism, writing, wisdom, mental prowess,
books/computers, reading, gossip, vocal music, travel,
correspondence, diplomacy, mathematics, the sciences,
history, school/education, mass media, visiting, libraries,
teachers, students.

Venus

Love/romance, family matters, husbands/wives,
sweethearts, peace, fashion, architecture, light
amusements, intimate social gatherings, shopping,
close friendships, gardening, fidelity, emotions, music,
pets, acts of kindness and generosity, art, sculpture,
poetry, beauty

Mars

Anger, power, lust, construction, war/combat, sex,
courage, banishing, medicine, passion, the military,
aggression/conflict, fear, police/soldiers, disagreement,
physical exertion, competition, group strength,
machinery, carpentry, bargaining power, needle crafts

Jupiter

Prosperity, money, employment, good fortune/luck,
fair judgments, friendship, investments, ambition,
wealth, prestige, success, courtrooms, gambling,
foreign interests, attraction, astronomy, social events,
psychology, the clergy, self-improvement.

Saturn

The hidden, past lives, transits, rebirth, self-undoing,
lies, mental and emotional distress, losses, the elderly,
completion, spirit communication, excavations,
archaeology, death, morality, meditation, accepting or
changing bad situations, protection from psychic attack

In addition to the planets already mentioned, our solar system also contains Neptune, Uranus, and Pluto, which were discovered long after the medieval system of planetary days was set. While they do not have specific days of the week they solely rule, they still have days they are more keenly felt. They also have arenas they govern either alone or in tandem with another planet.

Uranus

(Wednesday)—Spiritual pursuits, higher consciousness, stagnation, scattered energies

Neptune

(Monday or Friday)—Psychic efforts, dreams, intuition, divination, sea travel

Pluto

(Saturday)—The otherworld, death, transformation, generational issues

The Planetary Hours

A more precise way to harness planetary energy is by calculating the planetary hours of the day and night. This system dates back to the early medieval period and divides the hours of daylight and the hours of darkness each into twelve equal divisions so that day and night planetary hours are calculated separately.

To calculate these you will need a chart of the exact sunrise and sunset times for your locale. These times vary by latitude and a chart reckoned for a city more than an hour to the south or north of you will be useless unless you plan to drive all that way simply to work your spell. Charts for sunrise and sunset times can often be obtained through your local weather service, departments of fish and game (in the U.S.A.), or from local synagogues who use them to calculate the starting and stopping times of their holy days.

Take the total number of hours and minutes of daylight and divide by twelve. This will tell you exactly how long each planetary hour will be from sunrise to sunset (in other words, a planetary hour is not going to be a standard sixty minutes, but will be half of the total amount of daylight). Likewise, take the total number of hours and minutes of darkness and divide by twelve and you will get the length of each planetary hour from sunset to sunrise. In other words, there are twelve hours in every day (from sunrise to sunset) and twelve more every night (from sunset to sunrise). At the spring or autumn equinox every planet has exactly one hour of uninterrupted influence. At the winter solstice the night is longer and every planet has about an hour and twenty minutes during the night and about forty-seven minutes during the day.

The Planetary Hours Charts on pages 109 and 110 will show you the sequence of planets that govern each planetary hour. For example, if you are doing a spell concerning money during the daylight on a Sunday and want to add the influence of Jupiter which governs money matters, you would want to do it during the sixth planetary hour of the day.

Working with Storms

Another aspect of magickal timing involves working in tandem with weather patterns. Weather manifestations were considered a magickal phenomenon until surprisingly recent times, and seeking to control, change, or deflect weather was a cherished magickal art, one that many Witches spent lots of time learning and perfecting. Most of us are familiar with the rain dances of the Native Americans or the legends about the Druids of sixteenth-century England calling forth the storm that foiled the Spanish Armada's attack. But even when we are not adept at shaping the weather, we can still use the weather that comes our way as a powerful energy source for boosting our magick.

One of the greatest shows in nature is the electrical storm, and many of us have experienced the tingling of static electricity when one is very close. This is pure energy waiting to be channeled. Magickally speaking, the storm provides us a balance and a blending of the four elements: fire as lightning, water as rain, air as wind, all pounding the earth. Earth can also be represented in a storm as hail stones.

Daylight Hours

	Sunday	Monday	Tuesday	Wednesday	Thursday	Friday	Saturday
1	Sun	Moon	Mars	Mercury	Jupiter	Venus	Saturn
2	Venus	Saturn	Sun	Moon	Mars	Mercury	Jupiter
3	Mercury	Jupiter	Venus	Saturn	Sun	Moon	Mars
4	Moon	Mars	Mercury	Jupiter	Venus	Saturn	Sun
5	Saturn	Sun	Moon	Mars	Mercury	Jupiter	Venus
6	Jupiter	Venus	Saturn	Sun	Moon	Mars	Mercury
7	Mars	Mercury	Jupiter	Venus	Saturn	Sun	Moon
8	Sun	Moon	Mars	Mercury	Jupiter	Venus	Saturn
9	Venus	Saturn	Sun	Moon	Mars	Mercury	Jupiter
10	Mercury	Jupiter	Venus	Saturn	Sun	Moon	Mars
11	Moon	Mars	Mercury	Jupiter	Venus	Saturn	Sun
12	Saturn	Sun	Moon	Mars	Mercury	Jupiter	Venus

Nighttime Hours

	Sunday	Monday	Tuesday	Wednesday	Thursday	Friday	Saturday
1	Jupiter	Venus	Saturn	Sun	Moon	Mars	Mercury
2	Mars	Mercury	Jupiter	Venus	Saturn	Sun	Moon
3	Sun	Moon	Mars	Mercury	Jupiter	Venus	Saturn
4	Venus	Saturn	Sun	Moon	Mars	Mercury	Jupiter
5	Mercury	Jupiter	Venus	Saturn	Sun	Moon	Mars
6	Moon	Mars	Mercury	Jupiter	Venus	Saturn	Sun
7	Saturn	Sun	Moon	Mars	Mercury	Jupiter	Venus
8	Jupiter	Venus	Saturn	Sun	Moon	Mars	Mercury
9	Mars	Mercury	Jupiter	Venus	Saturn	Sun	Moon
10	Sun	Moon	Mars	Mercury	Jupiter	Venus	Saturn
11	Venus	Saturn	Sun	Moon	Mars	Mercury	Jupiter
12	Mercury	Jupiter	Venus	Saturn	Sun	Moon	Mars

When I was first taught to work with storms I was with a coven whose members would, at the mere approach of a storm, grab up all their magickal accoutrements and head outdoors. Common sense has since taught me that this is not always wise. Hoisting a metal sword up toward a stormy sky is more likely to make you a human lightning rod than a successful magician. Approached with caution and common sense—and indoors if need be—you can use your meditative techniques to align yourself with this powerful energy (see chapter 2). When you feel this has been successfully done (trust your instincts on this, they are probably better than you think), you can focus and send that energy where you wish it to go: into a tool or cord for later use, into a current need, or into someone who needs healing. Since you have the power of the four elements at your disposal, you can use an electrical storm to fuel virtually any kind of spell and, as long as both the storm and your own willpower hold out, you can send one spell on its way and then turn right around and draw on the storm's energy yet again to either boost the same goal or make another spell.

Be Sure of the Ethics of Your Goal

Once you have the spell constructed to this point, you need to stop and make sure of the ethics contained in your spell. You want to make absolutely sure that nothing in it, from visualization to wording, is going to bring harm to anyone. Simply looking at it on paper will not reveal these hidden aspects, nor will it tell you the future. This is why Witches have always relied on their divination devices to help them assess the harmful potential in any spell.

Divination is the art of reading signs and symbols that tell us about past or future events. Through divination we can assess potential outcome to certain events based on the energies currently in motion around the wheel of life. This is why you must construct the spell before you can get an accurate reading of its harm potential. You must first set those energies in motion for them to be readable by divinatory means.

If you do not already have a divination method you are proficient in, now is the time to start learning. This is one of those basic tools of Witchcraft that is indispensable. You can choose tarot cards, rune stones, pendulums, automatic writing, ogham sticks, or any other method. Books, decks, kits, and instruction books are readily available that can take you from novice to master in a relatively short time if you are willing to put in the effort to learn. If you are not sure which divination device is best for you, take a stroll through the metaphysical section of your local bookstore or ask in any occult shop. Someone will be glad to show you what is available and let you peruse the books and kits so you can decide which one most appeals to you.

What follows is the layout, or spread if you prefer, for a cards or stones divination that looks at all aspects of your spell's outcome. I have made similar layouts public before, and each of them varies little. This is because there are certain things you need to know about your spell before jumping blindly into it, and the questions these readings seek to answer cover them all. By reading each position carefully and critically, you will know which areas, if any, of your spell are potentially harmful, or which ones just need some work in general to balance out the energies to make it more successful. If you do not have tarot cards or rune stones you may substitute black and white markers or pebbles. The white represent positive energies or outcomes and the black ones negative. While this will not give you an in-depth look at the problems in the spell, it can help steer you in the right direction and show where some reevaluation is needed. In either case, where and how you make your corrections is solely up to you.

Cut the cards or stir the stones in your usual pre-divination manner. Be sure to focus clearly on your need to discover the outcome of your spell before you lay down the first card or stone. Interpret the positions in the following manner by assessing the meaning of each card or stone in relation to these influences:

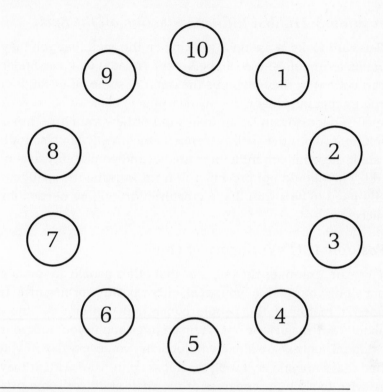

The Wheel Divination: a Tarot card, rune, or stone spread for learning about any harmful elements in a spell.

Position 1: The Need

This card defines the need or desire on which the spell is based. This may turn out to be exactly what you expect, or it may offer you new insights into your goal.

Position 2: The Hidden Underlying Need

This card looks at the root of your desire. This may be an issue or event you are already aware of, or you may find that your real agenda is quite different than you first expected. If this is the case, then you should seriously rethink your goal just to make sure you really want what you think you do.

Position 3: Hidden Influences Acting on the Spell

This card looks at energies working on the spell that you may not be aware of. These can be karmic (related to a past life or past action) or they might be the input of some other random energy that may inadvertently be trying to block or boost your spell. This card can be an indication of how your true inner self feels about the spell's intended outcome. It can also indicate if these hidden influences are beyond your ability to control. This should not prevent you from working the spell, but you need to be aware that a greater effort will be needed for success.

Position 4: The Influence of Others

This card examines the energies that other people are tossing out along your path to your goal, either positive or negative. It doesn't matter if the people concerned consciously know about your magick or not; their feelings about you and your eventual success are already influencing you every day. If you find that someone is putting roadblocks onto your path, it may be wise to slow the progress of the spell and take some psychic self-defense measures (see chapter 7).

Position 5: The Spell's Weaknesses

This card will show what aspects of your spell are in need of refinement. (Pay attention to these as they may be subtle!) This does not mean that any part of the spell is wrong or harmful, only that there is room for improvement. If the spell is worth doing at all, you should make every effort to alter it as needed so that it can be as effective as possible. My experience has shown that if this card makes absolutely no sense in relation to the issue at hand, then the spell has no major weakness.

Position 6: The Spell's Strengths

This card is your ego booster. It tells you what you are doing right with the spell you have constructed. Use this card as a gauge by which to measure your progress in the magickal arts. I have found that if the card makes no sense in relation to the issue then the spell is fine as is but it has no outstandingly brilliant qualities.

Position 7: The Inner-World Outcome

Because your spells must first go into the unseen or astral world, the place where thought forms live, you need to be aware that your spell also has the potential to do damage in that world as well as in the physical one. Causing harm in the astral is just as much of a no-no as causing it in the physical, and you will be made to pay for any transgression. This card indicates what blessings or havoc your magick could cause on the astral because of the thought forms you will be creating there.

Position 8: The Physical World Outcome

This card indicates what blessings or havoc will be wrought on the physical plane by your spell. This includes both the mundane results and the harm potential to both living things and the environment.

Position 9: The Final Outcome

This card tells you the probable culmination of your actions, the success or failure of your spell, the harm or help that will be left in all worlds, and if you will be happy with the end results or not. Between this card and cards 7 and 8, you should be able to tell if your spell will be beneficial to all concerned, if it will bring harm to anyone, and if it will yield what you desire.

Position 10: What Comes Back to You

This is the karmic card, the one linking the beginning and end of the wheel of life in relation to your spell and showing you what type of energies you will be placing on that wheel with your magick. If you have so far chosen to ignore the niggling evidence that some aspect of your spell might be harmful, this tells you how severe your payback will be. As already mentioned, a divination can only read potential already set in motion. If you change your actions now, you will change the energy you send onto the wheel, and this will alter the potential outcome for everyone. Take steps now to negate the harm potential both to others and to yourself.

If you see potential harm in your spell, this does not necessarily mean that your goal is wrong and that you should give it up. It just may mean you need to change only the part that is harmful. To find this, first check to make sure that you are not trying to dictate to the universe the manner in which it produces your goal. If you are trying to force this you may be taking from someone else against their will. If you are sure that it is not the case, refer back to the divination to help you pinpoint the problem area. It may be as much as a single word amiss. Try rewording the spell, its visualization, or its catalyst, and then do the divination again.

If after repeated efforts at modification you still do not get a divination you are comfortable with, you have one of two choices: one, you can cancel or postpone the spell to a later date, or two, you can add a line to your words of power such as "as it harms none," or "as all freely will," or "by the free will of all," or some similar vow to ensure that you are not violating the Rede. Including this may negate certain aspects of the spell's success, but it will be worth it if it keeps you free from unpleasant karmic entanglements.

Gather All Equipment and Go to Your Magickal Place at the Appropriate Time

It goes without saying that before you take off to your magickal place, whether that is a trek out to a local woods or a retreat to a corner of your own bedroom, you should have with you everything you need. While it is permissible to stop what you are doing and go in search of missing items, this is inadvisable. First of all, doing this will break your concentration on the task at hand. Instead of visualizing your goal, you will be trying to recall where you left your jar of basil leaves or your willow wand. Secondly, if you are working with a specific astrological factor your window of opportunity may be limited, and taking time out to search for missing items may throw off all your careful calculations. Thirdly, when you step out of sacred space in a highly charged state, such as a magickal one, you leave yourself vulnerable to attack by malevolent entities who are attracted by your strong energy field. In either case, the power you have available to put behind your spell will be siphoned off either through scattering your concentration or by having to put it into psychic self-defense (see chapter 7).

There are three ways to help you avoid forgetting things. One, have a permanent magickal space in which you can keep a cabinet with all your magickal catalysts, tools, and other items readily at hand. Two, on a separate piece of paper keep a running list of materials you need as you construct the spell. As you list each tool or catalyst during your construction of the spell, think in terms of what you need to take to make these items work properly. For example, when you write down that you will need one yellow candle, you should not only add the candle to your materials list, but also matches, a candle holder, and a snuffer. Three, you can also do a dress rehearsal for your spell, walking through it step by step. Not only will this ensure that all needed items are at hand, but for novices it is a great confidence builder too. It fixes in your mind exactly what you plan to do and how you will do it. Constantly referring back to written instructions to make sure you are on the correct step is distracting and will only serve to siphon off energy that could be better used to build up your spell. This is why many Pagan/Wiccan rituals are memorized ahead of time.

Prepare Your Magickal Space

Magickal space should be made sacred before it is used. These preparations can be as elaborate or simple as you like, but all should involve purifying and blessing the area and protecting yourself.

Even for simple spells and divinations, many Witches like to cast a complete ritual circle (see chapter 6); others do not. Many simply opt to psychically cleanse the area and do a brief self-protection rite.

When you have all your needed items and are at your magickal space, take a few moments to close your eyes, breathe deeply, and allow yourself to mentally connect with the energy pattern of the area. Even if you have used this same space before, you should still purify it anew because all sorts of minor occurrences can cause a change in energy patterns. People, arguments, illness, weather, animals, and unseen spirits can all leave their psychic imprint on a location.

Once you feel in tune with the area, mentally draw up from Mother Earth a ball of radiant white light. White is a traditional color of purification. Direct this to the center of the area and set it spinning counterclockwise. This is the direction traditionally associated with acts of banishing. In this type of purification, the goal is to banish all negative energies that may have settled in the area. When you feel this has been accomplished, allow the remainder of the ball to sink back into the earth.

You may also want to light a purifying incense such as frankincense, cinnamon, or bay. You can set it burning in the center of your space or carry it to the perimeters of your magickal work space while visualizing the vibrations of the area rising, taking on higher spiritual qualities, and becoming incompatible with those low-level entities and negative energies. I also like to take an herb known for both its purifying and protective properties and scatter it about the sacred space. My usual choice is basil, though bay, black pepper, cinnamon, or table salt work just as well. The drawback to salt is that it destroys carpets, and using too much will scorch any ground it hits.

As you work with the incense or the herbs, you can strengthen your visualization by chanting. As mentioned in chapter 2, chanting is an excellent way to center and focus magickal energy. You may write your own or use or adapt one of the following:

Incense, air of high refine,
Purify this space of mine.
Purged and purified be this place
That I have chosen as magickal space.
Herbs of Mother Earth give blessings here
To me, this rite, this sacred sphere.
Protect and cleanse this sacred place,
Hallow it now as my magickal space.

You must also offer yourself some type of psychic protection as you begin to do your spell. If you have cast a formal circle, then that protection is already in place (see chapter 6 for discussion and instructions). Keep in mind that any visualized circle can serve both as protection for you and as containment for energy you have raised even if you do not fully call the quarters, et cetera, as is done for a full-blown ritual circle. You can mentally draw a small protective circle around you just by willing it to be so with visualization.

If you choose to work without a circle you can protect yourself by:

- "Bathing" yourself in the smoke of a protective incense. The Native Americans frequently employ this method and refer to it as smudging. It is usually done with sage to purify, but can also be done with frankincense, cinnamon, thyme, or bay to protect.

- Mentally drawing down a protective white-gold light from high above you. See this as the universal power of the divine energy entering you, raising your inner vibrations, and making your spell an unwelcome event to troublesome entities.

- Mentally drawing up another ball of white light from Mother Earth and allowing it to encase you.

- Asking protection of your patron deity, or of the God and Goddess, by means of a prayer.

Ground, Center, and Begin Clearly Visualizing Your Goal

When your sacred space is ready and you are adequately protected, you should begin to focus solely on the task at hand. Firmly affix yourself, through visualization, at the center of all time and space, able to reach out to any world at will. Center yourself by drawing your personal energy into either a line running through your chakra centers or at your solar plexus or heart chakra centers (see chapter 2). Take a few deep breaths and feel yourself making a connection with the creative powers of the universe. Feel their energy filling you, merging with your own, and making you able to achieve anything you will.

Clear your mind of all other thoughts and begin clearly visualizing your goal. This is probably the most important step in the spell casting process and you should invest the mental image with as much power as you can muster. Recall your need in vivid detail and make your emotional connection with it as deeply and on as many levels as possible.

Raise Magickal Energy

Raise energy within yourself (see chapter 2 for a discussion of methods for doing this) and pour it into the magickal object(s) in whatever way feels right to you. This can be done as a mental projection, through dance, drumming, song, intense visualization, et cetera.

Do Whatever Physical Actions Your Spell Requires

Though you actually began making magick the second you started thinking how to go about creating your spell, it is this physical action most think of as the "real" spell. At this point you will work the main body of the spell, using the words, gestures, actions, et cetera, that you have worked so long and hard to prepare. Do whatever physical actions you have decided your spell requires (i.e., candle lighting, doll making, dancing). Use your words of power, light your candles, bury your herbs, mentally charge your stones, et cetera.

Release the Magickal Energy Toward Its Goal

When the physical actions are over, you should not rush to end the spell but rather revel in your feelings of success. See yourself as having now achieved your goal. Get as excited about it as you would if someone walked up to you at this moment and handed it to you on one of those proverbial silver platters. This is part of believing in yourself and your efforts.

You can also continue raising energy, perhaps creating what Witches have referred to for centuries as the Cone of Power. This name comes from the way this mass of power is shaped— as an inverted cone of energy rising over your working area. Many Witches believe this once-secret magickal practice to be the origin of the pointed hat seen ad nauseum in drawings of wizards and Halloween Witches. As you employ your energy raising techniques, mentally send them into a swirling cone around you. Send it clockwise if your spell is involved with manifesting and counterclockwise if you are seeking to banish. The cone is more effective in a group setting where many people can add their energy to the cone, but it can be done effectively alone if you don't try to make it too big. Remember that it is quality, not size, that makes it work.

When you feel the cone has peaked over your circle, and that you cannot possibly add any more strength to it, release it to do its job. Mentally and visually send it out toward its task. You should physically back up this effort by a releasing gesture such as the relaxation of your muscles, flinging wide your arms, spinning, throwing up your arms, raising a tool, kneeling or prostrating yourself, or doing whatever else makes you feel the energy is being sent.

End the Spell and Close
Your Sacred Space

You should finish your spell with words such as the traditional "So mote it be" or some other words or sounds that signal your deep mind that the energy projection is being shut down. Because these statements should always be phrased positively and in the present tense, they also affirm that you believe you know your magick is successful.

If you have been inside a fully cast circle, you will need to close it (see chapter 6). If not, simply visualize the excess energies you have released being grounded. If you have been outdoors, thank the spirits that dwell there for allowing you to use the space. You may even wish to leave a small gift, such as a coin, a stone, or some food if you are in the wild.

Ground Excess Energy into the Earth

All magickal energy does not leave you when you send it out to work on a spell. It can linger on and around you, causing you to feel jittery or even haunted. Ground it by placing your hands palms-down on the earth, into a bowl of soil, or on the floor of your home. Physically and psychically feel the excess energy draining out of you and know it is being safely absorbed and dispersed into Mother Earth (see chapter 2 for more on grounding).

Naturally if you are not in a place where your hands can actually touch the ground, this exercise can be done through the soles of your feet (even while wearing shoes!) or through careful visualization.

Record Your Effort in Your
Book of Shadows

Record your spell in your Magickal Diary or Book of Shadows with the date, time, weather conditions, and any astrological data you wish to include. This will be useful later when you have done enough spells to look for patterns. You may find that your most efficacious spells were done on Sundays, or when it was cloudy or snowing, or when you worked with a particular deity, when you burned green candles, or when the moon was full. Everyone has different affinities. These patterns will help you pick the best times for future spellwork.

Back Up Your Magick on the Physical Plane

Backing up your desire on the physical plane is a must! For example, if you have done a spell for healing, don't avoid seeing your doctor. You will need all the help at your disposal to overcome your illness, and magick and medical science make great partners. If your goal is a job, hit the streets and put in applications. If your goal is fertility, buy an ovulation detector kit or make an appointment with a reproductive endocrinologist. Even the Judeo-Christian spiritual traditions have a saying that teaches "God helps those who help themselves."

If you have followed up in every way you can think of, and nothing else you can do physically comes to mind, you can still spend as much time as is practical each day focusing on it by clearly visualizing your goal as a fait accompli. These added boosts of daily energy can often mean the difference between success and failure.

Rework the Spell as Needed

Some spells ask that you repeat them three, seven, or even nine nights (or days) in succession. This is sometimes done to take advantage of several astrological influences or to incorporate a sacred number into the spell. Sometimes it is simply to help you throw the full effort of your energy behind it. Some spells do not ask outright that you repeat them, but you may feel you need to do this to make them successful.

Break the Spell When Necessary

Some Witches do not like to allow the energy from a spell to continue indefinitely and will pick a time to break the spell by formally stopping the flow of magickal energy. They do this whether the spell has been successful or not.

I have never felt that most spells need to be broken since without a sustained input of energy, they die a natural death. The one case in which I feel that spell breaking is necessary is when another being has been involved with it such as a deity, a faery, a human spirit, or another astral creature, none of which are dealt with in this book. I further believe that most spells are broken as soon as thanks are given for its success. For me this automatically grounds any excess energy that may be running about from the magick.

If you feel you want to break a spell, simply stop the flow of energy into it and then visualize the energy you have projected into it breaking apart and fading into Mother Earth to be grounded. Then open your arms to symbolically gather up any stray energy that may be floating around you. Allow it to collect in the palms of your hands. When you feel that it has all been gathered up, place your hands flat on the earth or floor and ground the rest.

▼

5

A Sampler of Spells

This chapter provides a few simple spells to help you fully understand how the steps explained in the previous chapter are made to work. As you will see, it is much easier to put it all together than it may appear on paper. The trick is, as always, throwing the weight of your will behind the effort. When in doubt about what items to use or what things to do, don't forget to fall back on your elemental knowledge. This will immediately help you find the right tools and other correspondences best suited to your need.

Any spell you find in a book, or any other source except your own head, should be viewed as an outline, a map for getting you from point A to point B. What detours and side trips you take while traveling that road are up to you. I have used many spells taken from other sources, but rarely in the precise form in which I found them. When I was first learning to use magick I admit to following the recipes more closely. Then, as my confidence grew, I began to tailor them to my needs and affinities. For instance, if a spell required a fruit acid to cause a chemical reaction and it recommended an orange, I would substitute an apple because they are often used in Celtic magick, and my Craft tradition is a Celtic one. If it called for a watery herb, like lotus, I sometimes substituted moss because it is still a water herb, but one with which I have an affinity (and one much easier to locate!).

When substituting catalysts you should—as always—rely on your elemental teachings gleaned through your meditations and personal insights, as well as through any reading you may have done. Allow your magickal intuition to tell you which herb, oil, stone, or color fits which spell, and trust it to be correct. After spending a few months meditating with the elements it should not be hard to think in terms of earth/prosperity = brown, green, earthy herbs, dark stones, et cetera; or love/romance = water, pink, red, hearts, rose quartz, wine, et cetera. The ruling element of each spell in this chapter is provided so that you can work with these correspondences and/or substitutes if desired (or needed).

All the spells in this chapter pick up in the middle of the step-by-step spell construction guide given in the previous chapter. Prior to stepping into the spell as written you will need to have already completed steps 1–7. Studying the construction of these sample spells will show you much about how this was done:

Step-by-Step Spell Construction Guide

1. Clearly understand and define your magickal goal
2. Plan your visualization and other wording
3. Choose your catalysts and begin to empower them
4. Decide when you want and need to do the spell
5. Be sure of the ethics of your goal
6. Gather all equipment and go to your magickal place at the appropriate time
7. Prepare your magickal space

   Steps 8–12 will be illustrated within the written spells themselves. The way in which the closing steps (13–16) are handled will be up to you:

13. Ground excess energy into the earth
14. Record your effort in your Book of Shadows
15. Back up your magick on the physical plane
16. Rework the spell as needed

A Spell for Peace in the Home

Ruling Element: Water

Defined Goal: "To bring a sense of calm and peace to my
home and those who live here; to stop quarrels before
they begin so that my home is a pleasant and safe
place to be, and to neutralize all negative energy in
my home caused by past arguments."

Best Time: Friday, waxing or full moon, at dawn or dusk,
moon in Libra

Materials: A non-metallic bowl of blessed water, a
projective tool like a wand or athame (only if you
already have one), and a few grains of salt or a
rose quartz crystal. The quartz may be harder to
come by than salt, but the stone is recommended
for this spell since using salted water on your
home furnishings can cause damage to them. If
you choose or have to use salt, keep the amount to
only a few grains. The spell will still work since it
is not quantity that counts, but energy and intent.

Take a non-metallic bowl and fill it with water. This can be
plain old tap water; it doesn't matter since you will be charging and blessing it to turn it into the kind of water you want it
to be. When you are in your magickal place, begin stirring the
water with your bare hands in a clockwise motion. The clockwise turning of the water is compatible with your goal of increasing peace. While your hand is in the water, you should be
charging and empowering it as a catalyst for your goal. You
can do this in any way that appeals to you, or that was outlined in chapter 2. Your hands and your will alone will do just
fine if you find you are unsure what else to do.

When it is as charged as you feel it can be, take your forefinger or any tool and hold it over the water. Bless the water
by saying something like:

> Powers of water, flowing and peaceful,
> I bless you by my will, and charge you
> to send your loving energy into this
> spell. So mote it be.

Touch your tool or finger to the water to seal the blessing. The image of a projective masculine item, like an athame or finger, uniting with the receptive feminine water is a very old method of Craft blessing. Symbolically it brings together the masculine and feminine polarities of creation into one place and makes for very potent magick.

Next, take the salt or the rose quartz and charge it to your goal. You can stir the salt as you did the water, or you can use another method. The quartz can be charged in your hands by visualization or with the energy of one of your chakra points. When you feel the salt or the quartz is ready, hold it over the water and visualize the grounding and peaceful energies inside them waiting to be pulled out by you. When you feel ready, place the salt or quartz into the blessed water with these or similar words of power:

> Salt (or Quartz) and water.
> Water and earth united.
> Peace may they bring to this dwelling.
> By my will, so mote it be.

Beginning at the point in your home where you feel the most discord occurs (living room, bedroom, kitchen, et cetera), take the bowl of water and, with your fingers, begin sprinkling it about your home. Move clockwise throughout the house, sprinkling and visualizing a calming peace descending over your home and those who live there.

Chanting is a good way to keep your mind focused on this goal and to help maintain the energy flow. Try writing your own couplet, or try this one:

> Salt and water clears the air,
> Peace and calm to all in here.

Be sure to give extra attention to those other places where quarrels or problems often begin, and don't stop until you have reached your starting point. When you get there, send out the excess energy you may still be carrying around into the bowl of water. Place it in the kitchen or bathroom to continue pouring out its peaceful influence in the days ahead as you back up your spell on the physical. When you feel the bowl has done all it can for you, offer your thanks to the powers that have assisted you, then pour it either down the drain or against the outside foundation of your house.

A Spell for Home Protection

Ruling Element: Fire

Defined Goal: "To ward my home so that it is protected from elemental harm such as fire and flood, and from intruders both astral and physical. I want all current negativity that may be attracting other negative aspects to be gone, and I want it sealed against future attacks of negativity."

Best Time: Sunday or Tuesday, waxing or full moon, planetary hour of the Sun or of Mars, moon in Leo or Aries

Materials: Basil or cinnamon herbs, and incense made from cinnamon, frankincense, or other fiery protective herbs, matches, incense holder

You may begin this spell at any place in your home you wish to start, though I always like to start as close to the center as possible when doing a protection spell. You will not have to purify your magickal space because your whole home will become your magickal space and be cleared of its negative energies during the course of this spell.

Start by centering yourself. With your goal fixed clearly in your mind, mentally reach down deep into Mother Earth and pull up a ball of intense white light. Bring it into yourself without breaking the link to the earth. Then draw down the same light from high above you, bringing in the protective blessing of the divine universal. Also bring this into yourself without breaking the connection.

As you stand there with the divine light from above and below linking you to all time and space, begin to expand the energy. Visualize the white light radiating outward until the giant ball of white envelops your entire home. As it pulsates, visualize it neutralizing any negative energy there. See any unwanted entities who are hanging around fleeing in terror from its brightness. Keep this up until you feel your home is purged of all negative influences.

Without shutting down the ball of light, but without continuing to feed it, light some protective incense such as frankincense or cinnamon. These are relatively easy to obtain in any store selling novelty or gift items. Even many drug stores now carry stick or cone incense in these popular scents. Both frankincense and cinnamon have the ability to raise the vibrational rate of any area they are in. This means that they elevate its spiritual aspects, making a place incompatible with the low-level entities you wish to banish.

Take the incense into each room of your home, including closets, while you visualize the vibrational rate increasing and placing a mantle of protection over your home. Think of this as both driving out any astral beings you don't want around and also setting up warning vibrations to any physical intruders who might be contemplating entering your home. You should also visualize it as banishing the uglier aspects of the elements that could hurt your home. This includes flood waters, earthquakes, house or brush fires, winds, and storms.

As you make your rounds, you may talk about what you want to have happen using any words of power you have constructed for this spell. Be sure they are in keeping with "harm none" and with your defined goal. Even repeating your defined goal over and over to yourself is useful for keeping you focused, and these make excellent choices for your words of power.

Next, you will ward your house at all vulnerable points, such as doors and windows, by using the image of a fiery pentagram. A pentagram is the five-pointed star that has come to symbolize most Wiccan traditions. It is also a protective symbol, especially so when combined with the imagery of fire.

Allow yourself a moment to feel lots of fiery outrage that any being, physical or spectral, would dare to enter your home without your permission. Carry that passion with you as you move clockwise through the house stopping at each vulnerable point and, with your hand or finger, drawing the image of a large pentagram on its surface. Visualize that pentagram flaming with protective fire, burning anything that dares to enter uninvited, and frightening away other intruders. As you draw each one, reaffirm your effort with words such as:

> *By my will and this pentagram of fire,*
> *None may enter here but by my desire.*
> *Blessed be this dwelling space,*
> *Nothing harmful may enter this place.*

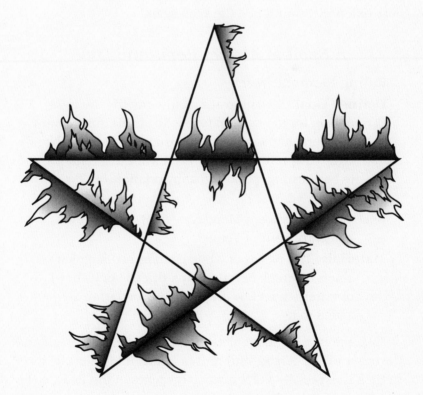

A flaming protective pentagram with its apex up

End the spell by grounding the white light and charging some protective herbs, like cinnamon or basil, and sprinkling them clockwise around the outside foundation of your home. If you are having trouble choosing a protective herb, remember to think fiery! If you live in an apartment, you may place these in a glass jar as close to the center of your apartment as possible.

You may wish to renew this spell once a month to keep it strong, or you may only want to do it as you feel the need. The choice is yours, though I heartily recommend a monthly renewal. I renew all my protection spells on the new moon. I have lived with these energies for so long now that I am used to the way they feel, and whenever I have forgotten to renew them I can sense their waning power and it makes me feel very defenseless until I do the spell again.

A Spell to Attract Romantic Love

Ruling Element: Water

Defined Goal: "I want to attract into my life the right person for me to be in love with at this time. I want this person to love me in return because I am the right person for him (or her). I want this romance to be a lasting, positive, happy relationship for all concerned."

Best Times: Friday or Monday, waxing or full moon, planetary hour of Venus

Materials: Two pieces of white cloth or two handkerchiefs, a length of red or pink thread, and a bowl of water with a few drops of blue food coloring added to it

Take the two handkerchiefs and name one as yourself and the other as the person you want to attract into your life. Love magick is especially vulnerable to breaches of the Rede, so be careful not to visualize an actual person or you risk violating someone's free will. You may think about the qualities of a person you admire, but not that person specifically.

Spend as much time as needed beforehand investing the two handkerchiefs with the energy of your goal. Then, when you are in your magickal space and actually doing the spell, you can truly see them for what they represent.

Visualizing your life merging with that of someone you love and who loves you in return, begin twisting the two handkerchiefs together. This does not have to be done tightly or beautifully, they just have to be joined. Be sure to keep your visualization up as you do this!

Again, chanting is a good idea. If you don't know what to say, sing a love song. There are certainly enough to choose from since romance has always been, and still is, the songwriter's bread and butter. Just be sure to carefully plan out which one you will use beforehand to make sure that all the wording in it is fully compatible with your goal. You don't need any songs about broken hearts or cheating souls to come into this spell.

When you are done, wad the braided handkerchief up into a small, loose ball and tie it with the red or pink thread. Red and pink are popular colors for love magick, as witnessed in their profusion around St. Valentine's Day (in actuality the old Roman Pagan holiday of Lupercalia, which celebrated love, faithfulness, and commitment). As you bind them, think of red's passion or pink's romantic qualities as the initial point of attraction.

Place the wad of cloth into the blue water. Blue is the color of loyalty and endurance. You want this relationship to endure as the two of you continue to grow closer.

Set the bowl aside where it will not be disturbed. Every morning before you leave your house stir it clockwise a few times and notice how the string is loosening, and the cloths unwinding, all of them blending into oneness in the water of fidelity. Keep this up until you meet someone with whom you can start a serious relationship, then throw out the water and allow the cloths to dry, keeping them as talismans of luck for your new union.

A Spell for Prosperity

Ruling Element: Earth

Defined Goal: "I want to bring prosperity into my life
now in the form of a cash flow large enough to meet
all my current needs so that I don't have to worry
every week about paying my bills and so I have a
little left over for security."

Best Time: Sunday, new moon, moon in Leo

Materials: A bowl of earth or clay, seven coins, a handkerchief or small piece of cloth in gold or green

Prosperity takes many forms and has different meanings
for many of us. For some of us it means simply money, for
others it means having food on the table and a roof over our
heads, for still others it means having a life full of friends,
family, and love. For the example in this spell, prosperity will
mean monetary security. In your magickal space, empower a
bowl of earth to your goal. Think of it as the fertile womb of
Mother Earth, your Goddess, from whom all blessings flow.
Know for certain that anything you plant in that soil will grow
and flourish.

Take seven coins, which you should have been charging as
you prepared this spell, and give them another boost of your
energy. See them as talismans of your new wealth.

One by one, press the coins deep into the bowl of soil with
words such as:

> *Coin of silver (or gold) shining bright,*
> *Needed by me so much this night,*
> *I plant you in the soil of earth,*
> *The Mother Goddess to give you rebirth.*
> *Blessings and more she gives to me,*
> *Money threefold returns to me,*
> *As I sow so shall I reap,*
> *Needed money for me to keep.*

Spend some time visualizing the goal once again, then place the bowl in your bedroom. Each morning before you leave your house, dig through the soil and pull out one coin. Place this in the gold or green cloth and carry it in your pocket (or purse) as a talisman to attract money. Continue doing this for a full week until you have extracted all the buried coins and are carrying them, happily jingling, in your pocket.

The imagery here is twofold. First, it gives you the feeling of being able to get money when needed by pulling it out of the earth where you planted it. Second, the coins themselves act as a form of sympathetic magick. This is a situation where a force or item is expected to attract a like force or item; in this case, money will attract money.

A Spell to Increase Mental Powers

Ruling Element: Air

Defined Goal: "To increase my intellectual capacity and assist in keeping my focus and concentration on my mental pursuits so that I can function to the best of my intellectual ability throughout the weeks to come."

Best Time: Wednesday, moon in Gemini or Virgo

Materials: A handful of ground rosemary and an east wind

I first used this unbelievably simple spell when I was in my last year of undergraduate school at the University of Texas. It was getting close to final exams and my best friend and I were a mess. We hadn't slept well for many nights, and besides our schooling we had several other projects in the works that required our attention. Thinking clearly was a rarity, and focusing our mental selves on any single task for more than a superficial minute was almost impossible. We looked to magick to help us get through those last trying weeks of the semester.

To work this spell, you will need only a small handful of ground rosemary (rosemary needles will not give you the pleasant effect of flying away on the breeze that the ground herb will). When you have determined that the wind is blowing from the east, the direction associated with air and the intellect, take the rosemary and empower it. Then go outdoors where you can feel the east wind blowing on you. Still clutching the rosemary in your hand, face the wind and allow yourself to mentally connect with the powers of the air element. Feel the intelligence of the wind and know that you can tap into its power. Visualize it as a catalyst for your own mental powers that need a boost.

When you feel the time is right, turn from the wind to face west and gently blow the herbs from the palm of your hand into the wind. Allow them to be carried away from you, knowing that they take your will into the unseen world to work on your behalf.

Back up the spell in the physical with lots of study and hard work.

A Spell For Personal Transformation

Ruling Element: Fire

Defined Goal: Open

Best Time: Sunday or Saturday, moon in Gemini

Materials: A candle in any color you choose (match it to your ultimate goal as best you can), matches, a candle holder, a snuffer, some energetic non-vocal music, something to play the music on (tape or CD player, et cetera), and a drum (only if you already have one)

This spell can be used to change anything about yourself you do not like. It can help you break a bad habit, lose or gain weight, be more compassionate, et cetera, but you must truly have the will to change, and only then can this spell give you the strength you need to make those changes in your life.

In your magickal space, light the candle. As it starts to burn, see it representing what you want to change in yourself. See the old burning away with the melting candle and the new desire being carried into the unseen world with the candle's flame. Spend as much time as you need making this mental connection.

Set the candle where it will not be knocked over, as the rest of this spell is going to get very energetic.

Turn on your energetic music. The reason it needs to be non-vocal is so that the words and mental images you use are your own, and not those supplied by a lyricist, whose agenda in writing the song is decidedly different from your own goals. You may drum along with the music if you have a drum. This helps build an intense energy field, as does magickal dance.

Begin by dancing in a counterclockwise manner while you visualize the unwanted habit, look, or problem waning. Take an occasional look at the melting candle to help fix in your mind that your unwanted aspect is indeed being driven out. You may chant in time with the music or sing lyrics you created yourself for this spell. It is best to pre-plan these words rather than try to make them up as you go. First of all, you will be concentrating on conjuring up good words rather than on the goal they are supposed to enhance, and, secondly, you may slip up and create verbal images you don't really want to have.

Keep raising this counterclockwise energy until you feel you can do no more, then release it. Allow it to sink into the earth harmlessly away from you.

Now start the dance again, this time in a clockwise manner, while you envision the good qualities you want to bring in to replace the ones you just eliminated. Again you may use whatever chants or lyrics you have created for this. They do not have to be beautiful, they just have to convey the imagery you want to your subconscious mind.

Allow the energy to build, raising a cone of power if you wish. When you feel you have done all you can, release the energy to its task in the unseen world.

If you have the time and are able to supervise, allow the candle to continue to burn itself out. Don't even think about leaving it burning if you cannot be there to supervise! If it is not possible, spend as much time as you can meditating on the spell and gazing at the candle's light. Snuff it out before leaving the area.

▼

6

Pagan Ritual Magick

When one hears the term "ritual magick" it is customary to think of ceremonial magick, the highly structured system used by Kaballists and Gnostics. But this is not the whole definition. Long before the mystic teachings of the Hebrews were codified, Pagan people were incorporating their basic religious rituals with their magick. Granted this was largely the province of priestly classes, such as the Vestal Virgins of Rome or the Druids of the Celtic cultures, but in modern times Wiccans and other Pagans have successfully reclaimed this art.

A ritual is loosely defined as a set pattern of actions enacted to achieve a definable end result. These actions can be formal or informal, but they remain a prescribed set of rites whose purpose is to imprint a lasting change on the life and psyche of the participant. When combined with magick, the end effect can be a startling and potent change.

> Ritual magick is the creation of a specific ceremony . . .
> to create or force a change to occur in accordance with
> your will. The only reason for doing ritual magick is to
> change something, even if the change is only one of
> personal attitude.[1]

---

1. Lady Sabrina. *Reclaiming the Power* (Llewellyn, 1992), 38. This is an excellent guide to Wiccan ritual forms, one I highly recommend.

Ritualizing any spell puts us in direct and immediate connection with the creative forces of the universe. Inside a ritual circle, all elements are present (remember in the introduction I mentioned the elemental theme underlying all magickal operations) as well as the deities and all time and space. Performing magick in a ritual setting connects us more deeply with the symbolism inherent in each word and action. These symbols trigger our deep mind to move in certain directions, which is why ritual form necessitates a certain amount of repetition.

Ritual magick can be done very effectively by a solitary Witch, but its organized nature allows it to work within group settings as well. Spells that might otherwise be able to be performed well *only* when done by individuals (even by many individuals at different locations) can become excellent group efforts when formally ritualized. In ritual, everyone participating knows his or her function, and the spell can flow effortlessly as it is charged by many minds all of one accord.

The Ritual Circle

The ritual use of the circle for religious rites and magick is ancient. The circular shape is a symbol of completion, eternity, and containment. In magickal traditions it represents our world view that all things—the seasons, our lives, et cetera—are cyclic in nature, each being born, dying, and then being regenerated once again in a never-ending circle of time.

In Pagan practice the circle has three functions: one, to protect the person(s) inside it from unwanted outside forces that may be attracted to the energies raised; two, to contain raised energy until it is deliberately directed towards its goal; and three, to mark off a place in between the worlds of matter and spirit, a space lying outside the confines of our normal perception of space and time.

Circles are cast anew each time they are needed. Though they usually remain unseen, except to the psychic eye, they are very real, and their boundaries must be respected. Some traditions allow for the cutting of a doorway in the circle should someone need to pass in and out, though such comings and goings are usually kept to a minimum. Animals and small children seem to be able to move freely across circle boundaries without disturbing their energy field. No one really knows why, but it may be because they have not been taught to think about the world in terms of what is or is not real. Like animals, young children see psychic phenomena all the time and seem quite comfortable with it until society teaches them otherwise.

Children seem to have an enviable sensitivity to magickal energy. A friend of mine, who used to run a Wiccan study circle, told me about inviting a couple with children to a sabbat (solar festival) ritual. The children were old enough to entertain themselves for a while, and were in the priestess' living room watching television while the circle was being cast outdoors. At some point in the ritual the youngest of the children wanted her mother and headed outdoors; the older child followed. Just as they reached the outside perimeter of the circle they slowed to a halt, then the oldest grabbed the youngest, telling her to stop and wait right where they stood. Though they had never been to a Wiccan ritual before, they both waited patiently while a door was cut so the mother could get out, not seeming to find anything odd about seeing the priestess cut a doorway in front of them.

Oftentimes newcomers to Paganism do not see the necessity for a circle and will try to fumble through complex spells and rituals without one. This is a serious mistake that will only have worse repercussions the longer it is ignored. With practice you will improve your energy-raising skills substantially, and the higher vibrations emanating from your aura will begin to attract an increasing number of entities that will want to come and feed on it. This oversight could also leave you vulnerable to psychic attack, a very rare but quite real occurrence (see chapter 7).

Before you cast a circle, you should have inside its area *all the items you will need for your ritual/spell.* Specific tools are not absolutely necessary for many rituals, but do help provide a focus, especially during spells focusing heavily on the use of one element. If you are still new to Paganism you may not have collected a lot of tools as yet, and this is fine. Don't be bullied into thinking oodles of accoutrements are necessary for successful spell or ritual work. The power driving any magickal operation ultimately comes from you, not from your working instruments.

Many Witches like to place an altar of some kind inside the circle, but this, too, is not an absolute necessity. An altar serves as a focal point for ritual, and provides a convenient place for arranging tools, decorations, or other items you have on hand. It is a place to honor the deities with statuettes or candles and where their energies can rest during your rites. The altar also provides a focus for the elements, as it will be oriented to a specific direction, and any elemental tools you have will be placed in their corresponding sections on its surface.

Virtually anything with a flat top can become an altar, even a special spot of cleared ground. You can use a flat stone, a table, a portable cloth, a dresser top, a box, a bookshelf—whatever suits the time, place, and mood. You may wish to have something serving as a permanent altar, either one in a fixed place or one that can be transported to different sites. Or you may choose to wing it with whatever is at hand. No one way is inherently right or wrong.

Where you place the altar within the circle is a personal choice. Sometimes these placements and directional orientations are dictated by specific traditions, other times by an individual or by the coven with whom one works. Some Pagans like to change the orientation of the altar with the seasons or with the specific type of ritual they are doing; others use a fixed location.

Elemental Rulers and Directional Attributes

No matter in which Pagan tradition one works, each of the four cardinal directions is designated as the realm of a particular element and has its own elemental beings and rulers. In most of the Wiccan traditions these directional attributes are earth to the north, air to the east, fire to the south, and water to the west. For ease of reading, and to keep down confusion, this book will use the Wiccan attributes, but you should always feel free to change these to suit your personal world view or that of another tradition. Some of these Wiccan directional associations were determined by watching nature, others through mythological references. For instance, water in the west comes from the Celtic myths of the Land of the Dead being to the west under the sea, which was the end of the known world at the time Celtic civilization flourished. Fire was given to the south because it is the home of the sun in the northern hemisphere.

In European-based Pagan traditions, the element of spirit generally has no home direction but is known to be there all the same, omnipresent, in and of all the other elements. In many Native American traditions spirit is honored in the direction of above, below, or center, and these can—and have been—adopted into many Pagan ritual traditions.

From the Middle Eastern traditions, and through Pagan contact with ceremonial magicians, we adopted elemental rulers or kings into our circle practices. These rulers are faery or elemental beings who embody the essence of the element they represent, and who come to our circle when the corresponding direction is evoked. Pagans are less likely to use labels for these elemental beings than are ceremonialists, but when we do, we generally—but not always—follow their model of calling on gnomes for earth, sylphs for air, salamanders for fire, and undines for water.

Either just before, during, or after the circle is cast, the elementals are called on to witness the ritual. This practice of invoking the elements at each direction is referred to in several ways, including calling the quarters, summoning the elementals, invoking the watchtowers, evoking the elements, calling the elemental kings/rulers, or summoning the guardians. Custom also dictates the elemental rulers must heed your call, at least in their most rudimentary form. This means that if they feel insulted by your invitation, or if your powers of evocation are still weak, you will not get the full benefit of their presence. You can strengthen your link to them by meditating on each one and being open to their teachings.

When we learn to view these elemental rulers as real, and not as mere projections of raw energy, we will find our working relationship with them much improved, and the success of our magick will improve proportionally as well.

Ritual Tools

In Witchcraft we have what are commonly referred to as "tools," accoutrements that symbolize a specific elemental energy. We usually place these on our ritual altars, and they are sometimes employed in our magick. All together they symbolize balance and completeness, and are used to direct magickal energy or to offer blessings to people, objects, and spirits. They can also be used as defensive tools to protect and banish unwanted spirits, energies, and manifestations by directing raised energy through them toward an intruder.

Many of our modern tools came into Witchcraft during the Middle Ages through Witches having contact with ceremonial magicians. Other tools come from the myths and legends of the early European people. An example of this is the hammer, adopted by many Nordic traditions due to its association with the God Thor.

Some tools are more commonly used throughout the Craft than others, and most long-time practitioners of Pagan religions are familiar with these regardless of which ones they or their traditions choose to use. *A full set of ritual tools is not essential to performing natural magick,* but they can be helpful, and you will find many references to them as you continue to study the Craft.

It cannot be overemphasized that, in magick, these tools are merely a focus for our power. They function as extensions of our own energies that work only as we will them, and they contain little magickal power of their own. What they do contain are affinities to a particular element and a vibration rate that ideally is compatible with our own inner vibrations. Both of these factors can make a tool more and less useful to you.

The way to decide if a tool is right for you is by holding it quietly and allowing your inner self to commune with it. From this contact you should be able to intuit compatibility. With repeated use the tool becomes more and more in tune with your own personal energy patterns, and this makes it a true working partner, perhaps for a lifetime, so you want to choose wisely.

There is no need to rush out and spend lots of money collecting tools. If you feel you need something to help you direct raised energy, a simple wand is all that is necessary, and you can obtain one by walking through a park, a woods, or your own backyard looking for a friendly branch that has fallen from a tree. I know many Witches who have found very good wands this way, and many would have no other even after many years in the Craft.

The following is a list of Craft tools and the element with which they are thought to share an affinity. You will note some overlap among the elements, particularly between air and fire. This is because different Witches and Craft traditions assign some of their tools differently. The point to remember is that each system works and neither is inherently right or wrong.

Earth

Disk, carved wood block (sometimes called a pentacle, or bearing the pentacle symbol), hammer, stones, clay, bowl of soil, salt, sand, double-headed axe, shield, wheel, necklace, club, roots, drum, bronze, bow, animal fur/pelts, mallet

Water

Cup, chalice, cauldron, hollow horn, bowl, pitcher, goblet, ring, barrel, trident, any cool liquid, wine cask, silver, convex shield, tea kettle, sea shells, paint brushes, bolline, sickle

Fire

Candle, hearths, athames/swords (and all blades forged in fire), wand, iron, red or orange stones, pike, claymore, matches, flint, ashes, torch, bracelet, solar disk (equilateral cross in a circle), broom, gold, spear, lariat, scourge, whip

Air

Staff, trident, stang, athames/swords, wand, feather, incense, sling, claymore, pike, single-headed axe, dagger/dirk, spear, javelin, earrings, broom, wind instruments, scourge, whip, broach, ram's horn, smudge stick, letter opener, pen/pencil, lariat, fan, smoking pipe, copper, arrow

The names of some tools, even ones commonly used, can be confusing to new Witches. It is important to understand their functions and symbolism. Five in particular that need further definition are the the athame, the besom, the bolline, the chalice, and the wand.

Athame

The athame is a double-sided blade that is never used to cut any physical surface. Traditionally it has a wooden handle painted black, but many Witches choose to decorate natural wood bases to their taste with paints, carvings, or woodburners. Athames can be fairly costly to obtain, and the market is currently loaded with all sorts of decorative athames, many finely crafted by Pagans at astrologically beneficial times. Ads for these can be found in many Pagan/Wiccan publications (see Appendix B).

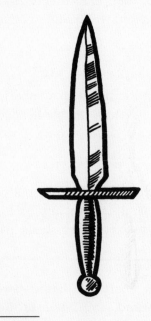

The athame is usually considered to be a tool of air, but some traditions assign it to fire. Its function is to direct energy, particularly that of the element with which it is associated. It also represents the masculine principle of creation

Athame

when used in the Great Rite ceremony, which commemorates the sacred marriage of the God and the Goddess.

For some Witches the athame is their most important tool, one chosen to fulfill a variety of magick and ritual operations, such as the blessing of ritual wines, drawing in/ down divine energies for evocation/invocation rites, directing all personal magickal energies, and casting the sacred circle.

The athame can be charged with magickal energy and held there until needed. (This is done largely by empowering the blade, as explained in chapter 2.) The myths and legends surrounding the heroes and deities of western Europe often make use of this magickal operation. One well-known example is seen in the Arthurian legends where the famous sword Excalibur is charged with much of the power that permits Arthur to rule his kingdom. He becomes king only when he has removed the magickal sword from its large stone base, representative of the feminine creative principle (i.e., Mother Earth).

Besom

Besom

The besom is a Witch's broomstick and it combines the feminine and masculine creative aspects. The staff of the besom represents the phallus, and the bristles represent the Mound of Venus, which guards the opening to the feminine reproductive organs.

The besom has a long and valuable history as a magickal tool, especially for fertility spells. Women would ride them hobby-horse style over newly planted fields to encourage growth, and it is from this image that the notion of the Halloween Witch riding around on a broomstick was born. Swatting animals with the broom as they were passed between ritual fires served the same function with livestock. The sexual imagery made the besom a natural tool for sealing marriage rites. The image of Pagan couples "jumping [over] the broom" together after exchanging vows is one known even in mainstream culture.

Besoms have been placed under beds for both protection and for fertility magick, and have rested near hearths and doorways to guard and protect. Two crossed besoms prevent unwanted people and spirits from entering the protected area.

Besoms are also used to sweep negative or mundane energies from a sacred area, such as one where a circle is to be created, and to sweep positive things into a household. In seventeenth-century Ireland, a woman named Dame Alice Kyteler was condemned as a Witch because a neighbor caught her out in the street at night sweeping toward her doorway while chanting a charm to bring prosperity to her home.

If you want to use a besom for your magick or ritual, go out and find one you like, then save it exclusively for this purpose. A besom is not your kitchen broom, and it should never be used in this mundane manner or you risk losing any magickal power you have stored in it. If you ever do use it on your kitchen floor there must be a magickal need behind your actions.

Bolline

Bolline

The bolline has been a very popular tool in Gardnerian and English Traditional Witchcraft, but is less well known in many other North American circles. The bolline is a white handled knife with a curved blade that gives it the appearance of being a small sickle. It is primarily used to harvest magickal herbs and plants, but it is sometimes used in lunar rituals.

The curved blade is symbolic of the waxing and waning phases of the moon, and is therefore considered a tool of feminine energy. Those not used solely to gather herbs are sometimes employed in a ceremony known as Drawing Down the Moon, during which the essence of the lunar Goddess is invoked

Chalice

into the physical body of a Witch, usually a priestess. In lesser instances, the bolline is used to direct energies during other types of moon magick.

Chalice

The chalice is a cup or goblet, often made of silver, which is deeply associated with water and Goddess energy. Archetypally it represents the womb of the Great Mother from whom we are all born and to whom we must return to await rebirth. Archaeological excavations in India have found evidence of ritual chalices used for Goddess worship which date back to 7000 B.C.E.

We read in the Arthurian legends of how King Arthur and his knights go on a quest to find the Holy Grail, the chalice used by Jesus during the Last Supper (in reality a seder meal celebrating the Jewish feast of Passover). The chalice was one of the many tools/images/rites of Paganism adopted into Christianity when the Church fathers could find no way of eradicating their use by the common people. The Grail still flourished as a Goddess symbol, and the obsessive need to find it may be a carryover of an earlier Celtic belief that a king needed a queen, a representative of the Earth Goddess, to legitimize his rule.

Cauldrons are sometimes used in place of or in addition to the chalice in many Celtic traditions, and the imagery is virtually the same.

Wand

Wands are stick-like tools that can be made of a variety of materials. Some of them are made of branches cut from trees, others are cast of silver or copper and topped with a crystal of some sort, others are made from wooden dowels found in hardware stores and decorated to taste. Their energy is masculine and they are considered to be tools of either air or fire. They are used to direct magickal energies and, like the athame, are often chosen to fulfill a variety of magick roles, including that of casting the ritual circle.

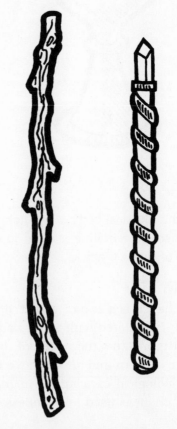

A twig wand, left, and right, a metal wand wrapped with leather and tipped with a crystal

Wands are symbolic of the Witch's power to mediate between the seen and unseen words. Medieval kings and queens are often portrayed as holding a scepter, another form of the wand, to symbolize both this power and their sovereignty.

Many Witches have more than one wand. One might have a willow wand for lunar magick, an oak wand for fire magick, and an apple wand for love magick. Those who follow a Celtic tradition may possess thirteen different wands, one for each lunar month of the Celtic Tree Calendar.

One variation on the wand is the staff, a larger version of the wand serving the same symbolic and elemental functions.

The Cleansing and Blessing of Ritual Tools

It is customary and wise to cleanse and bless tools before we use them in any magickal situation. The cleansing process is both a physical and a psychic operation that removes any previous programming or former energies that have become attached to the tools, either during their creation or through former use.

The old doggerel that states "cleanliness is next to Godliness" is one most Witches will agree with. Any longtime Witch can tell you that dirt, dust, and other filth is not conducive to good magick. To begin the cleansing process, take each tool one at a time and examine it for evidence of physical uncleanliness. This might be tarnish clinging to silver or dirt that has embedded itself in the crevices of other metals or carvings. Wooden items may need a good coat of varnish cleaner, or they may need to be sanded down and refinished altogether.

After the physical filth has been dealt with, you will need to deal with the psychic dirt. Spend as much time as possible with each of your newly cleaned tools, allowing yourself to get to know the feel, texture, and energy they possess. This will also allow them to attune to your own energy patterns, making them a true extension of your magickal will.

Take each tool one at a time and visualize them being filled with your own positive energies. You may see this as coming from you directly, or from a deity above, or from Mother Earth (see the directing energy instructions in chapter 2 if you are unsure of how to go about this). See this process as a purging that drives out all previous energies that might have been intentionally or unintentionally programmed into the tool.

Next you will need to purify each tool by using one of the elements as a cleanser. You can either use the one you associate with that particular tool or one you often use to purify and that speaks of cleansing to you. For example, you may want to pass an athame through the smoke of an incense or flame, or you may want to hold a chalice in a stream of clear running water or under a water tap. Other tools could be buried in earth, clay, or salt. The method you pick should be compatible with the condition and needs of the tool. Common sense should help dictate the procedure. Wooden items should never be placed in water and sensitive metals or gems should not come into contact with corrosive salt.

While you do the final purification, you might want to state aloud a blessing on the tool to affirm your intent for it as an instrument of positive magick:

> *Blessed be this (name of tool), in the name of the Lord*
> *and Lady of all. I charge you as an instrument of*
> *spiritual growth; an extension of my personal energies,*
> *used for only positive ends. If I forget my vows and use*
> *this (name of tool) in violation of the Rede to which I am*
> *sworn, may the powers I have invested in this tool turn*
> *against me, and all my magick be for naught. May the*
> *Lord and Lady bless with fruitfulness the work we shall*
> *do together, in accordance with the free will of all.*
> *So mote it be!*

No one can be sure where the admonition to the tools to turn against the magician should he or she work negative magick came from, or how old it is, but it has been around since at least the late Middle Ages, when it began appearing in oral teachings and grimoires. Today many Pagans include these or similar instructions when blessing their tools or when taking initiation vows. It is a good way to keep yourself away from the negative path since, even if you attempt to do evil, the tools will not allow you to do so and, in keeping with our Law of Threefold return, will send the harm back to the sender . . . you!

The final step is to dedicate each tool to its task and to the God and/or Goddess whom you serve. If you have no patron deities at this time, you may substitute the terms Lord and Lady or God and Goddess. An example of such a dedication would sound like this:

> *I hold in my hands the (name of tool), which I*
> *dedicate as a tool of the (name of element) element.*
> *I dedicate it to positive uses as I walk the path of*
> *the wise throughout this lifetime. By the Lord and*
> *Lady whom I love and serve, I make this pledge:*
> *that this (name of tool) shall be used only to the*
> *greater good of all. By my will I vow this; so mote it be.*

You can seal the vows by adding a small drop of your blood to each tool. This is another very old custom designed to further link your own energies with those of the tool. Blood was viewed as the essence of all life by many ancient cultures, and was thought to possess a small part of the uniqueness of the individual. With what we know today about DNA, samples of which can be obtained through blood, it seems the ancients knew what they were talking about.

The safest way to add blood to a tool is to go to a pharmacy and purchase the lancets diabetics use to prick their fingers to test their blood sugar. They are relatively inexpensive and, most importantly, they are sterile. Naturally in this age of AIDS common sense and a concern for the safety of others who may be with you during this process should be a consideration as well.

As you use your tools, more and more you will find that their own personalities begin to emerge. In the Celtic myths we read about warriors who named their most prized tools or weapons. They believed that knowing the true name of the tool, gleaned through long and good association, gave them the power to command it fully.

Casting the Ritual Circle

The basics of circle casting remain pretty much the same throughout Paganism, but there are many, many ways to vary the details. Some of these reflect personal tastes, others are based on cultural or traditional practices. For the sake of simplicity the most common version of casting and grounding circles will be presented here. This is so that if you are new to Pagan ritual forms you will be sure to learn the basics. Once these basics of circle casting are mastered and a firm knowledge of elemental energy is obtained, further experimentation is highly encouraged. Solitaries of experience create many unique circle castings, and some of these find their way into group practices. For example, when I am alone I use a variation on the standard casting involving a fountain of golden light showering from my crown chakra, or else I use a shower of sparkling white light emanating from the tip of my wand. I take these energy projections and mentally form them into a private circle.[2]

To cast a standard ritual/magickal circle, you will need only yourself and some uncluttered, private space in which to work. If you are following the step by step spell construction guidelines found in chapter 4, this would be number seven, "Prepare your magickal space as needed." You may choose to use a ritual tool, such as an athame or wand, but the projected energy from your own body or hand will work just as well. If

---

2. If you feel ready to experiment with some more advanced forms of circle casting, Silver RavenWolf gives complete instructions for some interesting variations in *To Stir A Magic Cauldron: A Witch's Guide to Casting and Conjuring* (Llewellyn, 1996).

you already have purchased or made tools for each element, they add a nice touch to your quarter calls and can help you to more deeply connect to each element, but remember they are not an absolute necessity.

The first thing you will need to do is find some ritual space. Even working all alone you will need a private area about four feet in diameter, or more if you want to dance or employ other sweeping movements in your workings. If you are not sure of your directions, then you will also need a compass to point them out for you. When you have pinpointed north, south, east, and west, mark them in some way so that they will be easy for you to find again during the rite. You might do this by placing a candle or stone at each point, or you might orient your altar in the direction of your choice so that it will be a marker to show you which direction is which. I recommend using a method that clearly marks the directions at the end boundaries of your circle since it is wise to know just where your circle ends so that you can remain inside it until the rite is complete.

Wiccans and Pagans usually purify the area they will be using for their circle before they begin casting by either blessing the area with lightly salted water, smudging it with smoke from a sage stick, or by using some other incense. This clears out negative and other unwanted mundane energies in your ritual space and raises the vibrational rate of the immediate area to a higher spiritual level that is incompatible with lower level entities who may be attracted to your working. Incenses serving a purifying and cleansing function include frankincense, sage, cinnamon, sandalwood, bay, and clove. I find frankincense especially good for this, and it is inexpensive and easy to obtain.

Some Witches like to take a besom and sweep out negative and unwanted energies from the circle area or scatter salt or another purifying herb, such as basil or thyme, around the immediate vicinity. If you wish to do either of these things, do so now while focusing on the meaning of the ritual you are about to undertake.

When you are ready to begin the ritual, stand quietly for a moment in what will be the center of your circle, allowing yourself to become centered and mentally prepared for your ritual. Raise your arms skyward and feel yourself filling with energy drawn down from the deities, or up from Mother Earth. Allow yourself and the area you are working in to be charged like a battery with this positive flow of power. Visualize it projecting out of you and filling the area to overflowing.

Walk to the edge of your circle and stand at the point where you or your tradition has deemed the proper place to

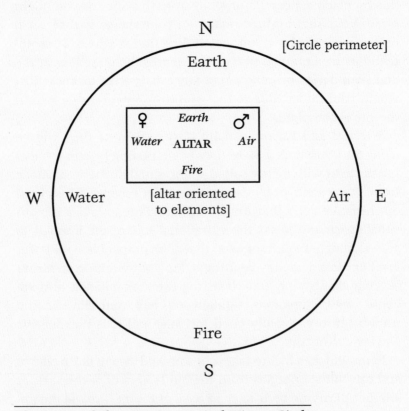

Placement of Elements in a typical Wiccan Circle

begin casting the circle (the eastern quarter in this example). Center yourself and point your finger or tool at the ground. The tool can actually touch the ground if you wish, but it is unnecessary.

Visualize energy coming from the end of your finger or magickal tool, creating a wall of intense blue-white light. Blue-white is one of the traditional colors of protection and higher spirituality, and a color many people report the circle to be. Clockwise is the traditional direction associated with growth, increase, construction, gain, et cetera. Most circles are cast in this direction and closed by moving counterclockwise. However, in some cases the opposite is true. For example, banishing rituals—those designed to remove some influence or problem—are often cast in a counterclockwise direction and then closed clockwise. This does not mean that the act to take place inside them is negative. Negative rituals can just as easily take place in a circle cast clockwise. Many things can be decreased that have positive results, such as banishing a bad habit, and many things can be increased, like bad will, which have negative results. Only the intent of the ritualist makes the difference.

Continue moving around the circle clockwise until you are back at your starting point, all the while visualizing the energy rising and surrounding you, and know that you are protected. Send as much energy into the creation of the circle as you can, continuing to draw it from the divine above you or the earth below you. Make it real and then respect its reality. Witches accept that the mind is capable of doing anything and everything, and the things it creates are as real as anything we might create with a hammer, nail, and block of wood.

There is more than one way to visualize the completed circle. Some like to see this as a wall, some as a dome growing over them, and others see it as a sphere encircling the entire area, including below the surface on which they stand. Choose the imagery that works best for you. You are free to change it later on if you like.

Calling the Quarters

After you have raised the perimeters of your circle you will need to make the circuit again, this time pausing to evoke the elements at each quarter.

If you have a tool for each element present inside your circle, you should *return to the altar between each quarter call and get that tool to carry with you to the direction whose presence you are invoking.* This helps you further connect with the element you are calling on and strengthens the link between your tool and the element it represents. This sample ritual is written *presuming there are no tools present,* but have no doubt that circle casting and quarter calling will work just as well with or without them.

You will also note that the wording of this evocation is that of an invitation, though you may change it to be a summons or command if you like. If you do, keep in mind just who and what you are calling on. It is generally accepted that the watchtowers, the guardian spirits of the directions, can be commanded. The elementals coming on command are the ones who have become traditionally associated with a particular element through contact with ceremonial magick. Other elemental spirits, such as other faery folk, discarnate human spirits, and all deities should always be given the courtesy of invitation and never be commanded.

If you are in a group situation, such as with a coven, it is likely that different people will be given the honor of calling each quarter. These may be either arbitrary or rotational assignments, or ones made based on perceived personal affinities between group members and certain elements. As you begin experimenting with circle casting, you will discover the strengths and weaknesses of your own connections to each element. Some of them will simply feel more responsive to you than others. After the quarters are called there is usually a unison response from the group offering welcome or blessings. When you are alone you will take on all these roles yourself.

Some traditions like to have you sound a bell as each quarter is called, a practice I am not fond of since I feel it frightens away certain types of spirit life that may be beneficial to your rites. On the plus side, the sound of the bell is thought to be purifying and to help take one up into a higher consciousness, and may chase away undesirable lower level spirits and elementals from your circle area. Since the proponents of each school of thought are pretty equally divided in Paganism, the choice is yours to make based on what makes you feel most comfortable.

You may begin calling the quarters in any direction you like. In most Wiccan traditions this is usually the north or east. Other traditions have different starting points or may even change directions depending on the season or the type of rite they hope to enact. For the sake of clarity this example will begin with the east, the direction most often associated with new beginnings.

Facing the east, say the following while visualizing your voice carrying out to the farthest reaches of that direction, covering the vastness of time and space, connecting you with the spirits of the element of air:

> *Watchtowers of the east—sylphs, guardians, spirits,*
> *and elementals—hear my cry. Whispering powers*
> *of the east and of air, I ask your breezy, reasoning,*
> *transitory presence at this circle tonight (or today).*
> *Join me in this place that is out of all places, at this time*
> *out of time, as I cast the sacred circle to worship and*
> *weave magick (or state other purpose when it is relevant).*
> *Guard, protect, witness, and worship with me this*
> *night/day, adding your powers and blessings to this*
> *working. Welcome powers of air which come to*
> *balance this sacred place. Blessed Be.*

Different traditions and individuals have ritual gestures or postures they use for each element. None of these are standard, and many Pagans forego them altogether. If you like the idea of invoking with a gesture, try adopting the invoking pentagram. This is a pentagram drawn in the air in front of you to help "bring down" what you are calling—in this case, an elemental presence—and then it remains as a protective barrier, helping to strengthen the perimeter of that quarter of the circle.

After you have called on air, stand still for a minute or two facing east and visualizing the powers of air and all its attendant spirits. You may even wish to close your eyes to help you concentrate on peering into the astral world lying just beyond the circle's boundaries. With your mind, feel air rushing at you, filling you with its energies and attributes, truly becoming a part of this quarter of your circle. If you are outdoors you may actually feel a small rush of wind respond-

An invoking pentagram

ing to your call. Do not move on until the imagery becomes too hard to hold clearly in your mind any longer. As long as air is still vivid in your mind, and you feel you are forging stronger connections with it, it is best to remain where you are.

When you are ready to call the next quarter, walk to the south edge of the circle, continuing clockwise. Raise your arms to the quarter, saying:

> *Watchtowers of the south—salamanders, guardians,*
> *spirits, and elementals—hear my cry. Passionate powers*
> *of the south and of fire, I ask your fiery, transformative*
> *presence at this circle tonight (or today). Join me in this*
> *place that is out of all places, at this time out of time,*
> *as I cast the sacred circle to worship and weave magick.*
> *Guard, protect, witness, and worship with me this night*
> *(or day), adding your powers and blessings to this*
> *working. Welcome powers of fire, which come to*
> *balance this sacred place. Blessed Be.*

Remain standing and facing south, visualizing the powers of fire and all its attendant spirits. You may even wish to close your eyes to help you peer into the astral world just beyond the circle's boundaries. With your mind, feel the heat of the astral inferno lying just outside your circle. Allow it to fill you with its energies and attributes. Invite it in and allow it to truly become a part of this quarter. If you are outdoors in the light of day, allow the sun to fall on your upturned face and feel its heat. Do not move on until the imagery becomes hard to hold clearly in your mind any longer. As long as fire is still a vivid presence in your mind, and you feel you are forging stronger connections with it, you should remain there.

Next, move to the west quarter, facing outward and saying:

> *Watchtowers of the west—undines, guardians, spirits,*
> *and elementals—hear my cry. Fertile powers of the west*
> *and of water, I ask your psychic, purifying presence at*
> *this circle tonight (or today). Join me in this place that is*

out of all places, at this time out of time, as I cast the
sacred circle to worship and weave magick. Guard,
protect, witness, and worship with me this night (or day),
adding your powers and blessings to this working.
Welcome powers of water, which come to balance
this sacred place. Blessed Be.

Stand quietly for another minute or two while still facing west and visualizing the powers of water and all its attendant spirits. You may even wish to close your eyes to help you mentally focus on peering into the watery realm just beyond the circle's boundaries. Let yourself feel the dampness in the air and the rise in humidity water brings. With your mind, feel its astral waves beating against the shore that is the edge of your circle. Allow it to truly become a part of this quarter.

Occasionally one hears of a Witch who was evoking water at the same moment it began to rain. Such a "coincidence" can be very moving, and this imagery will add a strong dimension to your ritual.

Do not move on to the next quarter until the imagery becomes hard to hold clearly in your mind any longer. Remain where you are as long as water is still vivid in your mind and you feel you are forging stronger connections with it.

When you are ready, move to the north quarter:

Watchtowers of the north—gnomes, guardians, spirits,
and elementals—hear my cry. Stabilizing powers of the
north and earth, I ask your sturdy, comforting presence
at this circle tonight (or today). Join me in this place that
is out of all places, at this time out of time, as I cast the
sacred circle to worship and weave magick. Guard,
protect, witness, and worship with me this night (or day),
adding your powers and blessings to this working.
Welcome powers of earth, which come to balance
this sacred place. Blessed Be.

After evoking earth, remain facing north while visualizing the powers of earth and all its attendant spirits. You may even wish to close your eyes to concentrate on peering into the astral world just beyond the circle's boundaries. Sense the presence of stability, love, and support, all qualities earth brings to your sacred space. Feel earth beneath you, rising through you like sap rises in a tree trunk, filling you with its energies and attributes. Allow it to fill the space around you, becoming an integral part of this quarter of your circle. Do not move on until the imagery becomes hard to hold clearly in your mind any longer. As long as earth energy is still vivid in your mind, and you feel you are forging stronger connections with it, remain still.

After the north quarter has been called, it is customary to walk back to the east to complete the full circle before returning to your altar for the rest of the ritual. Some traditions even call for the circle to be walked at least one more time, for a total of three times around. Three is a magickal number in Celtic and Norse Craft traditions, ones which are followed by a large number of modern Pagans.

Invitation to the Divine

It is also customary at this point to invite the God and Goddess into your circle. Notice I said "invite." Deities are never to be commanded. If you have patron deities, you may call on them by name. If not, it is perfectly all right to substitute the terms Lord and Lady, or you can just say God and Goddess. Trust that those powers of creation, both the masculine and the feminine, can and will respond to you.

If you are using an altar, it is customary to have some symbols placed upon it representing the God and the Goddess. Many Witches use candles to serve this function, one each for the God and the Goddess. These are lit as each deity is invited, symbolizing the light of their presence.

The color of each candle is dictated in many Wiccan traditions, but if you are working alone you may choose any color(s) you deem appropriate. If you are unsure which to choose, plain white is always acceptable, or try one of these if it appeals:

God Candle Colors	Goddess Candle Colors
Red (a fire color)	Red (for blood of the mother)
Orange (a fire color)	White (traditional color of the maiden Goddess)
Gold (a solar color)	Black (traditional color of the crone Goddess)
Brown (a woodland God color)	Silver (a lunar color)
Purple (a royal color)	Purple (a lunar color and a color of royalty)
Blue (sometimes used for father deities)	Light Blue (sometimes used for maiden Goddesses)

If you are not using an altar, have no fear—a heartfelt invitation without candles is just as effective. The deities know their own, and are much more accommodating than humans when considering your monetary shortcomings.

The invitations need not be lengthy, only sincere. Like the quarter calls, they can be done with or without a tool in hand. Some Witches like to call on the God with an athame or sword in hand and to call on the Goddess with the chalice. Blades and wands symbolize the power of the phallus of the God, and the chalice symbolizes the womb of the Mother Goddess. The choice is yours to make. With or without a tool, stand facing whatever direction you or your tradition deems to be the home of the deities, take a few deep breaths, and mentally reach out to that land to connect with the divine archetypes dwelling there.

An invitation should be issued separately for each deity. You may start with either the God or the Goddess as your personal beliefs or those of your tradition dictate.

Invitation to the Goddess:

> *Blessed Lady of life, of death, and of rebirth, mother*
> *of all creation, I humbly ask your presence at this circle*
> *this night. Witness my magick and lend it your creative*
> *energies. Welcome and Blessed Be!*

Invitation to the God:

> *Blessed Lord, God of this world and the world to come,*
> *spirit of the greenwood, I humbly ask your presence at*
> *this circle this night. Witness my magick and lend it*
> *your blessings. Welcome and Blessed Be!*

If you are using candles, light the corresponding one as you intone the last words of each invitation.

Ritual for Blending and Uniting with the Elements

This short ritual is an excellent way to connect with the power of the element prior to ritual magick. It may be used, altered, or discarded as you see fit in future workings. If you are a beginner, taking time to work with the elements whenever you can is the best way to spark your intuitive magickal creativity.

Pause, take a few deep breaths, and partially close your eyes. You want to take your consciousness down to an even deeper level, but still remain able to see. Begin walking very slowly clockwise around the perimeter of your circle. Do not pause at the quarters, but as you walk around and around, take note of the atmosphere in each quarter. Try to feel the essence of each element as you come into its quarter, sensing how one blends into the other as you pass through them and how each one resonates with your inner self. As you pass the east you might feel the wind. Notice how it blows warmer as you approach the south, and how the humidity of the heat rises when you move on toward water. You may walk around the circle as many times as you like, stopping only when you are ready.

I find that this ritual walk usually turns into a dance, one that evolves naturally from the rhythm of my steps. If you wish to try dancing your way around the circle, note how you feel compelled to move differently at each quarter as your body tries to express physically the power of the elements. For example, you may find you want to dance low to the ground through earth, to leap through air, use lots of hand motions through fire, or move more fluidly through water.

When you are finished, move to the center of your circle and stand with your feet together and your arms straight above your head. Think of your body linking the traditional "directions" of spirit: below, above, and center. You are now a pole of spirit energy poised at the very center of the universe. As you assume this position and sense your power, allow yourself to open to the natural pull each of the elements has toward this quintessence that links and unifies them and is part of them all. In this center space—in you—they can all meet and blend in their most beneficial forms. Allow yourself to be a conduit of elemental energy, with all the elements flowing harmoniously through you at once, all unified in spirit. You are spirit—you can draw from each element as you need it, and command it at will.

Remain in the center for as long as you feel the experience is beneficial to you. When you are ready to move on to other aspects of ritual work, or if you just wish to close the circle at this point, lower your arms and visualize the link between below, above, and center being broken. When this is done the elements will start to withdraw from you, back toward their own quarters.

Ritual Spellwork

At this point you may work your spell. If you are following the step by step spell construction guidelines found in chapter 4, this would be number 10, "Do whatever physical action your spell requires." Be sure to use lots of grand gestures, lavish words (or thoughts), and spend lots of time in visualization. Ritualized power raising through dance, song, et cetera, also works well.

Take your time in doing this spell, pouring into it as much energy as you can and allowing each of the elements you evoked to offer blessings to the effort. This can be done by touching each of your tools to the other catalysts (herbs, stones, et cetera) or by walking to each quarter and asking their aid.

As with any other spell, you may need to repeat your efforts more than once. This does not mean that you did something wrong the first time. Sometimes spells simply require more than one effort, such as ones that specifically call for doing them several days in succession or that simply need the extra boost. This repetition can be done within this circle, or you may choose to recast your circle at a later date and redo the spell.

Closing the Circle and Dismissing the Elements

When your purpose for casting the circle is completed, the energy you raised to create it should always be grounded to prevent it from causing you to feel frazzled or from "haunting" you. This is a time-honored occult custom and standard Pagan practice. If you are following the step by step spell construction guidelines from chapter 4, this would be both number 12, "End the spell and close your sacred space," and number 13, "Ground excess energy into the earth."

You will close the circle by the same method you cast it, only doing everything in reverse order. Begin by walking to the last quarter you called to begin dismissing them. In this example, you would start dismissing in the north. The word "dismiss" is one traditionally used to refer to the practice of releasing the quarters, but its tone of command can be confusing. As when you called the quarters, the tone is not one of command, but of thanks and release:

Thank you, powers of the north and earth, for your
presence here this night (or day); for lending your stable
energies to this circle and the magick that was made
herein. Go now with my blessings. So mote it be.

You may opt to dismiss the quarters with a ritual gesture
such as a banishing pentagram, drawn in the air in front of
you to help send away something you have in your presence.
This is not a requirement, merely a choice you can make. You
may also wish to use a bell as you dismiss each quarter, even
if you did not use one to call them. Bell sounds tend to raise
the vibrations of an area, purifying it and banishing unwanted
beings. Using bells at this point makes much more sense to
me than using them to call the quarters in the first place,
since you usually want the area cleared of spirit life, both the
pleasant and the unpleasant, before you dismiss your circle. If
you choose to use a bell, sound it now after the quarter dismissal is complete, and do the same at each released quarter.

Next, move counterclockwise to the west quarter. Counterclockwise is the traditional direction for banishment, release,
decrease, and endings:

Thank you, powers of the west and water, for your
presence here this night (or day); for lending your fertile
energies to this circle and the magick that was made
herein. Go now with my blessings. So mote it be.

Then to the south:

Thank you, powers of the south and fire, for your
presence here this night (or day); for lending your
passionate energies to this circle and the magick that was
made herein. Go now with my blessings. So mote it be.

Lastly move to your original starting point in the east:

Thank you, powers of the east and air, for your presence
here this night (or day); for lending your transitory
energies to this circle and the magick that was made
herein. Go now with my blessings. So mote it be.

If you have evoked the element of spirit in any ritual, you must thank it too. Since spirit lives in and around all things, and does not have any elemental guardians whom you have evoked, it does not require a formal dismissal as so the other elements. Simply stand in the center of the circle and say something like:

> *Spirit, ether, quintessence—force that brings all things together, which lives in and around all that is—thank you for your presence here this night (or day), and for blessing this circle. Blessed be.*

Starting in the east again, take your tool or forefinger and begin walking the perimeter of the circle counterclockwise. You are now grounding or closing the circle, and should be visualizing the energy you raised to create it either being sent

A banishing pentagram

into Mother Earth or being reabsorbed into your finger or tool. You may choose to do this only once, or you may walk the circle again as many times as you did to cast it.

Once the circle is closed you may wish to make a statement acknowledging this. Try a simple phrase such as, "The circle is closed but always part of me," or use the traditional Wiccan closing, "Merry meet, merry part, and merry meet again."

▼

7

Psychic Self-Defense

Psychic self-defense is the art of deflecting unwanted beings, energies, or spells that are sent your way either intentionally or by accident. These tactics are a part of the general repertoire and regular magickal routine of many Witches. Either daily, weekly, or monthly, many of us go through the ritual of protecting ourselves, our loved ones, and our homes. This does not mean that we are always expecting psychic attacks to occur. True psychic attack is defined as a focused, deliberate attempt to cause serious mental or physical harm, and can come from a person or a spirit. Such occurrences are relatively rare, but they can happen, especially as your magick becomes more and more successful and you attract the jealousy of others. When we go through our routine protective rites we are simply using common sense, sealing out random negativity or problems before they get to us and cause major difficulties.

A very, very small portion of negative energy sent your way comes from a conscious source. Psychic undermining is best done by those who are completely unaware they are projecting this damaging force your way. All people project energy; its condition (i.e., negative, positive, or neutral) depends on the frame of mind in which it was sent out. Untrained jealous minds are the worst offenders because they often do not realize that they are capable of such destruction, whereas people well trained in the occult have learned to control the content of their energy output.

The Basics of Psychic Self-Defense

In Witchcraft, psychic self-defense is sometimes referred to as "warding yourself." The term warding comes from the Anglo-Saxon *weardian* meaning "to keep watch," and refers to any act of protection that incorporates a maintained defensive perimeter around you (or anyone/thing else you seek to protect) to repel problem energies. (An example of a warding spell for a home is given in chapter 5 and uses the image of flaming pentagrams.)

The techniques you will use to protect yourself build on what we have learned so far about raising, manipulating, and directing energy. There are some very traditional "Witchy" methods for doing this, as well as some others that put a new spin on old tricks.

Standing in a Pentagram

Whenever you feel that your energy is being drained or threatened, immediately trace a pentagram on the floor underneath you and step inside it. It will act like a small sacred circle, repelling these forces that are eating away at you.

If you are ever in a position where you feel you need a pentagram beneath you but cannot trace one without being seen and thought mad, remember that you can do this purely through visualization. This idea of making magick without tools is sometimes thought of as an advanced magickal working, but I feel it is really no more than a stretching of your skill at energy projection. If you can feel at one with the energies you raise and send them successfully out toward your goals, there is no reason you cannot make magick solely with the power of your mind when you need to.

You can increase the effectiveness of the protective pentagram by mentally coloring it red, gold, or orange. These are fire colors, and fire is the ruling element of protective magick.

The Veil of Gold

One of my favorite ways to instantly protect myself is by creating a protective spray of golden light that I draw up from the
earth and project out from my crown chakra. I visualize this
as a foundation of protective light forming a circle that sur-
rounds me, repelling any negative beings or energies with
which I do not wish to be in contact. As with the aforemen-
tioned pentagram protection, gold is selected because it is a
color of fire.

Increasing Your Auric Field

The aura is the energy field surrounding all living things. Occultists and Witches have made a science out of reading the
size, color, and shape of the aura to determine someone's
character or the state of their mental or physical health. The
aura is thought to be a projection of the subtle or astral body,
an etheric double of our physical selves we all possess.

Experimentation has shown that we can temporarily influence the condition of our aura at will by forcing a change in
our emotional state or by deliberately drawing in magickal energy to our bodies for the purpose of altering the aura's appearance. Any time you feel vulnerable to psychic attack, such as
when astral projecting (see chapter 9), you can increase the
size of your aura and strengthen it as a protective shell.

To do this, mentally draw energy up or down (as explained
in chapter 2) and visualize it all being transferred to your
aura. See and feel it expanding at your will, creating an egg-
shaped cocoon in which you are cradled and protected and
through which no uninvited entity may pass.

You can also add color to your aura for added protection.
Do this by mentally visualizing the color you want to add as
you focus on expanding it. Fire colors such as gold, orange, or
red are recommended. And you can never go wrong if you
choose pure white.

Shields of Power

Many of our Pagan deities are depicted as carrying shields. Shields represent protection and the power to deflect blows aimed at your physical self. When conjured up mentally they can work just as well to protect your psychic self. To visualize your shields into place, simply create a clear mental picture of them surrounding you—or your home, car, et cetera—and then empower them as you would a catalyst for any other spell.

Each Witch has a different area of the body he or she feels is most vital to shield from negative influence, but the most

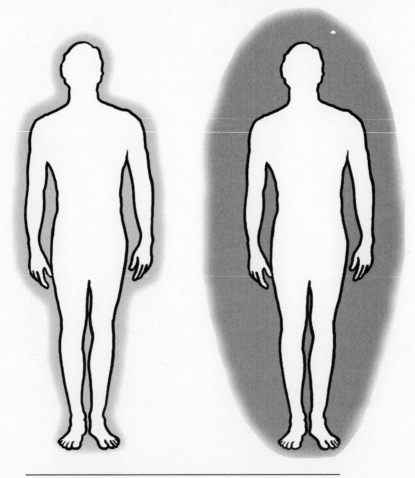

The normal range of the human aura, left, and right, a consciously expanded aura of protection

common seem to be the solar plexus and forehead areas—centers of strong psychic sensitivity. You may want to experiment with placing shields in different places to see which makes you feel safest. These points are not likely to remain static, and your protection needs may change with each new situation you face. For example, someone who is jealous of your beautiful singing voice may unconsciously be seeking to damage your vocal cords, and you will need to keep them well shielded. If someone is jealous of your resolve to get up each morning and jog five miles before breakfast, then it is your legs or chest area that might need the extra protection.

Psychic shields can bear any image you wish them to have. They can don protective symbols, a depiction of a deity, or a totem animal, or they can be visualized as ablaze with protective fire.

Closing the Chakras

The chakra centers you normally want open to allow for the free flow of psychic energy can be shut at will when you feel that the energy bombarding them is negative. To accomplish this, first think about how you drew in energy to open them, then reverse the process. Visualize a column of energy descending from your crown chakra down through your spine and flowing down into the earth. Mentally pour into the column the energy from your chakra and allow it to drain away.

It is not a good idea to maintain this completely closed state for long. The chakras not only balance your psychic and emotional energy, but also help regulate your physical self, and having them closed off for long periods can have ill effects on your health. Alternative and metaphysical healing techniques, such as therapeutic touch, focus on opening these centers as a means of holistically balancing the body to prepare it for self-healing.

You do not have to shut down all your chakras, but can choose instead to close only those chakras you feel need to be shut at a particular time (see the chakra chart in chapter 2 for color reference and location). For instance, if you feel your psychic attack is getting to you through your heart center, an energy point related to feelings, you can close only this one. Do this by envisioning all the chakras on your body fully open and glowing with their proper colors. Then mentally let the light in the one you want to close grow dim and begin to close up. You do not need to close it all the way; halfway will do until you feel any danger has passed.

To determine which chakra may be leaving you open to psychic attack, look through the following list and make a comparison between what disorders its imbalance is associated with and the nature of your current problem. Reading guides devoted to the chakras will give you a better indication of their functions, and this study is encouraged if you wish to work with the chakras on a regular basis. Naturally these imbalances are not listed here to prevent you from seeing a doctor or counselor if you need one. They are only to be used as guidelines for temporary problems you feel might be related to psychic attack.

Root Chakra

General instability, inability to center, sexual dysfunction, feelings of personal insecurity, paranoia, irritable bowels, spastic colon, constipation, diarrhea, weight swings, arthritis

Navel Chakra

Desire, willpower, feminine power, blood disorders, infertility, hormone imbalances, mood swings, eating disorders, urinary tract infections, vaginal infections, prostate disorders

Solar Plexus

Chronic indigestion, masculine power, flatulence, indigestion, hot flashes, violent outbursts, temper tantrums, diabetes, lactose intolerance

Heart Center

Dysfunctional romantic relationships, memory loss, lack of compassion, heart arrhythmia, anxiety attacks, allergies, respiratory problems, high or low blood pressure

Throat Chakra

Stuttering, fever blisters, tonsillitis, strep throat, sore throat, hoarseness, ringing in ears, a tendency to verbal abusiveness

Third Eye

Sudden blockage of psychic abilities, vision problems, dry eyes, panic disorders, sleep disorders, nightmares, headaches, dental problems, poltergeist activity (noisy spirit infestations)

Crown Chakra

Inability to think clearly, lack of good judgment, loss of interest in the spiritual, close-mindedness, bigotry, depression, chemical imbalances, neurological disorders, desire to withdraw from social contact

Be sure to rebalance and open your chakras when you feel the danger has passed so that all your energy centers are receptive to psychic energy and wanted psychic impressions. And if any of the above-mentioned symptoms persist for more than a week, please see a doctor.

Charging and Using Amulets

The word *amulet* comes from the Latin *amolior,* meaning "to repel," and the making and carrying of amulets is probably one of the oldest methods of magickal self-protection known to humankind. All the trinkets today's popular folklore says are "lucky"—horseshoes, rabbits' feet, et cetera—acquired their reputation because someone began carrying them around and started to feel fortunate. Those feelings gave confidence and soon the imagined became the reality.

In magick an amulet has two definitions that are not necessarily mutually exclusive. The first is that it must be a naturally occurring object, such as a stone or fossil, and not something humanmade (which is often referred to as a talisman). The second is that it grants protection to its wearer by having the ability to ward off negative energy or psychic attack.

Whether you want your amulet to be a stone you found on the beach or your diamond necklace, you must clean and charge it to its task as you would any other magical catalyst. Follow the steps for cleansing tools found on page 151, then charge the item to its task using the instructions on page 153. Be sure to clearly visualize your amulet as a protective device throughout its creation.

Making a Witch Bottle

No one knows just when the first Witch bottle was made and buried. It may have been five hundred years ago or five thousand. All we know for sure is that they are popular tools of defensive magick credited with creating a mantle of safety around the one who casts this spell through which nothing with harmful intent can penetrate.

The imagery behind the bottle harkens back to old beliefs about magickal substitution, a concept that one item is substituted for another you desire or is sacrificed to protect something even more important. The bottles were said to have been made and buried to protect Witches from death at the hand of the Witch hunters in the Middle Ages. They were buried to keep the Witches from ending up that way . . . thus, magickal substitution. The buried bottle also has symbolic links to the Mother Earth in her guise as protectress, her grounding abilities able to automatically ground any negative energy that comes your way.

The traditional Witch bottle is a small glass container into which needles, pins, broken glass, and other sharp objects have been placed. It sometimes contains a small portion of a protective or grounding substance such as salt or ashes. The rest of the bottle is topped off with the urine of the Witch, then is sealed and buried either just outside the Witch's doorstep or somewhere off the property, whichever suits you best.

I have seem some "sweetness-n-love" Witch bottle recipes over the years that contain fragrant herbs and flowers and strike me more as a love potion than a tool of protective magick. Naturally these bottles do not contain urine but are filled with blessed water instead.

If you really, really hate the idea of using your own urine (too many doctor's office images coming to mind!) then you can substitute vinegar, which has much the same acidity as urine and shares a history of usage in protective spells. However, do consider the mental imagery that comes with using your urine. It can be a very potent way to strengthen your ties to this spell, and the very thought of literally doing this act to your enemy can create the laughter and confidence required to make the bottle a success.

The first Witch bottle I made I created along with a friend. We both knew that we had inadvertently made a very bad non-magickal enemy, and we realized that her unwarranted hatred was having negative repercussions in our lives. We collected the glass jars and spent the better part of an evening digging through our garages, tool kits, and desk drawers, collecting the proper assortment of pointy objects. This in itself became a joyous magickal scavenger hunt.

When we were done gathering these items and had placed them in the bottles, we realized to our chagrin that it was not possible to produce on demand the other required ingredient, especially since we had severely overestimated the size of jars we needed. We brewed a big batch of iced tea and began to drink away while trying to focus on the Witch bottles as being able to defend us by immediately detecting and grounding any negativity sent our way. This was not easy as we had to keep interrupting the visualization process to make repeated trips into the bathroom, where our still half-filled Witch bottles sat waiting. After more iced tea than I ever again want to consume in one sitting, we both managed to fill our bottles.

Though I have become a believer in burying the Witch bottle by one's own door, that first time I was of the opinion that it should be buried somewhere away from my home. We took the bottles out to a rural stretch of Texas country road and buried them amidst chanting and visualization and a nest of fire ants, who made it clear they did not appreciate the addition of Witch bottles to their colony.

The bottles worked. We had little trouble from our enemy after that, and we learned a few valuable lessons about defensive magick.

Tradition says that the bottle will work for a year and a day unless it is broken.

Charging Your Inner-Warning Bell

It never hurts to have an added support system to warn you of trouble, especially when you are new to the psychic world and have not yet fully developed your psychic intuition to where it reliably works well for you. This intuition will come naturally in time to those who seriously study Witchcraft. There are also ways to speed up and enhance the process: through divination (reading the future through tarot cards, scrying, et cetera) or through exercises designed to help hone these skills, such as attempting to divine the shape of a hidden symbol. Another way to hone this skill is to work with a partner and, while one is trying to hold onto a mental image, the other can be trying to discern that image. This last method works exceptionally well because you are working with thought forms.

Thought forms are the etheric results of sustained visualization. On the unseen plane (see chapter 9 for full discussion) your thoughts have life and substance just as you have on the earth plane. In other words, your focused thoughts coalesce into energy patterns that you can charge and manipulate to work for you.

You can create a protective warning device from any bell by using your thought forms and the charging techniques you have already learned. To make one of these, empower the bell with your desire that it be a warning device for you in the event that you are approached by a negative being or by someone else's focused negative thoughts.

Hold the bell up to your third eye chakra (just above and between your eyes). This is your psychic center, and an excellent place for pushing a thought form out of your mind and into the real world. Visualize a small energy field growing behind your eyes, one that is a part of you but that still has a sentience of its own. See it as a protective sphere of dense light, and make it any color that makes you think of warning. Red is always a good choice, but white and orange can work well too. As it takes form, mentally charge it with its *exact task*. Speak or think out each word clearly as you charge it:

> *Sphere of perfect, protective energy, my magickal*
> *child—I charge you to enter and stay in this bell from*
> *where you will stand watch over me and my home*
> *until I bid you stop. Sound the bell loudly should*
> *any negative being, energy, or intent be directed*
> *this way. As you are part of me, and as I will this,*
> *so mote it be.*

Mentally project the thought form out through your third eye chakra and into the bell. This may take several minutes. Don't rush the process. You want to be sure you have transferred your will into the bell and not elsewhere. You also want to take the time to sense whether you have projected enough energy into this spell or not. A weak thought form will not be much of a protector. This is why it may be important to repeat this process several times to achieve the level of protection you want.

Hang the bell over a doorway or near your bed. Remember that it may not actually ring when it warns you; that is, it may not actually emit sound waves in the physical world. You may think you hear it—psychically—whether you are near it or not. Or you may see or hear it ring in a dream, or your attention may be drawn to it at an odd moment. Take all these as a warning sign of impending problems so that you can take steps to protect yourself.

Some Witches are fearful of creating thought forms or any other type of elemental being. These forms do have their drawbacks in that they can get away from you if you are not psychically sensitive or magically skilled enough to keep up with them. They can even turn on you if taken over by another "master" more powerful than you. But, in truth, the chances of either of these things happening is pretty slim.

The power of the thought form is going to be determined largely by your own skill level. In other words, you cannot produce something you do not possess. If your magickal skills are still weak, then your thought form isn't going to be a raging magickal genie-in-a-bell capable of moving mountains out from under you. Remember that it is *your* thought form and it is going to reflect the level of your power at the time it is created.

Creating thought forms to interact with you in the physical world is an act of great responsibility. You must act as a parent to this energy child you have created and be prepared to ground it if it goes astray or when its task is done. Never leave a thought form wandering unsupervised around the physical plane. Like your other magical energy, which must be grounded after use to keep it from causing your troubles, so should the thought form be grounded.

When you are done with the bell, or when you sense that its energy may be doing things without your consent, mentally draw it back out of the bell and into your chakra, and then send it into the ground. If not grounded it will eventually run its course and die from lack of nourishment. It will then make a home for itself in the astral as a weak pocket of unformed energy that astral travelers will be able to sense, but not before it has made your life uncomfortable.

To keep the bell functioning for you at optimum levels, you should plan to renew the spell once a month. Choose a time easy for you to remember, such as the full or new moon.

Sending Negativity Back Home

You can arrange to return any negative energy back to the one who sent it to you either by programming your warding methods to do this automatically or by casting deflecting spells. To turn any of the previously mentioned wards into automatic homing pigeons, simply add mirrors or other reflective elements to the visualization (except in the case of the Witch bottle, which already works this way). When you encase your aura in expanded light, see this as a mirror ball, just like the ones that used to hang in the old discotheques. When you trace the pentagram on the floor, make sure you visualize it as made of mirrored glass. It will be slippery and treacherous to those who don't know it like you do, and it will instantly reflect back any negative energy that was intentionally sent your way.

You can be creative with these reflective symbols and design one that is meaningful to you. I once knew a young Witch who was very involved in the sport of archery. He told me he liked to use the image of bows surrounding his body. Whenever someone fired a poison arrow at him, it would strike his bow and be fired right back. I always thought this was a wonderfully creative image and teased him about his Shakespearean "arrows of outrageous fortune" spell. But the bottom line was that it worked well for him as a magickal defense measure.

Spells to return negativity can be tricky in terms of the Wiccan or Pagan Rede. We never want to step across the line of harm by being the originators of negative energy. To avoid this I never do one of the spells with the idea of any one person in mind. Even if I think I know who may be wishing me ill, I could be wrong. It is best just to send it back in general. The energy knows who it belongs to and, when we deny it a resting place with us, will go home on its own. The only time I have broken this self-imposed rule is when I was receiving ugly letters and phone calls from someone (a non-magickal person, naturally) who was bent on carrying on a feud in which I had no interest. When I did not respond to his game, he increased his bullying and I knew it was time to bring out the magickal cannon. In his case, I was very clear about to whom the negativity should return. (By the way, the spell worked beautifully, and in only one shot!)

Some Witches will argue that any spell that turns negativity on someone else is always wrong and is against the Rede. Under any other circumstance I would agree, but not when the negativity you are being bombarded with is deliberately fired at you. No one has the right to do this to you—to upset your mental, emotional, and physical life simply to gratify some personal need for power or vengeance. This does not mean that you ever have the right to blast someone back with your own negativity, no matter what they have done to you. The wheel of life eventually comes around, and you do not want to be on the receiving end of your own whammy. Tormentors will get what they deserve due to their own efforts; you are just speeding up the process a bit, not adding to it. Think of it as simply returning something you happen to find to its rightful owner.

In my return-the-negativity spells, I avoid including any hint that I want the energy returned to the sender threefold. Whenever I tried using this imagery, it did not feel right and I would shut the spell down and start again without this codicil. Let the deities and the universe balance the karma threefold— all you really need to do right now is to get it as far away from you as possible.

As you read through this spell, consider the imagery involved and make notes on how you might want to modify this for your own use. I have several return-the-negativity spells I like. All include the idea of souring the benefits of the negativity that the sender may have accrued, of collecting it and firing it back, and of issuing mental warnings not to let it happen again. Think of this as the "speak softly and carry a big stick" corollary of your magickal ethics policy.

Returning the Negativity Spell

Ruling Element: Fire

Sub-Element: Water

Defined Goal: "To return any and all negativity that was deliberately sent to me back to the one who sent it, without sending out any negative intent of my own."

Best Times: On the dark or waning moon (spell will need to be done for at least three consecutive days)

Materials: Two white candles, one black candle, matches, a candle snuffer, three candle holders, a small mirror, a bowl of vinegar, some salt, three straight pins, a small nonmetal bowl, a small black cloth

Take all your materials to a place where your spell can sit undisturbed for at least three days. Place the mirror flat in the center of your working area. Place the black candle on top of the mirror, and on both sides of it place the two white candles. Place the bowl of vinegar in front of the mirror closest to you. Push the three pins carefully into the black candle, then light it. The pins serve to hold in the negative energy the candle will be collecting, and, as in the Witch bottle, add to the symbolism of defense.

As you light the black candle, you might want to make some statement of its purpose as a receptacle of negative energy. You may use whatever wording seems best to you. Continue collecting the negative energy around you, pulling it close to the black candle, all the while making sure you are not including any negative energy originating with yourself.

Contrary to popular opinion, black is not a color of evil. Black is a color of mystery and of the crone Goddess, and it has the power to absorb other energies we do not want around us. Think of how black acts in non-magickal situations (if there is such a thing). The black holes in space are said to be made of collapsed stars. In them the gravity field is so strong that nothing entering may escape—not even light! It absorbs and retains everything that comes into it. Within the world of color, black is the absence of reflected light, unlike white, which reflects all colors of the spectrum equally. Black absorbs light energy and holds it, which is why black materials are noticeably warmer to the touch than lightly colored ones. Your black candle is going to serve this same function in your spell.

Draw in your protection, then light two white candles. Visualize these as two pillars of protection standing watch over you and over the negative energy that is going to be absorbed by the black candle. You may even wish to speak out loud, stating what the candles represent.

Spend some time in quiet contemplation, focusing on the goal of the spell. Then center yourself (see chapter 2) and begin pulling your energy inward. As you do this you should be sensing the presence of the negative energy that has been sent your way as well. Allow it to draw in close around you. Now feel the black candle sucking up the negative energy around you like a huge psychic vacuum cleaner. Keep up this process as long as you can, or until you sense that no more negative energy is left to be absorbed.

If you get to this point in the spell and still have ethical considerations bothering you, do not visualize the energy leaving the candle and being reflected. Instead, allow the candle to retain the collected energy and bury it somewhere later. This way it is grounded but you have not actually returned it back to the sender.

You should also consider stopping at this point and changing the focus of the spell if you notice any anger within yourself. Anger can be, but is not always, a negative emotion. In this case, if you are feeling anger at the one who sent you the negativity, you may not be able to avoid mixing some of your own negative energy into what you are planning to return. This puts you in the position of being the aggressor, not the defender, and makes you as guilty as the one at whom you are angry. If you feel you cannot control this emotion, it is best to just stop now and bury the candle.

If you feel you are capable of safely sending the energy back, pause and visualize the black candle as being full of the negative energy it has collected. Watch the candle melting away as the flame burns it. As it disappears, see the negativity falling out onto the mirror. As it hits the mirror, picture it being reflected back to the one who sent it.

When you can keep up the visualization no longer, or when all your candles are about one-third burned down, pick up the black candle and dip the lighted end into the bowl of vinegar. Think of this as the quenching of the light of vengeance burning in the heart of your enemy and of the acidic vinegar souring any benefits that your enemy might have gained from harming you. That benefit was stolen from you, robbed from your peace of mind and well-being. It is your property and you can take it back if you like.

I also like to think of the blending of the fire and water elements as perfect partners in magickal self-defense. Fire burns away troubles and water drowns them. Together fire and water create steam, so think of this action as a steam cleaning for your psychic self!

Another good thing to do at this point is laugh. Laugh hard and loud! The power of laughter in dangerous situations is amazingly potent. I learned this trick from a Mexican *curandera* (a wise woman or shaman) many years ago. When I stopped fearing the power of my enemies and learned to laugh at them instead, I immediately gained the upper hand. It could be crucial for you to learn this art. It was for me. The curandera helped through the only battle in my life in which I was pitted against a formidable magickal enemy, and some of the weapons she hurled at me were quite daunting, since at the time I was still a relatively new Witch. I still use laughter when any situation, magickal or not, has the better of me, and it still works wonderfully well to turn things in my favor.

After three days, when this spell has run its full course, bury the stump of the black candle to ground any remaining negativity that may be inside. Allow the white candles to burn on as beacons of protection for as long as they last (and only while you are there to supervise). Pour the remaining vinegar down the drain.

Most return-the-negativity spells require repeated workings. I recommend starting with a three-day repetition, meaning that the entire spell should be repeated three days in a row at about the same time of day. These repetitions allow you to be sure you have gathered all the negativity surrounding you, both the original that was sent and what might still be filtering in as you begin this spell. It also allows you to focus your visualization more intently, to take advantage of variety of planetary hours (see chapter 4), and to incorporate any magickal numbers you or your Craft tradition hold sacred. The Celts and the Norse saw three as a sacred number—the origin of the phrase "three's the charm."

The Art of Banishing and Exorcising

Banishing means to send away someone or something permanently. In magick we banish to clear and purify a ritual area, our homes, or the immediate area surrounding ourselves. Negative energies/entities come in three orders: one, thought forms sent by other people, two, inhuman spirits attracted to the energy you create when you do a spell or ritual, and three, human discarnates, sometimes known as ghosts. It is number two, the inhuman negative spirits, at whom most banishing rituals are addressed. When a banishing is focused on removing from your presence a being rather than an undefined energy, it can also be referred to as an exorcism.

Banishing seems to be the preferred term in Wiccan/Pagan circles, probably because of the monopoly the Catholic Church has on the word *exorcism*. There is probably not one of us who has not seen at least one movie or read one book about a confused priest who finds himself pitted against demonic forces, and only the holy and approved exorcism rites of the Church can save him.

Negative spirits can be as different as negative people, and some are more or less bad than others. Usually they are attracted to you during magickal or spiritual rites when your positive energy output is strong and alluring. Even doing excessive divinations can draw them in. I once threw a Samhain party[1] at which someone was doing tarot readings for other people almost constantly. The following day I was aware of the presence of a being who had obviously found the energy raised during these readings very attractive. Other beings might follow you back from the astral, or unseen, world when you meditate, astral project (see chapter 9), or do other types of psychic work. New Witches experimenting with Wiccan/Pagan ritual will often find they get these trailers of beings who want to stick close just in case you do another one. They usually hope to be able to squeeze in between your protective barriers and feed off that energy.

---

1. Samhain is a Pagan solar festival with Celtic roots that is the origin of the modern Halloween celebration.

The first unwanted being I attracted seemed more like a playful nuisance than a threat. I could feel it sneaking around my house, peering at me from around corners, and it loved the vacuum cleaner. Whenever I swept the floor I could feel it hovering nearby, trying to decide what kind of energy was being produced and if it was useful. It usually did this at my back, which was very disconcerting. Yelling at it to back off helped for a while, but it just found the vacuum too irresistible. After banishing it from my home one night, I went to bed and was just about asleep when I heard scratching at the outside wall of my bedroom. In that hazy altered state of mind known as hypnogogic sleep I was well aware that it was the astral nuisance wanting me to let it back inside. It literally whimpered like a puppy. My husband woke up and heard it as well, and was not amused. I dragged myself out of bed and spent the time needed to extend my protective field to the edge of my property instead of just my home—another magickal lesson learned.

One other being that found its way in one night was less pleasant. The mental image I carry of its appearance still disturbs me, and I was very glad to have gotten rid of it. Like the nuisance spirit, I sensed it hanging around the far edge of the property for a while looking for a way back in, but I kept my defenses up and it eventually left to seek more willing prey.

One of my best friends, the daughter of a highly skilled Kaballist, was aware that such beings would find her own magickal interests attractive, but she was unprepared for just how distressful their presence could be. She attracted two creatures, one she could hear making a sound like raspy breathing and another that was initially attracted to her magickal energy, then attached itself to the negative energy of her alcoholic husband.

It must be emphasized that these beings are attracted to you, not the place where you do your magick and rituals or people around you, though it is through these rituals that attention is drawn to you. But you are the one raising the energy, and it is your aura and etheric self that the being wants to feed on. One of the first negative beings I had to deal with would have had to follow me back from a ritual site some six miles away from my home. Apparently my energy was attractive enough that it bothered to do just this.

I recommend using a fully cast ritual circle before doing any banishing (see chapter 6). This will keep negative beings from feeding off the energy you are raising as you attempt to get rid of them. It will also protect you if they choose to fight your edict rather than leave in peace. To put your mind at ease, I have never heard of a case where this happened, but it is always best to be prepared for anything when dealing with the caprice of otherworld entities.

After you have cast your circle and are sure of your security, you should know full well that these beings are hovering at the edge of that circle, attracted by its glow and by your energy that created it. The first thing you should do is face the being and, in a clear and firm voice, demand that it leave. Many astral beings, for reasons no one is completely clear on, must obey your command. Undoubtedly, many others will simply find your orders amusing.

Back up your command by using your hand or taking a projective tool like an athame or wand and making some gesture of dismissal, or a banishing pentagram, in the air in front of you (see chapter 6 for instructions on the pentagram). Fill the tool with your will to have this being leave, then mentally send it flying out of your circle to attack the being directly.

You can also draw up energy from Mother Earth to banish. Allow it to follow through you and into your power hand. Raise your palm at the being and visualize a stream of bright, white light blasting it, pushing it outside of your home and either off your property or forcing it into the ground to be dealt with by Mother Earth.

Another image that has worked very well for me is to picture a large, white, inverted tornado descending from high in the otherworld and coming down to engulf my house. I visualize it spinning counterclockwise and moving down through my home and on into the earth below, taking with it all negative beings, unwanted energies, or any other resident spirits that have not been expressly invited in by me.

Be sure to keep backing up your efforts with demands that the being leave. Even if the being does not choose to listen to you, your firm voice will strengthen your confidence, thus making your effort more effective.

When you have finished your banishing rite, mentally seal your home and yourself with positive energy. Do this before closing your circle just in case you have not been fully successful. This will prevent the being, if angered, from being able to attack you. After you close your circle, pause for a few moments and take psychic note of your surroundings. Once you feel your home is free of the being, go around and ward your house (see the house warding spell given in chapter 5). If you feel you have not been successful, recast the circle and do the banishing again immediately. Though it is likely that you will have a successful banishing, unless you are exceptionally sensitive to presences it pays to be thorough.

Exorcising Human Discarnates

The rituals surrounding the banishment of human discarnates, or ghosts, have been closely guarded Witch secrets for hundreds of years. The same is true for methods of contacting ghosts. Because Witches feared the repercussions of treading on the toes of the Orthodox religions, which claimed an exclusive possession on these rites, it has only been in the past half century that Witches have been more open about exorcism. It is an art I fear all too many modern Witches are unfamiliar with. Unfortunately this is one of the few Craft arts that cannot be satisfactorily or safely taught from a book. There is just too much involved, and to learn properly one really needs hands-on lessons with an experienced teacher who is actively involved in the banishing and can take you step by step through the process. I would probably never have learned, nor would my own teacher have thought to show me, had the situation not come up during my training. I am glad I learned something of this art, though I would not presume to think myself an expert, and I have to confess that it is a circumstance I would rather not find myself in again.

Just because a ghostly manifestation appears does not mean that it is malevolent, or that it is even aware of your existence. The first thing to be done is to determine what type of ghost it is.

- Is it merely a piece of magnetic recording caught in the air and being played back whenever atmospheric conditions are right? These energies can be grounded to some extent, but cannot be exorcised because they are not made up of the essences of sentient beings.

- Is it a peek at some living person in another time who becomes visible at certain moments because the veil of time grows thin at the place it is seen? In this case, the spirit may not even be sentiently aware of you or the "spirit" may be seeing you as well and be just as sure *it* is seeing a ghost.

- Is it a spirit who merely wants to remain near places or people he or she loved in life?

- Is it a transient spirit who is merely passing through your home, either from confusion or because it has chosen to wander around the earth plane for a time? These lonely spirits usually appear quickly, are harmless, seem to have no trigger that brought them in, and they usually go away on their own in a few months.

- Is it someone who is stuck on the earth plane, unwilling or unable to move on?

- Is it a friend or family member wishing to pass along a warning, trying to comfort, or wanting to stay around for a while just to make sure you and other loved ones are all right?

- Is it a loud or destructive spirit whose manifestation coincides with the presence of certain people? These

noisy ghosts are called poltergeists and they have
been associated with the presence of emotionally
disturbed adolescents.

- Do you see the spirit repeating an action over and
  over? This could be positive or negative, depending
  on how that person felt about the task in life. If it
  made the spirit happy, he or she may not be thrilled
  that you are trying to take away that pleasure. If it is
  a compulsion caused by a lack of realizing that, now
  dead, the task does not have to be continued, your
  interference may be seen as salvation.

Once you have determined what type of ghost you have,
you will have a better idea if it can be banished. Obviously a
living person you view through a rip in the time veil cannot
be banished. You will next have to determine if it is right for
you to try to banish this spirit. Human discarnate spirits
should be given the same courtesy of free will as are human
incarnates. If the spirit seems happy and is not threatening
you, it may be best—and most compassionate—to learn to live
with it. Sometimes these spirits will only be in your life temporarily. I once knew a family who had a ghost in their attic
they called Edward. When they arrived home at the end of the
day the lonely spirit would run back and forth across the attic
floor until someone greeted him. A cheery "Hello, Edward"
would silence him. This went on for almost a year, and then
he appeared to move on.

Certainly attempting to learn the name of the ghost is just
as important as trying to figure out what type of ghost he or
she is. In virtually all magickal/spiritual systems, knowing
something's or someone's name helps give you power over it.
It can also help you gain the spirit's confidence and put him
or her at ease, the same way someone who wants to gain the
trust of your watch dog tries first to learn its name. In the case
of a ghost, knowing the identity can also help you figure out
what the ghost is doing in the place you usually find it and,

hopefully, what it needs of you. If the spirit seems connected to a specific locale, you might try to research the history of the place to see if you can find any clues as to the ghost's identity.

You will also have to determine if and where there is a portal allowing inhabitants of the spirit world to enter your home. A portal is a thin place between the world of spirit and of form that allows the free passage of beings from one world to the other. These can best be located while in an altered state of consciousness. With your eyes closed, mentally travel to each part of your home, "feeling" out each part of your home, or by actually seeing a spirit pass into your home through one specific location. You can seal off this portal with a simple warding. A flaming pentagram of protection, renewed each month, should keep it closed permanently.

It is not recommended that you take your exorcism cues from badly produced horror movies and attempt to send a spirit elsewhere if you are not skilled at spirit contact or have some in-depth knowledge of parapsychology. Trying to coax a belligerent spirit, perhaps one who sees you as an intruder in his or her home, into the light may find yourself the recipient of an unpleasant outburst of ghostly temperament.

If you find you have a problem ghost in your home, look first for portals and seal them off at a time when the spirit seems not to be inside. This may keep it from being able to enter again. If the problem persists, seek out an experienced Witch who is willing to help or teach you, or find someone knowledgeable in the field of parapsychology.

▼

8

Techniques of Advanced Natural Magick

Many Witches, especially newcomers, wrongly assume that advanced natural magick is something like the magick of medieval wizards seen on television, involving the summoning and commanding of an ever-increasing army of spirits. They picture this like a scene from some old movie where combating magicians are forever pulling demons from a boiling cauldron. Natural magick does not work that way. Strengthening a natural spell's power comes from within, and requires superb control and execution of basic magickal skills.

Advanced natural magick involves one of four operations that can be used on their own or in combination to make them even stronger:

- Through using more catalysts, which require better skills of visualization to keep their added energies straight in the mind

- Through time-bending techniques, which take the magician outside the constraints of linear time so that the entire wheel of existence can be seen and acted upon at once

- Through advanced energy projection techniques, such as astral magick or sex magick
- Through sustaining magickal energy over a long period of time until the goal is manifested, utilizing everything touching one's life as a potential energy source

None of these techniques take long to explain, though they each do take a great deal of time to work through. This extra attention to magickal detail is part of the reason these work so well. All of them seem deceptively simple on paper. In fact, you may have already noticed that this is one of the smallest chapters in this book. This is because there is little to say about each of the techniques without becoming unnecessarily wordy. They are what they are, and only you can bring them to life with your desire and will.

Added Catalysts and Advanced Visualization

This method of advanced natural magick is pretty self-explanatory. It requires the addition of a greater number of catalysts, accoutrements, and symbols to a spell. Each one of these has to be individually empowered with its goal, and each one has to be carefully programmed for its own subtle contribution. For instance, where many forms of candle magick ask you to use one or two candles, advanced magick might ask for ten—each one's color, size, and shape contributing its own special power to the end result. Each of these has to be kept straight in the magician's mind. This requires a certain amount of magickal experience to be able to instantly associate these colors and symbols with their contribution to the outcome, and it requires greater powers of visualization to hold on to all these images at once and to allow them to coalesce in the ultimate result you desire.

An example of this type of advanced magick would be a spell for love requiring a rose quartz stone, two poppets (magically charged dolls), a bowl of water, rose incense, and rose oil to anoint seven candles. The rose quartz is a stone that has affinities with romance and peace, the two poppets represent the two lovers, the bowl of water brings in the water element, which governs romantic love, and the scent of roses, provided with the incense, is also a romance-related scent. The rose oil would be used to anoint the seven candles to further charge them to their goal. Six of the seven candles might include green (to bring in the powers of Venus, which govern romance), blue (for loyalty), red (for passion), one pink (for romance and peace), white (for truth in the relationship), and orange (which governs the areas of attraction and friendship). A seventh candle might be heart shaped to function as a symbol of the ultimate goal. All of these catalysts have been empowered individually with their special task and the end goal in mind. All of them have to be set in motion at the same time, which takes a great deal of concentration if for no other reason than that a spell with this many accoutrements will be a lengthy process requiring prolonged focus on the desired result.

A spell such as this might take an hour or more to work through, even after all the components have been empowered. The incense would need to be lit to set the tone for the working, and the rose quartz charged as a talisman of the goal that would need to be carried with the Witch until the goal is reached. It would probably be further charged in the smoke of the incense and the flame of each candle. The candles would have to be anointed, or dressed, in the proper manner, one at a time. This dressing is usually begun from the center of the taper and worked outward toward the tips when the spell involves attraction, and from the top and bottom inward toward the center when it involves banishing. All the while, focused visualization would have to be maintained. Each candle would have to be lit separately, probably from the heart-shaped candle that would likely take center stage as the primary symbol of the goal. The poppets would have to be psychically linked both to the Witch doing the spell and to the as-yet-unknown partner. The water would also need to be charged before being used on the poppets or any of the other catalysts.

Even after all the preparation for an advanced spell has been done, and the spell worked through with the utmost care, it may still have to be repeated several times to be effective. With this many accoutrements, a spell of this type could be quite costly.

Some Witches read the long ingredient list in spells such as these and toss them aside just as surely as some people would a recipe in a gourmet cookbook containing too many steps. They prefer to stick with the simple and known, and this is fine. Advocating this type of advanced magick as being very powerful is not to imply that doing a love spell with only one bowl of water and some rose incense cannot be just as effective. The advantage of doing a spell with lots of extra props is in the way it allows us to bring in so many other aspects of the goal and to tailor the goal more precisely.

Even in advanced magick the Witch still must go out in the world and act on the physical plane to assist the desire into manifestation. No amount of magick will bring Prince or Princess Charming to your doorstep if you never cross over it yourself. Again, care must also be taken not to infringe on anyone else's free will and to avoid dictating to the universe how the goal should be made manifest.

Working Backward and Forward in Time

Witches still believe, as our ancestors did, in the omnipresent nature of time.[1] While this is sometimes described as cyclic time rather than linear, "cyclic time" is not a wholly satisfactory description either—cyclic still implies movement along a pre-set course to single points—but it is the best term we have to work with in our limited vocabulary.

Time simply is. We only realize it linearly, flowing in a straight line from past to present to future, because we have been conditioned to think this way. The shamans and other priests and priestesses of the old tribes and clans were expected to divine the future by means of traveling to it for a firsthand look. Modern Witches phrase magickal goals in the present tense and not in the future tense to underscore our belief that, as the spell is done, the goal has already been attained—we just haven't caught up with it in the cycle yet.

Modern physics now supports these old beliefs that all time exists in one great omnipresent now, and this realization has spawned the first serious looks into and hypotheses about the possibility of time travel. One of the magickal uses of time bending is in altering "past" events to change our "present." In my previous book, *Lady of the Night,* I used the example of a car accident to illustrate this concept. What if you were in an accident that left you with a broken leg that would not set right? What if the only hope you had for walking properly again was to actually go back in time and relive the moment of the accident, causing it not to have happened? Granted that we are not yet magickally evolved enough to eliminate the results of the accident altogether,[2] but we can clearly lessen its severity. In the above example, the leg would mend properly over time.

Time study is one great paradox I find endlessly fascinating. The fact that all time is here and now seems at first to fly in the face of free will. If the future already exists, then how do we have any control over it? If the past is here, why aren't history books being constantly rewritten as the past changes and impacts our present? My answer is, who's to say that history isn't changing all the time and we just aren't consciously aware of it any more than we are of the omnipresent time factor itself?

To be able to bend time, you first have to absolutely believe that the past exists somewhere and that you can return to it just like you can return to places in your physical world, which you have left behind. In *Lady of the Night* I gave some

---

1. Two books I like that talk about time and time travel theories are Stephen W. Hawking's *A Brief History of Time* (Bantam, 1988), and John W. Macvey's *Time Travel: A Guide to Journeys in the Fourth Dimension* (Scarborough House, 1990).

2. There is a theory that the human mind has actually de-evolved over time, at least in terms of its metaphysical potential; that societal programming in western cultures has caused us to backtrack over the millennia so that we are actually less able to use all our magickal potential than we once were. Since we have no empirical way to measure the magickal aptitude of our ancestors, this will likely remain only a theory.

exercises for helping to overcome resistance to the time barrier, which can hamper this type of magick. These involve no more than attempting to peer past the veil into other co-existing time frames and being open to how various creative minds have viewed and presented time theories. It is a sad truth that our minds naturally resist the idea that the past and future are with us at this very moment. Even when we accept this intellectually, that killjoy chatterbox we call the conscious mind keeps up a running commentary of reasons this just cannot be so.

Start conditioning yourself to believe you can affect the past by thinking about how you can affect the future. You probably are planning on taking some action this very day that you hope will have some impact on the near future, even if it is just planning your grocery list. If you get to the grocery and suddenly decide to change your meal plan, you will have altered a future event. Presumably if you do a divination and see a future potential coming up that you don't like, you take steps to alter that as well. By doing this, what was once a set fact, as indicated by the divination, is altered when you put new energies into the event. The same can be done with the past to alter your present. I have had some success with time-bending techniques, both in the future and in the past, though I will admit that working in the past is much harder. I have managed to make one or two present-time problems less severe by working in the past, but I have never been able to completely change anything—at least to my conscious knowledge.

To work in the past, you must enter the deepest level altered state of which you are capable and project yourself mentally into the event you wish to change. Go through it step by step, over and over again, until the imagined becomes real. You will have to do this more than once—probably several times over the course of a few months. Eventually your mind will begin to accept your preferred version of past events, and you may even find it hard to recall the details of the other time line you have tried to eliminate. By doing this you make both sequences of events realities, which can impact your life.

Raising and Sending Energy
with Sex Magick

Many books have been written on sex magick, a subject that continues to fascinate us as much today as it did to the ancients. While a discussion of sex seems as if it ought to be pretty straightforward, even when related to magick, it doesn't take much research into the subject to discover that there are dozens of forms of sex magick, all of them fairly complex. There are the tantric arts and the raising of the kundalini, or inner-serpent power, of Indian mysticism, and the taoist sex magick practices of eastern Asia that are linked to prolonging the life essence. Then there are the more standard Pagan methods which, while less difficult to learn, can be almost as hard to master.

Because Paganism does not regard sex as a necessary evil, its imagery has been incorporated in many of our rituals for thousands of years. This is most keenly seen in the Great Rite of Anglo-Celtic origin, in which a blade and chalice symbolize the sexual union of the God and Goddess. In some circles this union is enacted de facto, though usually not with an audience. Because this aspect of the Craft has been so sensationalized it has worked against us by bringing into our ranks all sorts of folks who have little interest in the spiritual but lots of interest in sex. It is these and other bad elements who have been attracted to the Craft who use sacred sexual images to gratify their own egos and to gain control over serious students who come to them for guidance.

Like anything used in a sacred context, sex becomes a holy act, a sacrament. Because spiritually it contains potent symbolic messages, sex magick is a very powerful tool, one that is usually used sparingly. Sex magick can be easily misused, even unintentionally, simply because it is hard to control one's thoughts and intentions at the height of passion. Contrary to popular belief, many Witches never engage in the practice on a regular basis for just these reasons.

In sex magick, sexual arousal is used as a power-raising device. Naturally, prolonging this state makes the energy being raised all the stronger, providing the focus can be sustained.

Naturally, sending out the energy toward the goal must coincide with the moment of orgasm. There are two principal methods for making sex magick work. Only one requires that you be with a partner; the other can be done with a partner or alone. These methods are:

- Reciprocally viewing your partner as deity incarnate
- Focusing on an agreed-on symbol that has been charged with magickal intent

During our sacred rites it is assumed that the people involved in them contain some aspect of the divine incarnate. All women are Goddesses and all men Gods, aspects of the creative life force that, once united, sparks all things into being. In essence, working sex magick with the idea that the person you are with is a God or Goddess creates a Great Rite situation in which you are reenacting the moment when all creation began. Focused magickal intent is very powerful at this time, which is why care must be taken in molding it and in sending it out.

Keeping focused can be difficult when passions run high, a problem made worse because we have been conditioned to think that the spiritual and the sexual cannot coexist, therefore any lustful thoughts invading the mind must naturally counteract the higher aspects of the spell. This is garbage! The lustful desires of the God and Goddess toward each other are well documented in the myths and rituals of all cultures. Lust should be a healthy part of any loving relationship, and it would be sad for any couple if it were not. Passion will not negate a good spell; in fact, if it is carefully cultivated, its energy can add a great deal. Learning to control the focus of the energy is the hard part.

I have heard it argued that gay and lesbian couples cannot properly engage in sex magick, do the Great Rite, act as God and Goddess together, and on and on ad nauseum. In metaphysical terms, gender arguments are pointless. Inside each of us are both feminine and masculine qualities. At different times one may be more dominant than the other, but are both there just the same. As long as we are confined to a body of one gender, we may not be able to fully unite with a divine force representing our physical polarity, but it can be done with some degree of success. Gay and lesbian couples should feel free to work with these forces as would any other Witches.

Whether you are alone, or with a partner, you can increase your chances of having successful sex magick by simplifying your visualization. Focus on keeping a symbol in your mind that represents your goal. This is a much easier thought to hold on to when your attention is being pulled pleasantly elsewhere than trying to keep a mental movie playing through your head. The symbol will have to be chosen ahead of time and, if you are working with a partner, it will have to be agreed on to allow your energies to work in concert. Scattered sexual energy is as magickally useless as any other scattered magickal energy. After you have selected or created a symbol, spend lots of time mentally endowing the symbol as a representation of your joint goal so that when it is brought to mind during sacred sex, it is immediately flooded with magickal energy. The symbol can also be drawn on posterboard and placed strategically around the area where you will be making your sex magick so that if the image cannot be held mentally any longer, it can be projected into your subconscious just by gazing at the image.

The only thing unethical about sex magick is doing it without you partner's knowledge or consent. The person you are with has the right to know what you are doing with his or her sexual energy, and the right to be given the free will whether to participate or not. If you have an unwilling partner and forge ahead, you are violating the Rede and you will find the Law of Threefold Return coming back at you. If your partner is unwilling or uncertain, sex magick can be worked perfectly well all alone. Solitary sex magick can give you the opportunity to explore the depths of your magickal powers, and it will help train you to focus and visualize under the most challenging of circumstances.

There is also nothing wrong with working sex magick to assist your partner in something he or she wants. As long as you both agree on what the goal should be, there is nothing wrong with focusing the energy on only one of you.

Whom you choose to work your sex magick with is up to you. It can be a loving, long-term partner or someone else of your choosing who cares about your magickal desires. Sex magick between virtual strangers is not as potent simply because you must know someone and their energies before you can work in harmony with them. Since sex today can have deadly consequences, it should go without saying that a concern for the health and safety of both partners should be a factor in your choice.

The key to successful sex magick is keeping focused on the goal during arousal and foreplay when you are raising magickal energy and when sending it toward its goal at the moment of orgasm. Sex magick is not a tool everyone will want to use, any more than everyone wants to use an athame, but properly learned and executed it can be a powerful part of your magickal repertoire.

Sustaining Magickal Energy for the Long Term

Sustained magick can often succeed where one or two workings of a regular spell do not because it uses as a catalyst everything and anything that touches our lives to raise and send energy. It may seem a simple thing to do, but it requires an almost obsessive commitment to your goal and the willingness to let your life revolve around that goal for several months or more.

I have only made one long-term spell work because it was the only one I could stick with. Only one goal in my life has been so important that I was able to spend two full years focusing on it. My husband, Mark, was in a career he hated. He was miserable and, by association, I was miserable too. Every morning that he had to get up for work he would be nauseated and then he would come home with violent headaches. We knew we had to make a change, but doing so was not going to be easy. He had spent eight years of his life in university preparing for this career, and, by the time we knew we had to make some changes, he had already invested another seven years in his career. The money was pretty good, but we were struggling to pay off unexpected medical expenses that our insurance company denied and we knew that taking a pay cut would put a strain on us. Mark's education and career had not prepared him to do work in any other field that could hope to support us while we paid tuition expenses for him to return to school and prepare for another career, and also take care of living expenses. My situation was no more optimistic than his. I had been a freelance writer for nearly ten years, so I had no standard job history to put on a résumé, and I knew I would need to take a second job for a few years. My degree in history was useless as a selling point as well. We also knew that we wanted to settle down somewhere near family, which meant that before we even got started on the jobs and schooling we were going to have to sell our house and make a major move to another state.

It all seemed a pretty bleak picture until we decided to channel all the energy we were spending talking about what we wanted into a long-term spell for our goal. We clearly defined that goal, which given our situation had multiple levels, and we decided who would focus on which aspects. We threw our magickal and physical energies into the effort and, finally, two years later we saw the first part of our goal manifest.

We are living the results of that spell today. It has not been easy, and the physical effort (read *hard work*) we have had to do has been as intense as any spell. We live near my parents in Indiana, have a new home, and are working very hard to juggle school, work, and other responsibilities. But even with the hectic pace at which we live, I wouldn't trade the path we are on for anything we had in the past. We thank our Goddess every full moon for our blessings. The final outcome has yet to be realized, but the energies set in motion over four years ago are still manifesting and should conclude in the winter of 1997, when we will see the final result of our spellwork.

Advanced long-term magick works well because everything that touches your life becomes an opportunity for magick. The cycles of the spells and visualizations are deeply linked to the cycles of the moon. As a spell is initially worked, the lunar phase is looked to as a guidepost for how that visualization should be focused. For instance, if you are doing a long-term spell to improve your financial situation, you would concentrate on seeing your net worth increase as the moon waxed and your poverty and debts decrease as the moon waned.

Individual spells should be constructed for both moon phases and, whenever possible, worked as those phases are first beginning. The waxing energy spell should be done at the new moon, and the waning energy spell when the moon is just past full.

Other magickal techniques must also be used. Songs, chants, and affirmations (positive, present-tense statements about your goal) should be uttered whenever thought of; conversations and daydreams should flow around your goal, all infused with excitement; even the rhythms of the rhythmic tools and machinery you work with at your mundane job can be used to lull your mind into a magical state. Take advantage of these and focus on your goal. Catching these snatches of magickal moments each day is what keeps the energy of the long-term spell building.

Time-wasting tasks that are rhythmic in nature have been used magickally for hundreds of years. The old spinning and weaving songs were more than just ways to help pass time during a tedious chore. Listen to how many nonsense syllables are contained within them. These were there to help lull the mind into the alpha and theta levels, into the realm of the receptive and magickal. Though most of us no longer spin our own yarn or weave our own cloth, we can still sing about our goals in rhythm to our sweeping, dusting, or scoring.

Key symbols should be placed around you to keep reminding you of your goal. Mark and I kept a map on our refrigerator of where we wanted to ultimately live, and we cut out job ads and real estate listings from that city's newspaper and leafed through them on a regular basis. We devoted a part of each day to discussing our goals and feeding them our magickal will.

Keeping an eye on the phase of the moon, repeating the actual spells at each moon phase, and finding new and creative ways to focus your energy each day as you continue to work in the physical world toward your goal are the "secrets" to this type of very powerful advanced magick.

▼

9

Astral Magick

The astral world, or astral plane as it is sometimes called, is an important place for magicians and Witches to become acquainted with. It is conceptualized as an invisible other world that parallels and interpenetrates our own, but remains unseen in our normal states of consciousness. On this plane all thoughts, deities, spirits, and magick live, waiting to be called into the manifest world. All types of magick and ritual can be done in the astral with great efficacy since this is where your energies must go before manifesting. While there, you can find a likely place to cast a circle and work a spell or you can also travel to other places to work astral magick, such as appearing in your astral body at the bedside of a sick friend who has requested your help in healing.

Astral projection is best defined as the art of sending *consciousness* out at will to a location away from the physical body. While this projection ultimately remains in the mind, and thus is synonymous with the term "inner plane," it is no less a real place populated with very real beings and containing very real phenomena. This is the world where all our thoughts and dreams must first take shape before we can bring them into the physical plane through magick. It is also the home of the elemental powers and their inhabitant spirits.

People who are in a projected state do indeed have a part of themselves "out there" somewhere, though this is projection of consciousness, not of the soul. Some psychically sensitive people have been able to see these travelers and, when caught in a mishap, a few astral travelers have even come back bruised. I take this latter example as proof of the power of the mind to affect on the physical level what is seen on the mental one—magick in action!

Astral magick is usually considered an advanced skill, though merely projecting onto the astral plane is usually not. This is a terribly confusing concept for people trying to learn to project who are not succeeding. More than any other skill you will learn, astral projection takes repeated effort to be fully controlled by you. A readers' poll taken several years ago by Llewellyn's *New Worlds of Mind and Spirit* showed 63% of the respondents were able to consciously astral project. Some mastered the art in a few months, but it took others several years. Don't let anyone tell you that there is something wrong with you because you have trouble getting there. I had trouble as well, and would be willing to bet that so did most other people who now want to look down their nose at you and sneer because it was supposedly so easy for them. Granted, a few people are gifted enough to manage to astral project on the first or second try, but they are rare. Either these haughty people are lying to you about the amount of time it took them to learn or they are lying about their abilities altogether.

Even more confusing are the writings about astral projection that often lead the reader to believe it is something that it is not. This is not a deliberate attempt to confuse anyone, but is merely trying to put into words what people who have been successful have to say about an experience that is very hard to describe without a common frame of reference. We all experience psychic phenomena in slightly different ways simply because we are all different people, and there is absolutely no one definitive experience. A few people actually lose all sense of their conscious minds when astral projecting, though a great many retain some sense of both worlds. As magician D. Jason Cooper wrote, "They simply ignore [the physical] in favor of the vision they behold."[1]

---

1. *Esoteric Rune Magic* (Llewellyn, 1994).

Some claim to see their astral vehicle linked to their physical body by a silver cord that keeps the body alive while they venture out. I have never seen this cord and believe it to be an illusion the mind uses to convince itself that it is safe during an experience that can be frightening at first.

Defining Astral Magick

Astral magick is defined as the changes you cause to happen, both in the astral *and* in the physical, as a result of your forays into the astral world. Think of it as magick without tools. You can will absolutely anything into being on the astral, work spells and rituals, and create any sort of astral tool or environment you want in which to work. In the astral your thoughts take immediate form, and once you learn to shape and control these forms, you have a potent magickal skill at your disposal. That may sound simple on paper, but just wait until you try to control every single thought. It takes a great deal of mental discipline to shape astral magick at all, especially without unwanted side effects.

On the astral you can peer into the volumes of information usually referred to as the Akashic Records, a detailed account of everything that has ever been, is, or will be; and of every individual lifetime that has ever been lived and all their spiritual and karmic repercussions. With these records you can learn more about yourself, your relationships, and your habits in one evening than in many lifetimes on the analyst's couch.

You can also enter your dreams in the astral, dreams being nothing more than an uncontrolled astral experience in the first place. I find one of the most enjoyable aspects of astral projection is when I can send myself to the place where the thought forms of my best dreams live and enter into them to shape them the way I choose. It is pure bliss to be able to live those beautiful dreams in an astral state. And because those thought forms are every bit as real on the astral as my physical body is on the earth plane, I have the added thrill of knowing it was not "just a dream," but a very real and satisfying experience.

Less understood astral experiences involve any sort of divided consciousness techniques. This means that the mind, while the body is either fully awake or asleep, is able to separate itself into two separate spheres, each focused on its own task or issue. The conscious mind is fully aware of both of these simultaneous worlds and is able to follow events unfolding in each. These divided consciousness techniques include:

- lucid dreaming, a dream state in which the dreamer realizes he/she is dreaming and chooses to take conscious control of the dream
- using a watcher, an astral "spy" deliberately sent forth to a certain place to retrieve information
- dual consciousness in the awakened state, sometimes known as "awakened dreaming," in which the person, usually engaged in some mind-numbing mundane task, is literally able to keep half a mind focused on each without losing contact with either

Dual consciousness is one of my favorite types of astral projection. It is an excellent stress reliever, can make dull times pass rapidly, can help you constructively work out problems far ahead of their crisis point, and is just plain fun.

Each of the divided consciousness techniques is specialized. With the exception of the "watcher," they require strong powers of visualization (see chapter 2) and some expertise at basic astral projection.

Banishing Fear in the Astral World

Many people, some Witches included, have an unnatural fear of astral travel and the astral worlds. These range from concerns about what type of beings they will meet to becoming lost and being unable to return home. It is vital that you learn how to calm your fears when you astral travel. The astral is made up of thought forms, which is why it is often said that "thought is action on the astral plane." Astral entities that might wish you harm feed on fear, especially on their home turf where the slightest thought of bodily harm can open the door of opportunity they are waiting for.

We cannot escape the fact that negative beings live in the astral, and we must deal with them the same way we would deal with dangerous creatures we might encounter while hiking in the woods or walking the city streets. Being prepared and informed is the key to safety. You will minimize chances of attracting negative beings by entering their world with the best of intentions and with a clear and level head. This means that we don't enter the astral with negative intent, such as to spy on someone else, or with negative emotions tugging at us. In D. J. Conway's excellent book on astral projection, *Flying Without a Broom*,[2] she recommends allowing your astral self to stop at a well or pond to drop into it all your problems, concerns, or negativity before venturing into the astral world. Another way you can ensure that you don't project an aura in the astral that is attractive to negative beings is by beginning your efforts by visualizing all those negative attachments melting off you like ice on hot pavement and sinking into Mother Earth.

Another common fear is of getting lost or becoming stuck outside of your body. You cannot get lost in the astral. This is a mental state, and the same path that carried you into it will carry you out again. It is wisest to exit the astral by the same route you entered, meaning that except in cases where an emergency retreat is necessary, you should reverse any mental imagery you used to get into the astral. For example, if you entered through a tunnel, don't exit over a rainbow. Remember that your thoughts are very fluid and responsive in the astral, and often just thinking about your body will cause your consciousness to return.

Your psychic self-defense techniques are also useful here. You may also stop at any time in your journey and mentally surround yourself with protective light, draw a few pentagrams in the air about you, or call on a guide, totem animal, or deity you trust to help protect you (see chapter 7 for more suggestions).

---

2. Llewellyn, 1995, p. 22.

It is very rare that anyone becomes so deeply attached to their astral adventures that they cannot be reached by someone in the physical world who needs you to awaken. Only a few very deep-level hypnotic subjects manage this under the best of conditions. Rest assured that if some dire event arises needing your attention, you will be able to be awakened. This may seem very jarring, and it will not be pleasant, but it will not be harmful to you either.

If you have concerns about your physical body, which many people feel has been left behind as they project, you can leave on your body some physical token of protection such as a piece of jewelry, an amulet, or one of your magickal tools. You can also mentally encase it in protective symbols like pentagrams, shields, or circles. If you are still nervous, allow yourself to look back at your prone body before you travel on, and know that it is merely sleeping and well protected.

If you are just starting to experiment with astral projection it is best to keep your travels confined to small areas. This is not for safety reasons, but to help allay fears of being lost or running into bogeymen until you can gain more confidence. However, if on your first attempt at projecting you wish to visit some distant time or place, go ahead and do it. Chances are that if you manage to project at all, you will succeed.

Techniques for Astral Projection

There are several books on the market that teach astral projecting techniques and serve as maps of the astral world. The fascinating thing about them is how little they share in common, yet they all work.[3] They each teach different concepts of and techniques for traveling on the astral plane. It is wise for the student to try several of these to find which one works best.

---

3. I have three favorite books on astral projection that I often recommend due to their very practical nature. These are J. H. Brennan's *Astral Doorways* (Aquarian Press, 1986), D. J. Conway's *Flying Without a Broom* (Llewellyn, 1995), and Melita Denning and Osborne Phillips' *The Llewellyn Practical Guide to Astral Projection* (Llewellyn, 1979).

You can begin experimenting by using one of the following methods:

- Focused meditation
- Guided meditation
- Symbolic gateways
- The chakras

Focused Meditation

In focused meditation the idea is to bore the mind with so much inactivity that it goes elsewhere in pure self-defense. This takes up to thirty minutes to do, but the results can be startling.

I had never given much credence to this method before it worked for me, quite accidentally, during a past-life regression session at a psychic development seminar in Arizona. The session took close to an hour, and after about fifteen minutes I had managed to lose the train of thought. I remember wanting to squirm, but was sure this would be disturbing to others, so I tried to retain my altered state of consciousness and just drift along until we were instructed to awaken.

At some point I noticed that my fingers were numb and that I was losing all physical sensation in them, but I continued as I was. Suddenly I realized that I could see the room I was in from the point of view of the ceiling, even though I was sitting in an uncomfortable chair with my eyes closed. I was so startled that I "snapped back" into myself.

I was terribly excited as I realized I had just experienced my first conscious astral projection, and I almost broke out of my altered state. Knowing that to make this work again I had to emotionally detach, I took a few deep breaths and focused on that drifting feeling again. In a moment or two I was back at the ceiling, looking around at the conference room. I have no recollection of floating up to get there. I was just there, and that was that. While hovering over the room I took inventory of my surroundings so that I could verify them when I awoke. Sure enough, my physical eyes were able to confirm what my astral eyes had seen.

To bore your mind into projecting, place yourself in an altered state of consciousness, either by using a method you already like or by following one outlined in chapter 2. Once you
are in an altered state, simply let your mind drift. This doesn't
mean daydream about mundane matters; that is a sure way to
spoil your efforts. It just means thinking about nothing specific. When this method worked for me I remember I was
thinking of myself drifting over a giant time wheel looking for
an interesting place to land, but since there wasn't any I just
kept drifting above the wheel until my consciousness sought
other entertainment.

Guided Meditation

Guided meditation is a user-friendly entry point into the astral
world, one that often works before you realize it has happened
to you. Guided meditation, sometimes referred to as pathworking, is defined as an escorted mental journey into the unconscious, or astral plane, for the purpose of gaining knowledge and effecting a lasting change on both the conscious and
subconscious mind. It involves the use of a prewritten path, or
guiding story, which one follows along during meditation.
These meditations can be read to you by someone else who is
not embarking on the inner-world journey or they can be pre-
recorded and played back at a later date. Several prewritten
paths appear in popular Pagan books and periodicals, and they
are easy to find.[4]

If you want to try this method and have no guided meditation readily available, use a story from myth or legend. The
archetypal language and symbolism found in these make
them easy astral pathways for both the conscious and subconscious minds to latch onto. Faery tales and other children's
stories also have a heavily archetypal framework, or patterned
themes, which make them work well as guided meditations.
Just keep in mind that the type of astral experience you have,

---

4. I included three full-length guided meditations, with induction
and coming-home triggers, written from a Celtic prospective in
Celtic Myth & Magick (Llewellyn, 1995). I also included detailed
instructions for creating your own pathworkings.

the place you land, and the beings you meet there will be colored by the tone of the meditation. If the imagery you are following is dark and ugly, so will be your meditation. While at some point dark images need to be fully explored simply because they are a part of us and of the astral, they are not recommended for beginners.

With regular practice at guided mediation, you will eventually discover that you are no longer listening to the meditation being read to you. You will be able to venture off the prewritten paths and explore the world you have entered all on your own. By doing this, you should have no doubt that you are traveling consciously on the astral plane.

Symbolic Gateways

Symbolic gateways are another method I am fond of, and chapter 10 will present to you an entire system of these using the Indian tattwa symbols as catalysts. Like guided meditation, the area of the astral world you enter and the beings you meet there will be colored by the symbolic gateway you choose. Good symbols to start with are the alchemical symbols (see chapter 3), the tarot cards, or the rune stones. You can use a different one each time you enter the astral and land in a new place every time. For instance, using the Magician tarot card will present to you a completely different world than will the Tower card.

The basic technique for making these work is to gaze at them until a halo appears around the outside of the symbol (this is more fully discussed in chapter 10). Close your eyes and allow the image on the back of your eyelids to engulf you. With practice this will provide instant access to the astral.

After my initial success with the bore-'em-to-distraction method of astral projecting, I experimented with symbolic gateways and found them very easy to learn. I still use them frequently because they provide advantages other methods do not. The strong archetypes in the symbols involuntarily activate and involve the subconscious, and they have the ability to instantly create unique and interesting astral worlds to visit.

The Chakras

Probably the most popular method of astral projecting is exiting through one of the chakra centers (discussed at length in chapter 2). Opinion is divided on which one, or ones, make the best and safest exit point. One book I read says that exiting through the lower chakras propels you into the lower astral level, where nasty entities you do not want to meet live. In another book the solar plexus chakra is recommended, and in still another the navel chakra is recommended for women because of its association with the feminine creative power center (the womb). One friend of mine always claimed her exit point was through the back of her neck, probably at the back of her throat chakra, and another told me she always used her crown chakra and feared to try to use any other. None of these people were attempting to mislead anyone else by their teachings or assertions. They were simply reporting what had and had not worked for them.

You will have to decide for yourself which chakra point makes the best exit for you. I have never had much luck with the chakra method, so I will not try to advise you. Logically, you should choose the chakra you feel is your strongest, the one through which you can most easily send out magickal energy, or that is linked to an element with which you have an affinity. Suffice it to say that unless you think you will be harmed by using a "bad" chakra, you are going to be perfectly safe.

To exit from a chakra point, mentally focus your consciousness to that point. Visualize your inner self at that doorway, waiting for it to open. Allow all physical sensations to cease as you concentrate your whole being on that exit point. When you feel the time is right, mentally move yourself out of the chakra, think about where it is you want to be, and you should appear there instantly.

If You Have Troubles Astral Projecting

Witches have long known of reliable and effective methods for assisting astral projecting, most of them herbal in nature. These include burning jasmine incense, drinking jasmine tea, making a small pillow stuffed with mugwort (an herb long used to facilitate projections), or by using flying ointments.

Flying ointments are body coverings made from herbs and essential oils known to assist in helping the astral mind separate from the conscious mind.[5] Traditionally, these were mixed in a base of lard, then applied to the entire naked body. They usually included lamp black, the ugly carbon coating that collects on the inside of oil lamp globes. The lamp black probably had no magickal potency by itself, but was likely used to help disguise medieval Witches who met under the cover of darkness.

Other flying ointments were reputed to contain hallucinogenic or toxic substances. While hallucinogens can conceivably be useful in the short term, over the long term they lead to dependence, and one becomes unable to enter altered states of consciousness without them. Anyone can have visions while taking these drugs, but using them will not lead to the development of magickal skills. The purpose of your Craft study and practice is to be able to perform these changes in consciousness at will, using your own developed magickal powers. Hallucinogens are known to produce visions in and of themselves, and if you continue to rely on them, you will never be sure if your astral experiences are true rewards of hard work or an artificially induced psycho-drama.

Like hallucinogens, toxic substances also have the ability to alter our consciousness, but they do so by constricting blood vessels, producing histamines, lowering blood pressure, and

---

5. Many essential oils are irritating to the skin and should never be applied directly to the body. Others are highly toxic, even when the plant they are derived from is generally thought to be safe for ingestion. Books dealing with the magickal or medicinal uses of oils can help you learn which ones can be safely used in ointments, baths, or teas.

raising the heart rate, sometimes to dangerous levels. In other words, they produce symptoms known to be present in someone who is dying from a condition known as anaphylaxic shock. We are all familiar with the near-death visions reported by people who have nearly died in emergency and operating rooms, and know that there is reason to be suspicious of the visions even though they tend to follow similar patterns. Don't give yourself reason to doubt, and please don't put yourself at risk.

My opinion of toxic herbs in flying ointments, which is in line with a new theory being tossed around the Craft community, is that these ingredients were not generally a part of the original ointment recipes but were reported as such by Witches on trial as a means of getting back at their prosecutors. The astral world is so alluring that the condemned Witch could be reasonably sure that the bogus ointment would be tried by accusers, and the hypocrites would then get their just reward.

If you wish to try a flying ointment before projecting, the following recipe uses ingredients thought to be safe. Naturally, you should take your own allergies and personal affinities into consideration when you make it, and you should feel free to add, subtract, or substitute where needed. It makes enough for one person to apply liberally before one attempt. If you wish to make more, or make enough for more than one person, multiply the proportions accordingly.

Non-Toxic Flying Ointment

$1^1/_2$ teaspoons mugwort, well crushed

$^1/_2$ teaspoon parsley, well crushed

$^1/_4$ teaspoon catnip, well crushed

$^1/_4$ teaspoon orris root powder

pinch of valerian root, pulverized

1 drop jasmine oil (*not* a synthetic)

Combine the dried herbs and oils in one cup of unscented body lotion.

Using a Watcher

If you are sincerely working at astral projecting but just don't seem to be able to get the hang of it no matter which method you try, you may want to experiment with the use of a watcher. Using a watcher is one of the divided consciousness techniques of astral projection mentioned earlier, and it is one that may help jumpstart your efforts.

The watcher is astral material sent out from you to a specific place or person in order to retrieve information. It is sometimes referred to as an "astral spy," but its purpose should never be to pry into the lives of others. While the watcher is out and about, you can go on about your daily business, or you can remain in a receptive, meditative state seeking impressions. If you keep going about your business while your watcher is traveling, you may occasionally feel your psychic senses being stirred, but this should be a welcome feeling, one that lets you know you are succeeding.

To send out a watcher, simply allow your mind to slip into a meditative state and, when you feel centered and ready, focus a part of your inner self (a part of your astral "you") into one area of your body. Select a chakra point for this (see chapter 2) that feels like an easy exit point for your astral self. Then expel this astral energy, mentally seeing it come from you and taking the shape of a small eye. Mentally tell this watcher where you want it to go and what you want it to learn for you, then send it on its way with an admonition to "harm none." This may help keep it from spying on things that are none of its business. Though we refer to the watcher as an "it," as if it were a thing apart from us, it is not. It is us in the purest sense, and we are responsible for what it does.

You may recall the watcher after several minutes or several hours; the choice is yours, though if you are a beginner you may find the watcher's energy starting to dissipate if you leave it out unattended for too long. You need to bring it back to you while it is still strong in order to get the greatest benefit. Think of it as being the same as sending out a human courier on urgent errands; you can only push him so far before he becomes tired and less efficient. Push even further and he will collapse altogether.

To recall your watcher, simply go again into your meditative state and visualize the eye coming back to you and being taken back into your body from the same point at which it exited. Spend some time in this relaxed state mulling over any images or impressions the watcher has retrieved. Also be alert to any dream or psychic hot flashes over the next few days that may be the result of the watcher's efforts.

Working with a partner who is also experimenting with this technique can work wonderfully. Your partner will be able to confirm or disavow any impressions you get, and so he or she will know right away when you are on target and when you miss. However, be warned that keeping a close eye on the clock while doing this will not necessarily prove an accurate gauge of your success. Remember that time has no meaning in the astral, and though it may be 5 P.M. by your bedside clock, it may be later or earlier on your astral excursion.

I had an astral projection partner I worked with who knew that sometime in the late afternoon or early evening I would be sending my watcher to her home. The impressions I got were so vivid that when I woke up I immediately called her. In an excited rush I blurted out, "You were in the kitchen brewing something that looked like tea, and Jim [her husband] was sitting in front of the TV in a blue jacket eating an apple with the cat in his lap. Am I right? I'm right, right?"

I was devastated when she told me that Jim was working late and wasn't even home yet. Moreover, she was down with a cold and currently was not having any cravings for tea. That in itself was amazing since she is originally from England and, though she has been in America for decades, has never lost her English love of daily tea. To not have even one image correct was disappointing, to say the least. I was so sure I was right on target, but took my friend at her word and vowed to try again later that night.

Several hours later my friend called to tell me that when Jim came home he was chilled, so he put on an old blue jacket. Obviously in the process of catching her cold, he grabbed the only thing he felt like eating—an apple—and then sat down in front of the TV. Their big orange cat promptly took up residence in his lap. The tea? What I was seeing was my friend hanging her head over a boiling kettle of water trying to steam open her aching sinuses! And all this occurred approximately three hours after I saw it via my watcher.

Gaining confidence with your watcher can help your conscious mind—that old naysayer who has wrecked more magickal work than the whole Spanish Inquisition—realize that you really do have an astral self and that it can be sent out by you at will.

How to Judge an Astral Experience

If you are experienced in astral projection, past-life regression, or other trance-imagery work, you are familiar with the ambiguous feelings they often generate—the ones that make you think you just made the whole thing up. In the beginning you may be making up much of it, but with practice the imagery becomes harder to discount, and the knowledge you gain from your ventures will let you know that you are not the one behind it all anymore.

If you return to your normal consciousness and find that much more or less time has passed than you expected, you can take this as a sign that you have been successful. Time has no meaning in the astral world, and the elemental realms are especially noted for their lack of respect for the linear thinking of humans (see chapter 10 for discussion and methods of entering these worlds). You may even notice that everything you experience in the astral world seems to be happening at once, with images flowing into each other at a faster rate than you can comprehend them all.

Returning to normal consciousness and feeling as if you have truly been away is another indicator. One night when I was bursting with lots of positive emotions that I wanted to explore more intently, I went into the astral using the water tattwa as a gateway (see chapter 10) and stayed there for— believe it not—five hours! When I finally came out, I felt as if

I had been somewhere enjoying a long and lively evening with friends. I was exhausted and ready to go to sleep.

Many Pagans and occultists say that another way to tell if you are successfully projecting is by the point of view from which your mental or astral self sees the action. If you are successful they expect you to see everything the same way you see it in your normal consciousness. You don't see your own face, you just see your arms reaching out, your legs stepping beneath you, etc. It is as if a movie camera has been placed on your face and you view the world through its lens, but that lens is never turned on you.

Fifty years ago I would have accepted this "point of view test" as an accurate gauge of astral projection, but today's astral travelers were raised with movies and television teaching us how to view the world around us. Even though we closely identify with the protagonists of our favorite television shows, we do not view the action from their eyes only but rather from the remoteness of the camera, which allows us to see the protagonists from a distance and watch all their facial expressions and reactions. This constant bombardment of the remote point of view has strongly impacted the way we see things in the astral world. For those of us raised with the visual media, while we are in the astral it often seems natural to step back and watch ourselves.

A good way to decide if this test would be accurate for you or not is to look at the way you dream. If you always dream "traditionally," seeing the action as if a camera were mounted on your face, then you can use the old point of view test with certainty. On the other hand, if at least half the time you dream about yourself as the "star" of your dream, being filmed from outside yourself, then this test would have little accuracy for you.

Not all forays into the astral world yield profound results. Sometimes you will mostly have fun, other times you will wish for an astral notebook to capture all the insights bombarding you. It is generally accepted that each of us learns at the speed we are intended to learn, and that flashes of brilliance will come when we are ready and not before.

Even if you think that you have just had a pleasant trip and have nothing interesting to record in your Book of Shadows, you should write this down anyway. The value of good record keeping will show itself here as well. Some astral world experiences may seem pointless at the time you undertake them but, in retrospect, may prove valuable. As you go over past records you may notice patterns that lead to insights you did not recognize at first. These, too, help validate your experience and show you that it was indeed "real."

▼

10

Elemental Magick Through the Tattwas

The tattwas are twenty-five archetypes, or symbols, discovered in India hundreds of years ago that embody the power of the elements and provide entry points into the elemental realms. The word *tattwa* is Hindustani and literally means "element." Their use as a magickal tool spread throughout central and eastern Asia, and today the symbols can be seen adorning many Tibetan temples.

Over the past century the tattwas have been written about in some depth by ceremonial magicians, who apparently use them frequently as astral gateways, but the Pagan point of view has never been fully examined. As a result, most Pagan magicians have been left out when it comes to using these powerful tools of elemental knowledge and understanding. This is sad, since our archetypes live in these worlds too, and have much to teach us if we will let them. Instead of meeting archangels or demons through the symbols, the Pagan explorer in the elemental realms is likely to encounter devas, faeries, guides, numina (nature spirits), or even deities who can take us by the hand and show us those astral world places that have the most to teach us about the element we are working with. This makes the tattwas not only powerful tools for understanding the elements, but magickal ones as well.

The beauty of the tattwas is in their very basic shapes and colors that have no cultural bias but present elemental power in a very concise, attainable format. As Francis King and Stephen Skinner phrase it, "Because of this, visions obtained by working with the Tattwas portray the Elemental Forces in very basic terms, and experience of these visions gives the magician an understanding of the elements in a much clearer and more intensive way than would be the case if he neglected to work with the Tattwas."[1]

There are five principal tattwas symbolizing the four elements and spirit. All the others are formed by using combinations of these symbols:

Element	Tattwa Symbol
Earth	Yellow Square
Water	Silver Upturned Crescent
Fire	Red Equilateral Triangle
Air	Blue Circle
Spirit	Black Upright Oval

A quick perusal of the five primary tattwas gives us an idea of their archetypal origins. The silver crescent, long a symbol of the moon and the Goddess, naturally links itself to water and to lunar and feminine power. For earth we have the stable, solid square. Fire is a blazing red triangle, pointing upward like flames. Air is a vivid blue, like the daytime sky, and circular, like the sacred spaces we shape in the air around us. In a few magickal texts spirit is presented as a convex shape, more like a marquise-cut diamond, but the oval predominates in most systems. The oval is much better suited for Pagan use anyway since the egg shape is an archetype of birth and of the soul, and features prominently in Pagan myths and celebrations.

With the possible exception of the square, all of these symbols have a notable history in Pagan metaphysics and mythology. The circle is perhaps the oldest known sacred symbol.

---

1. Francis King and Stephen Skinner. *Techniques of High Magic* (Destiny Books, 1976), 54.

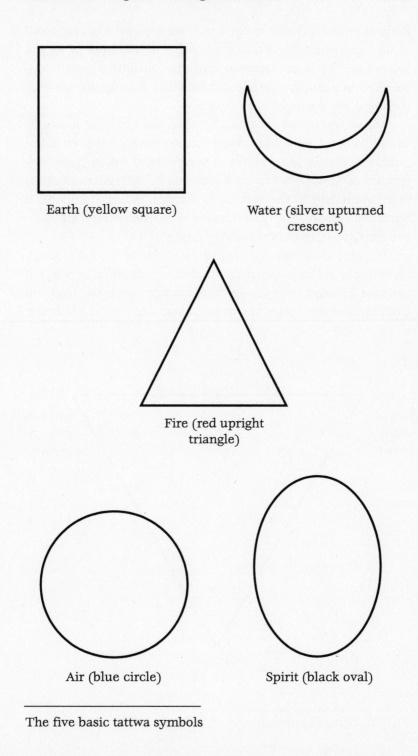

Earth (yellow square)   Water (silver upturned crescent)

Fire (red upright triangle)

Air (blue circle)   Spirit (black oval)

The five basic tattwa symbols

Early humans linked it to the cyclic nature of the seasons and of life, and in spiritual terms viewed it as a sphere of divine protection. In many ancient cultures, dwellings were constructed in a circular form due to a belief that square shelters inhibited the positive flow of energy.

As a spiritual and magickal symbol, the crescent is nearly as old as the circle. The oldest known examples of crescent renderings have been found in the ruins of the ancient civilization of Mesopotamia, dating to nearly 5000 B.C.E. Because of its similarity to the waxing or waning moon, it became a feminine symbol. Many Goddesses have been portrayed wearing crescent horns, most notably Egypt's Isis.

Triangles are often seen in old woodcuts of medieval magicians' garb. When pointing downward it is sometimes referred to as the Triangle of Manifestation and represents the God and Goddess and their joint creations. It also depicts the Mound of

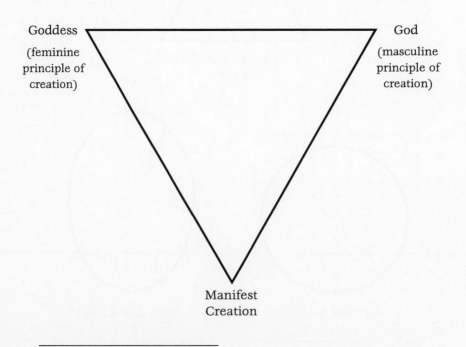

Goddess
(feminine
principle of
creation)

God
(masculine
principle of
creation)

Manifest
Creation

The Triangle of Manifestation

Venus on the pubic region of a woman's body, another place that births things into creation. Pointing upward it symbolizes the union of one's masculine and feminine sides, uniting as we each seek union with the divine. The triangle's three sides also link it to the world's many Triple Goddesses—one deity with three faces—maiden, mother, and crone.

The egg-like oval speaks for itself. Many creation myths speak about the world being born from an egg, or use eggs as a metaphor for reincarnation. Eggs feature heavily in modern Pagan rites of spring when they are given, buried, decorated, or eaten to symbolize rebirth and union with the divine.

The other twenty tattwa symbols come from combining the principal symbols with smaller versions of themselves super-imposed on the larger pictures. These twenty include:

The earth subset:
    Water of Earth
    Fire of Earth
    Air of Earth
    Spirit of Earth

The water subset:
    Earth of Water
    Fire of Water
    Air of Water
    Spirit of Water

The fire subset:
    Earth of Fire
    Water of Fire
    Air of Fire
    Spirit of Fire

The air subset:
    Earth of Air
    Water of Air
    Fire of Air
    Spirit of Air

The spirit subset:
    Earth of Spirit
    Water of Spirit
    Fire of Spirit
    Air of Spirit

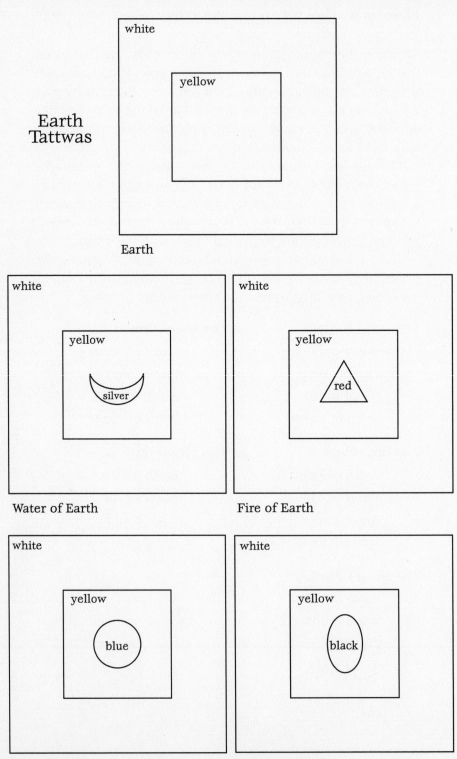

Earth Tattwas

white

yellow

Earth

white

yellow

silver

Water of Earth

white

yellow

red

Fire of Earth

white

yellow

blue

Air of Earth

white

yellow

black

Spirit of Earth

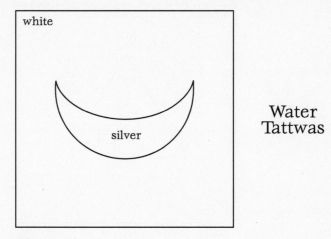

Water
Tattwas

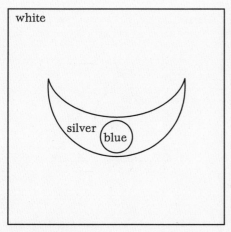

Water

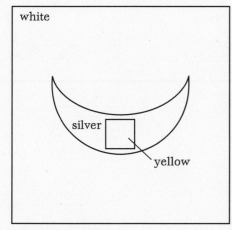

Earth of Water

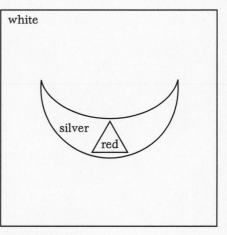

Fire of Water

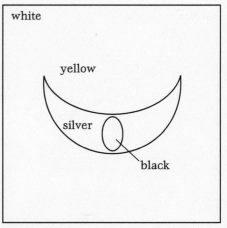

Air of Water

Spirit of Water

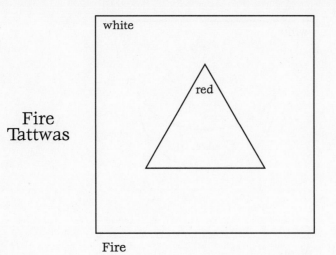

Fire
Tattwas

white

red

Fire

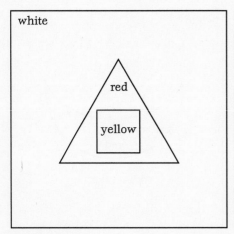

white

red

yellow

Earth of Fire

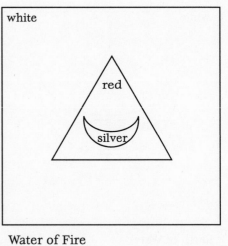

white

red

silver

Water of Fire

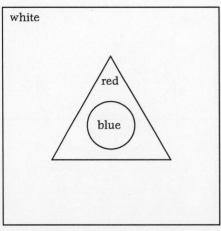

white

red

blue

Air of Fire

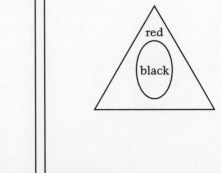

white

red

black

Spirit of Fire

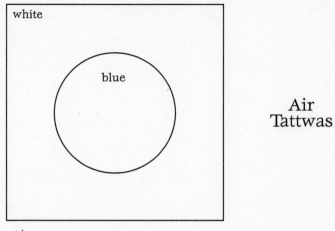

Air
Tattwas

Air

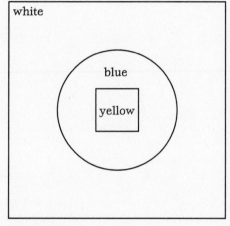

Earth of Air

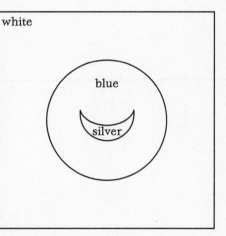

Water of Air

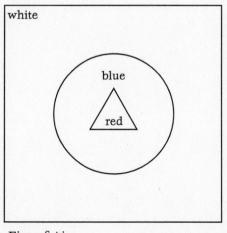

Fire of Air

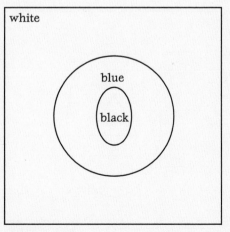

Spirit of Air

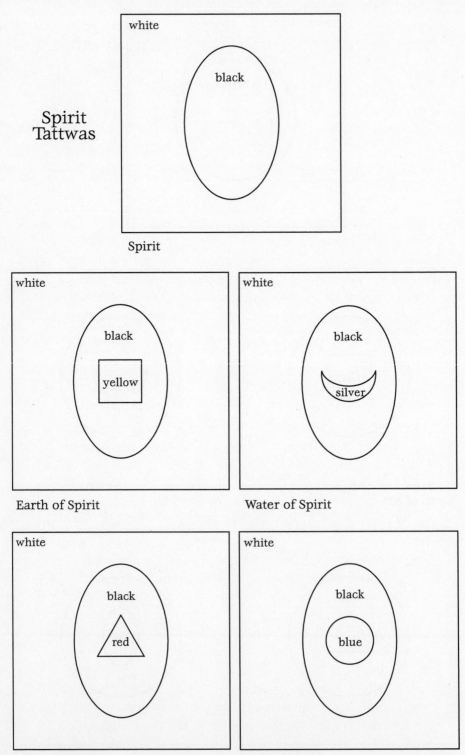

Spirit
Tattwas

white

black

Spirit

white

black

yellow

Earth of Spirit

white

black

silver

Water of Spirit

white

black

red

Fire of Spirit

white

black

blue

Air of Spirit

Making Your Own Set of Tattwa Symbols

It is easiest to work with the tattwas if you take the time to make your own set out of paints and posterboard so they are the exact right color and size to work with. I made my first set of tattwas with a friend in 1988 and I still have them. Though they are admittedly getting a bit yellowed and ragged, they nonetheless still provide me commendable gateways to the elemental worlds.

To make your own set, you will first need twenty-five sheets of standard-sized, white posterboard. Cut each of these down so that they form perfect squares (these will end up measuring 22" x 22" if you are using standard-sized posterboard). These squares will be used for your backgrounds, the pieces on which you will mount the actual tattwa symbols.

Using a compass, ruler, or other device that will enable you to make geometrically accurate figures, cut templates for your five primary tattwas. These need to be big enough so that you can easily gaze into them from about six feet away. Plan to make them larger if you will have to hang them much farther away than that when you begin to meditate on them. Mine are hung about eight feet from my meditation space. My earth square is 9" x 9", my fire triangle has a 9" base, my air circle and water crescent are 9" across, and my spirit oval is 10" x 7".

When you have the templates cut out, and are satisfied that they are as accurately drawn as possible, place them on another piece of white posterboard and trace around them to get all your basic tattwa symbols. You will need five of each for your complete set of twenty-five.

Next, you will need to make templates of smaller versions of the symbols, the ones that will be placed inside the larger ones to make up the elemental subsets mentioned earlier. Judge their size based on how big you have made the larger symbols. You want each smaller one to fit neatly in the center of the larger ones without being overpowering, so they remain fully inside their confines and are able to be clearly seen from whatever distance you will have them hanging when you start to meditate on them. My small squares measure $3^1/2$" x $3^1/2$", my circles are $3^1/2$" across, my crescents are

5" across, my triangles have a 4" base, and my small ovals are $2^1/_2$" x $3^1/_2$". You will need four each of these smaller symbols.

Carefully cut out all your smaller tattwas from your poster-board, trimming them as needed until you are sure that they are as accurate as possible.

The next step is to paint them. You want the colors to be as solid and vivid as possible, so watercolors are unsuitable. I tried using tempera paints when I first made my tattwas and found that they left too many brush strokes that later could interfere with the symbol's ability to function as an astral gateway. Oil paints would probably present a similar problem. I ended up using automotive spray paints. The colors are vivid, solid, and leave just enough of a reflective sheen to aid in their purpose. Reflective surfaces have long been used to induce an altered state of consciousness suitable for meditation or astral projection. Spray paints were also the only way I could get a true silver for the crescent. Tempera paints offered only a light gray substitute.

I confess that I had to compromise with the yellow paint. I simply could find no spray paints in a true yellow, and used a

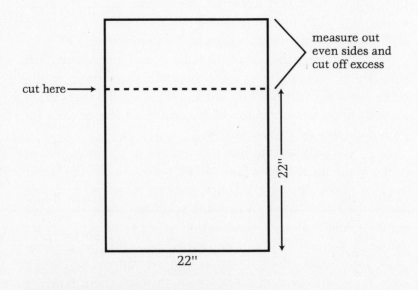

Cutting posterboard into a square

tempera paint instead. In my efforts to avoid leaving brush strokes, I applied at least five coats and, as a result, today my earth Tattwas have a crinkled look that the others don't have.

I used my garage floor, covered with several layers of newspaper, to spray my tattwas. To make it easier, group them together by shape so that you can use your spray paints all in one area and don't have to crawl around on hands and knees seeking the shape you want. Keep them well away from one another too. Spray paint particles can fly some distance away, and you don't want stray flecks from your black spirit tattwa landing on your yellow earth tattwas. You will also need to keep the area well ventilated while you are using the paint, and might even want to buy some of the small, inexpensive face masks sold in paint, hardware, or automotive stores.

Allow the tattwas to dry overnight, then spray them with another light coating. Examine them again the following day to make sure the color is even and that each symbol is completely covered with paint. Any areas that did not get a coating of paint need to be resprayed. It is imperative that you have a solid wall of color on each one if they are to function their best for you. If you need to touch up any of your tattwas, do so now; then allow them another night to fully dry.

The next step is to mount the five primary tattwas onto the white squares of posterboard. With a ruler or tape measure, attempt to center the symbols as accurately as possible on the posterboard. I used rubber cement to attach my large tattwas—a mistake I will not repeat! No matter how thinly and evenly I spread the glue, or how much pressure I kept on the tattwas as they dried, I can see the effects today of the glue's natural shrinkage, which has caused most of my symbols to become slightly wavy. This effect can interfere with their functioning, especially when you are learning to use them. When I remake my tattwas I will save the glue for the smaller symbols, and adhere the larger ones with the sticky foam squares easily and cheaply found in hardware stores. This will keep the symbols from rippling with time and, when the white backgrounds yellow—as they eventually will—it will make it easy to transfer the tattwa symbols I worked hard to make onto new backgrounds without having to recut and re-paint an entirely new set.

If you do decide to use glue to mount your primary symbols on the posterboard, place a heavy book or some other weighty, flat object on top of it for at least twenty-four hours to help press the glue down evenly. This will minimize the waving effect for a while, though it will not prevent it from occurring in the long run.

At this point you should have twenty-five white backgrounds, each containing one large, primary tattwa symbol for a total of five of each.

Remove one of each of the tattwa cards and set them aside. These are your five primary tattwa symbols, the ones that stand alone without any sub-element. They are now complete, and will be the ones you will want to explore first.

Using your ruler or tape measure, take your sixteen smaller symbols and center them on the larger ones, as shown in the illustrations. To attach them, use only a very small amount of glue evenly spread over the back of the smaller ones. To keep them from curling as the glue dries, place them under a heavy, flat object, like a thick book, for at least forty-eight hours.

Getting to Know Your Tattwas

Spend about a week looking at the symbols daily, especially right before you go to sleep (5–10 minutes should be sufficient).You do not have to stare or to think about anything in particular as you gaze at them. They will imprint their message on your subconscious in the same way a subliminal tape works. Your deep mind knows what they are, and will need this period of acquaintance to help you fully benefit from their use.

You do not have to infuse the symbols with your energy as you would need to do with most magickal tools. The difference between most other magickal tools and the tattwa cards is that these symbols are not acting as an extension of yourself or your will, therefore you do not need to "empower" them.

When you feel you are ready, you may begin to explore the elemental realms firsthand.

Entering the Elemental Realms

Very simply put, using the tattwas to enter the realm of the elements opens for us the astral world and all its wonders. As we scry into their depths and meditate on them, the symbols literally open themselves to us and we can astral travel directly into their world.

The elemental realms hold a dual place in Pagan cosmology. In keeping with the old occult adage of "as above, so below," we acknowledge that the elements live in both the physical world, as represented by nature, and in the astral world, as represented by the mind. By using the tattwas as a gateway to this world we not only discover the elements but the entire astral plane as well. In this projected state, the elements themselves become your teachers. While in their realms you can meet with faeries, guides, numina, or deities; you can listen as plants, lakes, rocks, and other natural formations tell you their tales; you can fly without wings, submerge without scuba gear, and cast natural spells of great efficacy.

Spells worked in the elemental worlds are very efficacious and quick to manifest. They also yield the most rapid retribution for misuse. Working earth-related spells in the earth world, water-related spells in the water world, et cetera, is always best. You may successfully work any subset elemental spell while in the primary tattwa since it is this element that is still the ruling one. For example, any spell you find in the Water of Earth or Fire of Earth chapters can be worked in Earth just as easily. In some cases your own inner senses or elemental world experiences may move you to assign a particular event or scene to a different tattwa. This is as it should be. Who is to say a lava flow is best learned from in Water of Fire and not Fire of Water?

Stepping Through the Tattwas

The basic process of entering the symbols is through scrying, the art of gazing *into* rather than at an object with the purpose of inducing visions. Whether or not you can consciously astral project yet does not matter at this point. With practice in scrying and visualization it will happen, and eventually the time will come when you have no doubt that your astral mind has separated from your physical one. For now simply mount your selected tattwa card at eye level in front of your place of meditation. You may sit or lie down, whichever is most comfortable for you. Take a few deep breaths and begin to relax your body and slow your mind into the receptive levels.

If you are one of those people who has trouble getting into the proper state of mind, or who is easily distracted by outside sounds and smells, you might want to play some soft New Age-type music, the kind that seems to have no cadence, or burn some incense in the room. I am fond of using sandalwood incense and playing any of the "inner harmony" albums produced by Valley of the Sun (see Appendix B for address). Teas, oils, or incense that help open the psychic channels or

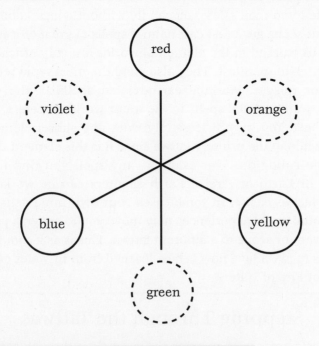

The color wheel. Solid circles = primary colors, broken circles = secondary colors

that are attuned to the specific element you want to explore are also useful (see chapter 2). You might also wish to employ methods that have been traditionally used to assist with astral travel (see chapter 9).

As you continue to scry the tattwa, close your eyes just far enough to give the symbol a hazy glow. Focus on looking into the tattwa rather than at it. Avoid staring. All this will do for you is give you eyestrain. Don't be afraid to blink when you need to.

After several minutes you may start to notice a colored halo around the edge of the tattwa. This is the reverse image of the card color reflecting off your retina, and it is the signal that you have gazed at the symbol long enough. The color you see will be the same color you would see on a color negative if you had taken a photograph of the tattwa. This reverse image roughly follows an artist's color wheel; each color has its opposite. In terms of your tattwas, these opposites are:

Tattwa Color	Reverse Image Color
Yellow	Violet
Silver	Black-Violet
Red	Green
Blue	Orange
Black	White

Don't be surprised when your eyes do not perceive true colors in reverse. Your violet may look a bit on the mauve side, and your orange a bit reddish. Think of, or look at, negatives from a color photograph to get an idea of how these colors might appear.

At this point there are seven different methods you can use to enter the tattwas, and you should choose which one seems easiest for you. You may even want to experiment with them all to see if they provide different images or experiences.

Image on a Blank Wall with Eyes Open

With this method you will not close your eyes, and because of this I find it the most difficult of all to use, but it seems to be the one most favored by the ceremonial magicians who have written about using the tattwas.

After you begin to see the halo of the reverse image, direct your gaze to a blank, white wall, or onto another "tattwa card" that is completely blank. Allow the reverse image to form in the center of the card. Hold it as steady as possible and direct your gaze into it, allowing it to pull your consciousness through it.

For the rest of the methods, close your eyes when you see the halo formed clearly around the tattwa. You will see the reverse image on the inside of your eyelids. Allow yourself to fully relax and work with this by using any of the following methods.

The Enlarged Image

Allow the reverse image to appear on the inside of your eyelids. You will find it wants to move about, and the only remedy for this is to hold your eyes perfectly still and force the image to remain fixed. Because it will begin to dissolve after you close your eyes, you will have to work rather swiftly with it.

Take advantage of the image's tendency to move about to enlarge it. See it growing to large proportions, big enough for you to imagine yourself stepping into.

Being Engulfed by the Image

Allow the image to come toward you rapidly until it covers the entire field of vision. This is best accomplished by moving your closed eyes apart as if you were trying to look past the reverse image on your lids. As it moves in, notice the clarity of the image blurring as if dissolving, becoming more fluid. As it engulfs you, you will find that you are inside it.

The Open Door

Hold the reverse image as still as possible. Think of it as a portal between worlds. Will that it become accessible to you. As you do this, visualize a door in the tattwa opening so that you can mentally enter. After you do this, shut the door behind you to keep the two worlds separated. Bleed-through between astral and physical world aspects is undesirable and can lead to ugly experiences for you in the astral and feelings of being haunted in the physical.

Parting the Veil

As in the open door method, hold the image as still as you can, all the while keeping in mind that this is a portal between worlds. Visualize part of the symbol becoming thinner and turning into a large curtain. Mentally step up to it, part this veil, and enter the tattwa. Be sure to close it behind you and visualize it returning to its former density after you step inside.

The Flying Self

The visualization in this method is much more like that of traditional astral projection. As you watch the reverse image dancing in front of your closed eyes, see yourself lifting from your physical body and flying into the image. At that point allow it to vanish until your mind calls on it again to be a portal back home.

Entering with the Aid of a Guide

As in the flying self method, visualize yourself flying from your physical shell and floating up to the "door" on the symbol. At this point ask a friendly guide, faery, totem animal, or one of your personal deities to come and escort you inside. The being may appear beside you, or it may step out of the symbol itself and invite you to follow it in.

If a being appears who is unfamiliar to you, or of whom you feel suspicious or uncertain, you do not have to go with him or her. You may ask for another guide, or you may return to your body and your normal consciousness and try again at a later date. It is also a good idea not to take the hand of any being who sticks it through the tattwa door and offers itself sight unseen. Benevolent spirits who have your best interest at heart will allow themselves to be seen by you before expecting you to travel with them. Remember that the astral is a real place, and its elemental worlds are real too. Never discount the entities you meet there, and never go against your better judgment and tag along with just anyone who stops for you. You wouldn't accept a lift in the physical world from just anyone, so don't do it in the astral either.

Returning Home Through the Tattwas

It is both customary and wise to exit the astral by the same route you entered it, unless there is an emergency that requires a hasty retreat. This is to avoid mental confusion and bleed-through between the two worlds and to keep your conscious mind, which requires order and logic to function properly, happy.

Regardless of which of the seven methods of entry you took into the elemental world, you should leave it by returning through the same tattwa in roughly the same manner. You can do this one of three ways:

1. Mentally retrace your entire route back to the place where you entered the tattwa. This is time consuming, but is often the best method for beginners.

2. Mentally will yourself to be back at the entry point, and you should be transported there immediately. If you have any doubts about your skill to do this, ask your guide or totem animal to help you.

3. Mentally ask the tattwa to manifest before you so that you can reverse your entry process. Form a picture of it (reverse imaged) in your mind, and it should appear shortly after you make the request. This method is usually best worked by those with lots of astral world experience.

When you are at the tattwa, reverse the process by which you entered. In other words, if you came in through a curtain in the tattwa, visualize it reappearing before you slip through it. Once you are on the other side, visualize the tattwa dissipating until you are floating alone in nothingness. Think of your body, remembering the feeling of being corporeal, and you should slip gently back into it.

Open your eyes and look again at the tattwa hanging before you, visualizing all the gateways you may have opened to it being resealed until you are ready to enter it again.

What to Expect in the Elemental World

Kabballist and ceremonial magician Israel Regardie was a firm believer in the tattwas as universal gateways, crossing the lines of all magickal systems and traditions, but wisely knew that what each of us experiences in those worlds can vary widely.[2] Part of this is due to just where in the elemental world we land, how much negative baggage we dragged in there with us, and what we need to experience at the time we enter.

Preconceived ideas about what you will encounter can help get you started on your journeys, which is why loosely constructed guided imagery, or meditations, appear in each of the meditations given in this chapter. These can help give you a feel for the quality of the element, particularly when working in the subsets, where the elements are subtly blended. For the most beneficial experience you will eventually need to move out on your own and explore areas of the element that do not

---

2. *The Golden Dawn*, fifth edition (Llewellyn, 1986), 462.

appear in any preprinted text (see chapter 3 for elemental correspondences that can help guide you). Further in this chapter will be suggestions to lead you safely through this process.

When my friend Sheva and I began our journey into the tattwas, we had no idea which one we should start with or what we should expect. We forgot the very basic nature of the tattwas and found ourselves pinned to the astral gateways by elemental forces too powerful for us to fight against. Sheva entered air first, rationalizing that its low density would make it an easy one to step into. As soon as she stepped through the circle she found herself buffeted by fierce winds coming from all directions. Some blew hot, others cold, leaving her blinded in a world that she likened to the white-out of a blizzard. I entered earth first, rationalizing that it was the closest one to the earth plane on which I lived, but when I stepped through the yellow square I found myself in total darkness. I waited patiently for my astral eyes to adjust, but they never did. Hesitantly, I began groping around in the darkness and felt the cool, slightly damp stone walls of a subterranean passageway, probably a cave. After stumbling around for a while with absolutely no illumination to assist me, and not realizing that I could probably have willed myself a torch or something, I came back out through what I hoped was my gateway to record my disappointing experience in my Book of Shadows.

After comparing notes, Sheva and I realized that we needed some guideposts to get us started. We worked out some very elementary guided imagery for each tattwa so we could land in the elemental world somewhere that would be navigable—pitch-black caverns and vicious whirlwinds not included! Once we had these markers in place, we found we could step fully into the elemental worlds without being pinned at the gateway by the worst aspects of each element. We could then call on guides and deities to help us venture further, and found we had much freer range in our explorations than if we went in cold.

Be prepared for anything in the elemental world, and feel confident knowing that you have the power to overcome, move on, or leave whenever you choose. This is important since, even with guided imagery and guides to assist you, you must keep in mind that all worlds have their positive and negative qualities, and you may find you do not like some places or manifestations in the elements. The gentle, people-helping gnomes live in the earth realm, but so do the jealous and baneful earth faeries known as the duendes. The beauty of nature and its caretaker spirits also live in these realms, but so do the spirits of earthquakes, gales, cyclones, conflagrations, and floods, and you can land in the middle of one of these as easily as you can in a calm spring meadow.

What the elements have to teach you will be unique to your experience, and no one else can write a complete script suited to your special needs. This is why you will need to take the information found in this book, and from any other sources of elemental knowledge you have at hand, and piece together your own journeys. Each time you enter a given tattwa, you will need to reevaluate your previous experience and decide how best to construct your new one. A typical prewritten/prerecorded meditation, which will keep you on track while still allowing for learning and growing, will have a very open format looking something like this:

- Introduction and entry, meeting a guide, and getting key words for returning home
- Pause to look around (five minutes)
- Journey into one part of the elemental world
- Pause to look, learn, or to receive messages from beings or objects (five–ten minutes)
- Movement to another place in the elemental world
- Pause to learn (five minutes)
- Pause for divinations or spellwork (ten minutes)
- Recalling tattwas and returning home

Before Entering Any Tattwa

Prepare mentally and physically for your elemental journey in any way you deem appropriate. Hang your tattwa where you can see it easily as you lie or sit in your chosen place of meditation. Take a few deep breaths and begin to relax your body and slow your mind. Following any of the methods outlined in this chapter, project into the tattwa. Be sure to visualize yourself picking up an elemental tool if you feel you would like to have it along.

You can ask your guide, totem animal, or deity to lead you somewhere in the elemental world that would most benefit you to explore at this time. To do this, mentally call out to your guide to come to you and he/she/it should appear shortly. If you do not have a guide or totem animal who is already familiar to you and with whom you have an established working relationship, you may call on any of the friendly guides, faeries, or animal spirits who inhabit the earth realm to assist you.[3] Do not demand their attention, but mentally call out and ask for the most beneficial being who is interested to come and guide you.

The steps for returning to normal consciousness are just as important. Before you leave the elemental world, plan to offer your thanks to any being who has assisted you. The exception to this rule might be with any faeries who have helped you along, as the convoluted rules of faery etiquette usually do not permit thank yous. Instead offer them blessings and good wishes.

Prepare to return home following any of the methods outlined earlier in this chapter. When the tattwa has appeared to you in reverse image, step through it, close it behind you, and

---

3. Spirit guides and totem animals are a study unto themselves, and there are several excellent books on the market available that teach how to contact and work with these beings. For learning to work with guides I recommend Ted Andrews' *How to Meet and Work with Spirit Guides* (Llewellyn, 1996), and for learning about totem animals I heartily endorse Jose and Lena Steven's *The Secrets of Shamanism* (Avon, 1988).

slip back into your body and awaken. Finish your elemental journey by gazing once more at the physical tattwa hanging in front of you. This firmly locks in your mind the fact that you are "back home" and helps seal the portal between worlds, which your travels have opened.

You can use the guided meditations as key points for creating your own journey, or you can prerecord the written ones presented here, or have them read to you by a trusted friend. You will find you have to do little work to shape them the way you want them. They are written to be customized by you and, as such, are very open-ended. They primarily provide entry and exit points, as well as a few key images that can help you into their deeper aspects. Also included in each meditation are suggestions for unusual elemental places you may wish to visit, and spells and divinations you can perform while there. You may use any or all of the suggestions in each one to make your meditation as long or as short as you like. Allow yourself as much time in them as you feel your skill level will permit, then have the reader or tape recorder take you step by step through the returning material. You may always return later to explore other aspects of the element.

Dealing with Fear in the Elemental Worlds

A trick of self-protection that works wonderfully when exploring the elemental world is to take in with you the magickal tool corresponding to that element. To do this, simply visualize yourself picking it up just before you enter the tattwa. You may also want to leave it on your physical self as well. Ceremonial magicians refer to their tools as elemental weapons; indeed, that is what they become when taken into the elemental kingdom they are linked with. As in the physical, they represent the power of the elements and your ability to manipulate them. For example, if while in the air realm a malevolent air spirit makes unwanted moves on you, wave your air wand at it and command it to be gone.

If you ever feel uncomfortable or are not confident of your ability to banish unwanted beings, simply visualize the tattwa you entered reappearing and then think of your physical self and allow yourself to be sucked safely back through the tattwa and into your waiting body.

Look back to the chapter on "Astral Magick" for a more extensive discussion of techniques that can be employed in any astral situation to ward off unwanted spirits, or just to make you more comfortable.

As mentioned in chapter 9, you cannot get lost in the elemental world. If you are using the guided meditations in this book, stick to the paths they provide until you feel sure enough of yourself to venture out on your own. These will provide you with the added confidence of trigger words and imagery for safely returning home.

Inside the Earth Tattwa

As your astral eyes adjust to your new environment, take time to memorize some of the features of the place you are in so that it will be easy to find again. Tell yourself that throughout this adventure, you will be the one in control. If at any time you need or wish to leave the earth world, all you have to do is command it to be so with the words TATTWA APPEAR. Instantly the tattwa will reappear to you wherever you are, and you may quickly slip out. If you find you need further help, think the words I AM HOME and you will find yourself back in your body, fully awake.

Take one last look at the earth tattwa, in its reversed violet color, standing before you. Allow it to fade, safely sealing off the portal you have opened between the worlds. If you have entered with the aid of a guide, ask him/her/it to accompany you on this meditative journey at this time.

Looking around once more, you notice that you are
in a dense, verdant forest. Everywhere you look the
world is brown and green and the scent of rich, virgin
earth invades your nostrils. You inhale deeply of it,
the perfume of Mother Earth.

Pause here to allow time to learn from your environment. Be
open to any animals, beings, or natural objects that appear to
you or that choose to speak. In this earth world, even the stones
will be able to converse with you or to move about at will.

If you are having the meditation read to you, or if you are
prerecording it, allow at least five minutes for this. When you
have finished, you may move on.

As you peer into the depths of the forest, you spot a
rocky wall just ahead, behind some trees. You walk
over to it and realize there is a fissure in the rock face
that is likely the entrance to a cave. It is dark inside
and, to your dismay, you see nothing with which to illuminate your way.

Just as you are about to give up, you hear a scrap-
ing sound from the trees behind you. You turn around
and see an animal coming toward you, pushing a
glowing crystal.

The animal who appears to you will likely be one associated with earth energies, such as a snake, a groundhog, or a
badger. Be open to it and its offering. If you have a fear of the
animal who appears, you have two choices: one, you can ask
it to appear in another form that is easier for you to relate to,
or two, you can stand your ground and see what you can learn
from the experience of facing your fear. In either case, pause
for a moment or two to listen to the animal in case it has
something to tell you.

Thanking the animal, you take the crystal and step
into the dark fissure.

Inside the cave are pathways leading off in several directions. You pick one and step into it. The crystal glows brightly, offering comfort and lighting your way. As you pass through this tunnel you see more rocky formations in small chambers off the passageway. Several of them seem to be trying to tell you something, and you stop at a few and wait to hear what they are saying.

Spend as much time in the cave as you like. When you want out, ask the crystal to take you back to the entrance. You should shortly find yourself there. Leave the crystal at the opening of the cave to be reclaimed by the animal who lent it to you.

You may now go on to explore other parts of the earth world. You may stop and work earth-related magick, cast a circle and hold a ritual, or gaze into a crystal and search for prophetic visions.

There are hundreds of places in the earth kingdom of the astral world for you to explore. You may rewrite the guided meditation so that you land in one of these to begin with, or extend it so that you explore these other places in addition. Some of the more pleasant earth-related places or events you can experience are:

- Fields of lush, growing grains, such as a summer cornfield, planted in rich, black earth
- The hollow hills of the Anglo-Celtic faery folk, particularly those of the gnomes
- The inside of tree trunks—easiest to enter are those that share earth energies, such as hedgerows of all types, ash, dwarf elm, or hawthorn
- Cavern passageways of all types, sizes, and styles
- The inside of stones, where you can meet with their resident numen

- Kivas, the underground ceremonial chambers popular in Native American traditions
- Encounters with friendly earth animals and nature spirits, such as spiders, groundhogs, gnomes, and brownies
- Encounters with other Pagans celebrating earth-centered festivals, particularly those surrounding planting or harvesting
- Encounters with earth archetypes from the tarot cards, such as the Empress
- A rock garden
- A deep canyon

Other events or scenes in the earth world where you might find yourself, or where you may choose to explore, can be less than pleasant to the novice. While many may seem violent or inhospitable, an experienced elemental world traveler can protect him or herself and make use of what these have to teach. In some cases, whether these places, encounters, or events are deemed pleasant or not is purely subjective. For example, someone who enjoys exploring burial chambers would not find it an uncomfortable place at all. Possible less-than-pleasant earth places and events include:

- Earthquakes, both below and above the surface
- Unilluminated caverns
- Subterranean burial chambers
- Encounters with unfriendly earth-ruled animals and beings, including poisonous serpents and trolls

Inside the Water Tattwa

As your astral eyes adjust to your new environment, take time to memorize some of the features of the place you are in so that it will be easy to find again. Tell yourself that throughout this adventure you will be the one in control. If at any time you need or wish to leave the water world, all you have to do is command it to be so with the words TATTWA APPEAR. Instantly the tattwa will reappear to you, wherever you are, and you may quickly slip out. If you find you need further help, think the words I AM HOME, and you will find yourself back in your body, fully awake.

Take one last look at the crescent water tattwa, in its reversed black-violet color, standing before you. Allow it to fade, safely sealing off the portal you have opened between the worlds. If you have entered with the aid of a guide, ask him/her/it to accompany you on this meditative journey at this time.

Looking around once more, you notice that you are ankle-deep on a sandbar in a large pool of silvery blue water. Looking around you note that the water is so wide that you cannot see the shore in any direction. In spite of your unusual predicament, you do not feel alone or abandoned here.

Pause to allow time to learn from your environment. Be open to any sea creatures, beings, or natural objects that appear to you or that choose to speak. A being may come along and invite you to come and explore under the water. Decide if this guide is trustworthy, then follow up. Have the guide return you to your starting point when you are finished. If you are having the meditation read to you, or if you are prerecording it, allow at least ten minutes for this. If you merely wish to look around and gauge your surroundings, three or four minutes should be sufficient.

As you stand looking around, you feel at one with the water and sense yourself melting away, droplet by droplet, until you no longer exist as yourself. You are in and of the water now, just another organism living within it, flowing with it where the current takes you. Experience life as water and learn from it. How does it feel, and how do those feelings change as you drift along? Feel the fluid nature of water as you flow from one place to another.

Allow five to seven minutes to explore this aspect of water.

Now you notice that the current is slowing, bringing you to rest in the stagnant waters of a shallow lagoon where your body begins to reform from the water droplets that have been carried there.

When you are whole again, you may go on to explore other parts of the water world. You may work water-related magick or cast a circle and hold a ritual. If you desire to do so, at any point in your water-world journey you can stop and gaze into the water in search of prophetic visions. You may do this with a clear mind, allowing the visions to manifest as they will or by first forming a question in your mind to which you need answers. Remember that the rules of nature in the astral are not the same as on the physical. If you are having trouble understanding the answers you receive, ask water to clarify things for you. You may be surprised at how this can be done.

Some of the more pleasant water-related places, scenes, beings, or events you can experience are:

- Oceans, rivers, lakes, and streams
- Gentle spring rains
- Encounters with friendly water spirits, such as some types of merpeople
- Encounters with water totem animals
- Encounters with Pagans holding river/sea festivals
- Meeting with water deities
- Encounters with water archetypes/characters from the tarot, such those in the Moon card

Events, scenes, or encounters in the water world you could possibly find to be less than pleasant include:

- Hurricanes, particularly the storm surge areas along coastlines
- Floods
- Rip tides
- Encounters with baneful water faeries and spirits

Inside the Fire Tattwa

As your astral eyes adjust to your new environment, take time to memorize some of the features of the place you are in so that it will be easy to find again. Tell yourself that throughout this adventure you will be the one in control. If at any time you need or wish to leave the fire world, all you have to do is command it to be so with the words TATTWA APPEAR. Instantly the tattwa will reappear to you, wherever you are, and you may quickly slip out. If you find you need further help, think the words I AM HOME and you will find yourself back in your body, fully awake.

Take one last look at the fire tattwa, in its reversed green color, standing before you. Allow it to fade, safely sealing off the portal you have opened between the worlds. If you have entered with the aid of a guide, ask him/her/it to accompany you on this meditative journey at this time.

Pause to allow time to learn from your environment. Be open to any animals, beings, or natural objects appearing to you or who choose to speak. If you are having the meditation read to you, or if you are prerecording it, allow at least five minutes for this. If you merely wish to look around and gauge your surroundings, three or four minutes should be sufficient.

Looking around once more you notice that you are in a world of heat and flames. You could be in a field or floating on air; it is impossible for you to tell the difference. From horizon to horizon, flames shoot from below you like sun flares, and the "sky" above you is orange with swirling flames. Dancing inside the flames about you, you notice tiny lizard-like creatures, the salamanders who are the rulers of the fire element. As you gaze at one particularly attractive section of fire, one of the salamanders comes forth from it to speak to you. It is a beautiful creature but so bright you almost have to shade your eyes, and you find it hard to see the separation of the salamander from the flames.

Allow approximately five to seven minutes for this communication, more if you think you would like to travel through the fire world with the salamander as your guide. If you do, have him bring you back to this point before embarking on other fire world journeys.

You may now go on to explore other parts of the fire world. You may work fire-related magick or cast a circle and hold a ritual. If you desire to do so, at any point in your journey you can stop and gaze into fire in search of prophetic visions. You may do this with a clear mind, allowing the visions to manifest as they will, or by first forming a question in your mind to which you need answers. Remember that the rules of nature in the astral are not the same as on the physical. If you are having trouble understanding the answers you receive, ask fire to clarify things for you.

Some of the more pleasant fire-related scenes, events, or experiences awaiting you are:

- Campfires surrounded by interesting astral world companions
- Sacred balefires with astral beings holding rituals at them
- Walks under a desert sun
- Encounters with figures in the Strength and Sun tarot cards
- Encounters with fire totem animals, such as lizards and other desert creatures

- Encounters with fire spirits and faeries
- Encounters with deities of fire, such as
  Brighid or Prometheus

Events, scenes, or encounters in the fire world that you could possibly find to be less than pleasant include:

- Grass or forest fires
- Other areas of spontaneous combustion
- Lifeless areas that are scorched so badly by fire or sun that they cannot support life at this time

Inside the Air Tattwa

As your astral eyes adjust to your new environment, take time to memorize some of the features of the place you are in so that it will be easy to find again. Tell yourself that throughout this adventure you will be the one in control. If at any time you need or wish to leave the air world, all you have to do is command it to be so with the words TATTWA APPEAR. Instantly the tattwa will reappear to you, wherever you are, and you may quickly slip out. If you find you need further help, think the words I AM HOME and you will find yourself back in your body, fully awake.

Take one last look at the air tattwa, in its reversed orange color, standing before you. Allow it to fade, safely sealing off the portal you have opened between the worlds. If you have entered with the aid of a guide, ask him/her/it to accompany you on this meditative journey at this time.

Looking around once more you notice that you are in an undefinable world in which wind is the predominant force. Its pressure on you is gentle but insistent, making you aware of who the boss is here. You almost feel as if the air is testing you, deciding if you are worthy to be here or if you should be blown back into your own world.

As you peer carefully into the air around you, you see the sylphs, the spirits of air, being carried on its currents. They seem to add a dash of color to this windswept world.

Pause here to allow time to learn from the sylphs. Be open to any other animals, beings, or natural objects appearing to you or who choose to speak. If you are having the meditation read to you, or if you are prerecording it, allow at least five minutes for this. When you have finished, you may move on.

One of the sylphs seems to notice your presence and hovers in the air in front of you, offering itself as a guide into the air world. It reaches out a wispy hand to you and, as you touch it, you are borne upon the air and into its world. Soon you realize that you do not need the sylph's touch to fly. You feel as if you have wings and, like a soaring eagle, you take off on your own, riding the wind currents as if you have been doing it all your life.

Spend as much time riding the air currents as you like. You may meet other flyers in this world, and you may attempt to interact with any you like. When you want to quit, mentally will yourself back to the starting point, or call the tattwa to reappear wherever you are.

You may also explore other parts of the air world, stopping to work air-related magick, to cast a circle and hold a ritual, or to gaze into the wind currents and search for prophetic visions.

There are hundreds of places in the air kingdom of the astral world for you to explore. You may rewrite the guided meditation so that you land in any one of these to begin with, or extend it so that you explore these other places in addition. Here you may also find:

- Encounters with wind deities and spirits
- Encounters with air totem animals, like birds
- The ability to mentally communicate over large distances

- Creatures who are fickle or two-faced
  (figuratively and literally)

There are negative places to beware of in the air world, and these include areas of cyclones and gales.

Inside the Spirit Tattwa

As your astral eyes adjust to your new environment, take time to memorize some of the features of the place you are in so that it will be easy to find again. Tell yourself that throughout this adventure you will be the one in control. If at any time you need or wish to leave the spirit world, all you have to do is command it to be so with the words TATTWA APPEAR. Instantly the tattwa will reappear to you, wherever you are, and you may quickly slip out. If you find you need further help, think the words I AM HOME and you will find yourself back in your body, fully awake.

Take one last look at the spirit tattwa, in its reversed whitish color, standing before you. Allow it to fade, safely sealing off the portal you have opened between the worlds. If you have entered with the aid of a guide, ask him/her/it to accompany you on this meditative journey at this time.

Looking around once more you notice that you are in a crystalline region shaped like the inside of an egg.

Pause here to allow time to learn from your environment. Be open to any animals, beings, or natural objects appearing to you or who choose to speak. In this spirit world, everything you will encounter has sentience and is able to communicate if it wants to. This is a world where spirit forms and essences, which have so far had no other way to connect with you, can make their interest known. If you are having the meditation read to you, or if you are prerecording it, allow at least five minutes for this. When you have finished, you may move on. Because the teachings of the spirit realm are going to appear to be more customized to your own needs than any other, where you go from here will have to be up to you. Some people find the world of spirit daunting and like to take along company. Until you are used to exploring in spirit you may wish to ask a trusted guide escort you in and out. He/she/it can help take you through the experiences you most need at this time. Here you may be allowed to burst from the egg-like environment in the manner of birth or be led deeper within it. You may be taken to a place where you can sense everything that is, was, or will be is colliding and coalescing, or you may be permitted to experience a void of nothingness, where even your mind has trouble functioning.

Other scenarios to begin your spirit explorations in are:

- Voids of all kinds
- Storms that naturally combine all the other elements—fire in lightning, water in rain, air in the winds, all pummeling the earth
- Webs, symbolic of the unity of all existence
- Encounters with the characters in the Magician, Universe, or World tarot cards
- Ancient sites of great mystic learning, such as the Oracle at Delphi

Exploring the Tattwa Subsets

Exploring the subset tattwas can be more difficult than journeying into the primary ones. Here there is a subtle blending of the elements in which one is still dominant. There is also more opportunity for havoc due to battling nature spirits, each with their own agendas, and to colliding energies caused by the merging of two very basic forces that are trying to blend yet remain apart. On the plus side, these same energies offer great learning opportunities to the intrepid traveler, and some of the most valuable astral world experiences you are likely to have may be found here. You will also have to refine your visualization skills to keep the reverse image of two symbols on the inside of your eyelids until you can get inside the elemental world. As you prepare your meditation, keep in mind that the larger element of the tattwas always dominates.

Possible places, events, and beings you might visit or encounter in the subsets are listed here, but do not allow this list to limit your imagination or cause you to reject a trusted guide who offers to take you into alternate elemental experiences.

Water of Earth: Jungles, marshes, creeks in caverns, the edge of beaches, riverbanks, quicksand, mud puddles, amphibious creatures currently on land.

Fire of Earth: Deserts, areas of hardened lava, earth spirits and faeries with a staunchly protective nature.

Air of Earth: Windy canyons or valleys, naturally forming underground wind tunnels.

Spirit of Earth: Labyrinths, cemeteries, dolmens (stone altars), cairns (rock burial mounds), protective spirits of burial grounds.

Earth of Water: Bayous and swamps, wide cavern lakes, the ocean bottom, riverbeds, rain forests and their wildlife.

Fire of Water: Hot springs, desert oases, ceremonial sweat lodges.

Air of Water: Sailing scenes, waterfalls, pouring rain, rain deities and spirits.

Spirit of Water: In the womb before birth, sacred wells, water-related sacred sites, such as the Aztec Temple of the Moon or the Greek Temple of Poseidon.

Earth of Fire: Forest fires, fireplaces, citrus groves, active volcanoes and their spirits.

Water of Fire: Active lava flows.

Air of Fire: Lightning, fires spreading through the force of wind.

Spirit of Fire: Sacred balefires, ovens, and fire-related sacred sites, such as the Aztec Temple of the Sun or Rome's Temple of Vesta.

Earth of Air: A breezy mountain top.

Water of Air: A humid day, a winter windstorm, waterspouts, faeries with watery attributes, which are sometimes viewed as able to fly, such as the wicked Unseelie Court of Scottish lore.

Fire of Air: The backdraft from blast furnaces or hearth fires, warm summer breezes.

Spirit of Air: Hot air ballooning, cloudy areas in unformed regions of the astral world.

Earth of Spirit: Pagan circle rites, standing stones and menhirs, the pyramids and other temples that honored earth deities.

Water of Spirit: Pools of blood, icebergs.

Fire of Spirit: The creative spark, the realm of ideas and creativity, the cleansing fires featured in some cultures' end of world/rebirth myths.

Air of Spirit: The winds of change.

▼

Afterword

Living a Magickal Life

Making *Magick* has been written from the perspective of someone who practices Witchcraft. Certainly magick can be made outside of a spiritual framework; it has been done, and will continue to be so. Sometimes these magicians are responsible people, other times they are too self-serving to realize that what they do will ill-affect others, and sometimes, sadly, they just don't care. For me, it is inconceivable to separate magick from the spiritual framework that shapes my life. Magick and the spiritual are intricately woven strands within my web of existence and they simply cannot be disentangled. I will continue to believe—and teach—that it is important to embrace a magickal lifestyle that includes a spiritual basis and values self-responsibility and service to others, not just a desire to have and have and have. In this balance we find inner peace and we are open to the good things that shall surely be returned to us threefold.

When we embrace magick as part of our life, it demands that we live a lifestyle that reflects our magickal thinking. This is the essence of living as a Witch. It is not so much the fact that we can make magick that sets us apart from the rest of the human herd, but rather that we see magick in all creation. When we see a flower opening to the morning sun, the shadow of the earth fall across the full face of the moon, or a spider spin a web of strength from hundreds of slender threads, we are forced to acknowledge that all life is magickal, powered by the energy of a divine will.

That is the macrocosmic view of magick. On the microcosmic level we know that we are able to create as well simply because we are a part of that universal store of energy. We have been born in the image of the divine and possess its gift of creation, the ability to shape our own realities just as the God and Goddess shaped the great reality in which we dwell.

Witches acknowledge this power underlying all acts of manifestation. And because we view ourselves as an integral part of creation, part of the web of all existence, we accept that we can draw power from other beings, things, or places in this web and shape it to what we desire. We consciously choose to harm none because we know that the web is strong only when held together, that any upset can break one of the slender strands linking it to the others, and this causes repercussions to vibrate all through the web. Each action, positive or negative, affects all.

Magickal living requires that we exist in harmony with nature and with all other creatures. Acting on your environmental concerns, a Pagan passion long before it became the fashionable thing to do, is a fine way to live magickally even if you never cast a single spell. We may not all come to the same conclusions about how this is best accomplished, but the important thing is that we try and that we avoid judging the efforts of others. For instance, debate often rages in the Pagan/Wiccan community about vegetarianism and whether this is or is not a prerequisite for magickal living. Each side makes a good argument for itself, but constant bickering only serves to divide us and put the negative energy of anger into our magickal lives—not a good energy to have vibrating about our web!

Being aware of the cycles of nature will also put you into the world of magick. Sensing when a storm is approaching, being intuitively aware of the phase of the moon, feeling the approach of snow, sensing the presence of elementals or animals as you walk through the woods, hearing a tree or herb speak to you of its power, all put you in tune with the great wheel of life—the web of existence. The closer you bond with these things, the easier it is to work with them in magickal partnership.

If you are new to the magickal life, I urge you to temper your magickal studies with spiritual ones. Don't think that this will detract from your magickal efforts, trust that they will only be enhanced by your connection to the spiritual.

Those of you who possess advanced magickal and spiritual skills might consider mentoring a newcomer to the Craft. It is true that not everyone enjoys teaching, and many Craft teachers have been badly burned by ungrateful students. But those of you who have learned to make your magickal aspects at one with your daily lifestyle and your spirituality have an invaluable experience to share with those sincere students who want to learn from you and, someday, pass along your teachings to others. It is a perfect chance for you to positively impact the web.

If you have read through this book, or any other book on magick, and have decided to pursue magickal study, I heartily recommend setting a specific working schedule for yourself. A practice schedule for developing basic magickal skills appears in chapter 2 and can be augmented with other aspects of magick. For example, after spending a couple of weeks on basic skills, you might add some basic spell constructions, then some ritual magick, then some astral exercises. If you are also working on your year and a day study of Paganism/Witchcraft with an eye toward initiation, you may want to blend your magickal studies with your spiritual. Talk to your teacher or mentoring coven, if you have one, about how to do this. If you are alone in your efforts, you may want to get a book on complete basic Witchcraft and plan which chapters of that book best correspond to the magical studies you have planned for yourself. You might mix your ritual magick practice with a study of festival rituals, or your elemental studies with lessons in weather magick, or any of many other combinations. Don't be afraid to trust your instincts on this.

Also keep in mind that everyone's needs are different, and everyone learns at a different rate. Don't compare your working plan with someone else's and find it lacking. To get the most out of it, you should work at the pace that is right for you.

Magick is a powerful tool for change that can enrich every life it touches. Use it in harmony and love, and it will enrich you too.

As it harms none, do what you will.

▼

Appendix A

Magickal Catalysts and Correspondences

In this appendix are listed herbs, plants, flowers, stones, colors, et cetera, and their magickal associations. This list will help get you started with spell construction, but be aware that it is far from being a complete listing. Each of these (i.e., magickal herbalism, stone magick, color magick) is a subject unto itself, and quite a few books discuss them solely and in detail. Please look to the Bibliography for some of the titles and authors from which you can choose.

Keep in mind when working with herbs and oils that many of them are toxic, volatile, or can severely irritate skin. Do not burn them, consume them, or put them in contact with your skin until you know exactly what they will do when mixed with your own body chemistry. Try dabbing a small portion on the inside of your forearm and leave it for twenty-four hours—you should have a good idea of how it reacts to your skin. Consulting a good botany text should tell you if a plant is safe to burn or ingest. Also, if you are prone to allergies, you will need to use extra caution.

Herbs, Trees and Plants

To Aid Astral Projection
Ash, Dittany of Crete, Jasmine, Lavender, Lettuce, Mugwort, Orris Root, Poplar, Rowan, Sage

For Beauty
Catnip, Hawthorn, Pomegranate

To Aid Divination/Psychic Work
Apple, Beans, Catnip, Dandelion, Holly, Lilac, Nuts,
Mistletoe, Moonwort, Oak, Peppermint, Rowan,
Valerian, Yarrow

To Break Curses
Pepper, Mistletoe, Vetivert, Snake Plant

To Induce Prophetic Dreams
Agrimony, Broom, Clover, Jasmine, Mistletoe,
Mugwort, Oak Leaves, Pussywillow, Rose, Willow

To Banish Nightmares
Anise, Hyacinth, Morning Glory, Myrrh, Tuberose

To Banish/Exorcise
Allspice, Angelica, Beans, Cedar, Elder, Garlic, Ivy,
Juniper, Leek, Mistletoe, Onion, Pepper, Ragweed,
Thistle

For Fertility
Acorn, Barley, Bistort, Carrot, Eggs, Grape Vines, Grass,
Hawthorn, Holly, Moonwort, Mugwort, Oak, Pine/Pine
Cone, Potatoes, Primrose, Reed, Rice, Saffron, Wheat,
Willow Leaves

For Happiness
Allspice, Sandalwood

For Healing
Angelica, Ash, Boneset, Cedar, Comfrey, Dill, Elder,
Fennel, Ginger, Ginseng, Honey, Lavender, Mint, Rosemary,
Rowan, Saffron, Vervain, Vinegar, Violet, Willow

To Stop Gossip
Cloves

For Grounding Assistance
Potatoes, Turnips

To Attract Love
Apricot, Apple, Apple Blossom, Birch, Coltsfoot, Dogwood
Flowers, Gardenia, Ginger, Hibiscus, Lavender, Lotus, Myrtle,
Orange Blossoms, Orris Root, Parsley, Reed, Rose, Rue,
Turmeric, Trillium, Vanilla, Vervain, Violet, Willow, Yarrow

To Increase Lust and Strength
Camphor, Damiana, Galangal, Hibiscus, Parsley

To Strengthen Mental Prowess
Celery, Eyebright, Rosemary, Rue

To Find Employment
Clove, Cinnamon, Dill, Marjoram, Thyme

For Money and Prosperity
Ash, Barley, Blackberry, Cowslip, Dill Seed, Elder, Grape Vines, Hawthorn, Hay, Nuts, Oats, Peas, Pine Needles, Potato, Reed, Rice, Sugar Beets, Turnip, Wheat

For Peace
Burdock, Huckleberry Root, Sugar Cane, Vanilla

For Protection
Apples, Ash, Ashes, Basil, Blackberry, Bluebells, Blueberry, Broom, Cloves, Frankincense, Garlic, Gorse, Hazel, Nettles, Oak, Orange Peel, Pepper, Primrose, Potatoes, Rosemary, Thistle, Turnip

For Purification
Birch, Burdock, Camomile, Cinnamon, Elder Flower, Frankincense, Funegrek, Heather, Linden, Peat, Salt, Termeric, Vervain

To Increase Spirituality
Alder, Blueberry, Gardenia, Mugwort, Saffron, Sandalwood, Violet

Stones and Metals

To Aid Divination/Psychic Work
Amethyst, Cat's Eye, Coral, Geodes, Lapis Lazuli, Meteorite, Moonstone, Obsidian, Opal, Pearl, Sapphire

To Induce Prophetic Dreams
Aquamarine, Azurite, Coral, Mother of Pearl, Moonstone

To Banish Nightmares
Chalcedony, Hematite, Pearl

To Banish/Exorcise
Bloodstone

For Binding Spells
Lodestone

For Courage
Lapis Lazuli, Ruby

For Fertility
Emerald, Geodes, Jade, Malachite

For Healing
Copper, Garnet, Lapis Lazuli, Opal, Quartz Crystal,
Ruby, Sapphire, Yellow Topaz

For Grounding/Balance Assistance
Calcite, Hematite, Quartz Crystal

To Attract Love
Emerald, Jade, Moonstone, Mother of Pearl, Olivine,
Red Jasper, Rhodocrosite, Rose Quartz

To Strengthen Loyalty
Apache Tear, Granite, Lodestone

To Increase Lust and Strength
Carnelian, Diamond, Iron Pyrite, Ruby, Yellow Topaz

To Strengthen Mental Prowess
Diamond, Fluorite, Zircon

To Find Employment
Copper, Gold, Lodestone

For Money and Prosperity
Diamond, Jade, Peridot

For Peace
Emerald, Moonstone, Rose Quartz, Silver

For Protection
Bloodstone, Flint, Granite, Iron, Lapis Lazuli, Onyx,
Opal, Tiger's Eye, Yellow Topaz, Tourmaline

For Purification
Amethyst, Sapphire

To Increase Spirituality
Amethyst, Obsidian, Red Sandstone, Sapphire,
Silver, Turquoise

Colors in Magick

Red
Strength, passion, lust, God magick, energy, anger, health, action, projection, courage, sex magick

Orange
Attraction, friendship, fire magick, justice, the law

Yellow
Mental magick, the intellect, wisdom, concentration, communication, travel, storytelling spells, air magick

Green
Fertility, wealth, prosperity, personal appearance, spells for children, peace, balance, earth spells, eco-magick, growth, nature spirits, faeries, fruition

Blue
Healing, sleep, inner peace, dreams, past-life work, music magick, Goddess magick, loyalty/fidelity, water magick, divination

Indigo
Healing, sleep, inner harmony

Violet/Purple
Healing, meditation, psychic work, prophetic dreams, connection to other entities, spiritual pursuits, divination

Black
Absorption, protection, banishment

White
Purification, protection, joy, truth, exorcism, spirituality, stopping gossip, justice

Gold
God magick, the sun, employment, energy/stamina

Silver
Goddess magick, the moon, psychic powers, dream magick, divination

Brown
Animal magick, home magick

Pink
  Peace, love/romance

Olive
  Illness, uncertainty, cowardice ‑

Planets in Magick

Moon
  Goddess mysteries, the home, children, childbirth,
  fertility, divination, motherhood, psychic powers, women,
  life cycles, dreams, growth, astral projection, the subconscious, water, sleep, reincarnation, private matters, the night,
  the home, animals, peace, tranquility, and nursing.

Sun
  God mysteries, employment, the law, leadership,
  prosperity/money, protection, strength, men, royalty,
  theater, entertainment/performing arts, heat, charity,
  volunteering, government, law, self-confidence,
  movement/dance, fire, personal power, physical self-
  defense, purification, public matters, and exorcism.

Mercury
  Communication, the intellect, fickleness, healing, herbalism,
  writing, wisdom, mental prowess, books/computers, reading,
  gossip, vocal music, travel, correspondence, diplomacy,
  mathematics, the sciences, history, school/education,
  mass media, visiting, libraries, teachers and students.

Venus
  Love/romance, beauty, family matters, husbands/wives,
  sweethearts, love/romance, peace, fashion, architecture,
  light amusements, intimate social gatherings, shopping,
  close friendships, gardening, fidelity, emotions, music,
  pets, acts of kindness and generosity, art, sculpture,
  poetry, and beauty.

Mars
  Anger, power, lust, construction, war/combat, sex, courage,
  banishing, medicine, passion, the military, aggression/
  conflict, fear, police/soldiers, disagreement, physical
  exertion, competition, anger, group strength, machinery,
  carpentry, bargaining power, and needle crafts.

Jupiter

Prosperity, money, employment, good fortune/luck,
fair judgments, friendship, investments, ambition, wealth,
prestige, success, courtrooms, gambling, foreign interests,
attraction, astronomy, social events, psychology, the clergy,
and self-improvement.

Saturn

The hidden, past lives, transits, rebirth, self-undoing,
lies, mental and emotional distress, losses, the elderly,
completion, spirit communication, excavations, archaeology,
death, morality, meditation, accepting or changing bad
situations, and protection from psychic attack.

Uranus

Spiritual pursuits, higher consciousness, stagnation

Neptune

Psychic efforts, dreams, intuition

Pluto

The otherworld, death, transformation

The Elements in Magick

Earth

Fertility, pregnancy, prosperity, grounding, stabilization,
children, money, planting, growth, the home, harvesting,
pets, cattle, serpents, burrowing animals, buried objects,
dancing, many stones, image magick, and drumming.

Water

Childbirth, pregnancy, cleansing, inner transformation,
psychic endeavors, divination, purification, the
emotions, romantic love, spirit manifestations,
death, rebirth, and past-life explorations.

Fire

Profound transformation, protection, employment, legal
matters, destruction/construction, acting, passion, war/
conflict, courage, strength/stamina, sex, sex magick,
strength, lust, cleansing, and exorcism/banishing.

Air

Intellect, study, writing, the elderly, astral travel,
communication, music, sound, changeability,
weather magick, and power raising.

Appendix B

Just for Fun:
A "Test" of Craft Knowledge

I developed the following list of questions to give me a general idea of the level of knowledge of my Craft students prior to their initiations. The test has gone through many incarnations, the most recent being autumn of 1995. Unlike your usual test, there is no grading of this one, and no passing or failing. I usually work with the student informally with these, then present a copy after initiation so that the new Witch can refer to the questions later on when self-introspection about their direction in the Craft is needed or desired. Since a good many of the questions deal with magick, I thought readers of this book might enjoy the challenge of a self-test of this type.

Some sample answers are given to many of the questions to jumpstart your own thinking about magick and Paganism. Most of the questions do not have right and wrong answers. Many of them may have as many answers as there are Witches. The original version of this appendix included no answers of any sort, but then it was suggested that it might be more useful if I provided some guidelines for the less subjective questions, ones that can help point you in the direction of resources from which you can conclude your own answers.

Just keep in mind that you cannot fail, and that you should enjoy yourself while going through these. You are free to use these questions in Pagan/Wiccan study groups to facilitate open discussion, and to adapt them to the needs of any students who may eventually come your way. You may also answer any question with a magickal riddle if one comes to mind (these are popular features of many mythic stories), or with another question if it seems appropriate. For example, an experienced friend of mine said she would have replied to the question, "Does the threefold law apply in non-magickal situations?" with the response, "Are there any non-magickal situations?" Hmmm . . . an interesting point to ponder.

▼

- **What is the difference, if any, between Witchcraft and Paganism?**

Paganism defines any earth or nature religion. Witchcraft is a term referring to specific Pagan traditions, usually from western European origins.

- **Can one be a Witch but not Wiccan?**

The word *Wiccan* originally referred to a specific tradition of the Craft. Though today it is used to broadly define a variety of western European-based practices, many call themselves Witches who do not consider themselves Wiccan.

- **What are the origins of Wicca and from where did the word derive?**

The word *Wiccan* is speculated to have come from either the Old English *wyk,* meaning to shape or bend, or the Anglo-Saxon *wit,* meaning to have knowledge. The word *Wiccan* was probably applied to a definable religious tradition no earlier than the late nineteenth or early twentieth century.

- **How did Witchcraft get its evil reputation among the mainstream religions?**

The word *Witch* was diabolized by the early church in a deliberate attempt to undermine the nature religions of Europe. The St. James version of the Christian Bible (seventeenth century) used the word *Witch* in place of *poisoner* in a key passage in Exodus in order to have church authority to carry out their Witch hunts. For more, see Vivianne Crowley's *Wicca: The Old Religion in the New Age* or Raymond Buckland's *Witchcraft From the Inside.*

- **What, if any, is the difference between religion and spirituality?**
- **Is Wicca/Paganism a religion or a spirituality?**
- **Explain the symbolism of the pentacle.**

The circle surrounding the star represents eternity, wholeness, and containment. The five-pointed star has two meanings, a microcosmic and a macrocosmic one. On the microcosmic level it represents the individual. At the top is the head, the seat of our connection to the divine. Underneath are the arms and legs, representing the human body. Taken together, the meaning is that of mind over matter, or of spirituality over flesh. On the macrocosmic level the star represents the five elements. At the apex is spirit. Each of the lower four points represents one of the other elements. All together they symbolize the power of the spirit over matter, or that of the divine over the physical.

- **What is the significance of a pentagram with its apex pointed upward? What about a pentagram pointed downward?**

The apex up usually symbolizes positive workings or working of increase. This varies somewhat by tradition as well.

- **Do Pagans ever use or wear the pentagram in a downward position? Why or why not?**

While the pentagram is usually shown with its apex up when used as a symbol for Wicca, many traditions have rituals in which this image is inverted. This is not because they are working negative magick, but because they wish to take advantage of the symbolism of the inversion as a catalyst to help their rite succeed.

- **Explain the symbolism of at least one other Craft icon such as the solar cross, ankh, labrys, et cetera.**

There are hundreds of ancient symbols representing various aspects of Pagan belief and practice. Three books that can assist in this study are Doreen Valiente's *An ABC of Witchcraft*, *Behold the Sign*, and Ernst Lehner's *Symbols, Signs and Signets*.

- **What is meant by the term "solitary" or "solitaire"?**

This is a term for a Witch who practices alone either by choice or chance.

- **By what honorary title are the priest and priestess of a coven sometimes called?**

There is some variation on this by tradition, but in many Wiccan traditions a priestess is called Lady and a priest Lord.

- **What is the traditional number of members for a coven and why?**

Thirteen is traditional but not required, and most covens seek quality rather than quantity. Thirteen is said to have been chosen to represent the number of lunar months in the solar year, or to represent the four seasons (three coven members for each) plus one priest or priestess.

- **What is the difference between a degree/hierarchical tradition or coven and an egalitarian/priestly one?**

A degree tradition is one in which members advance through a prescribed hierarchy of levels, called degrees. Priestly traditions have no degrees and encourage all to become leaders. I described this, and other aspects of coven life, in more detail in my book *Inside A Witches' Coven*.

- **What is the difference between a traditional and an eclectic Pagan/Wiccan?**

A traditional follows or practices within a specific Wiccan or Pagan tradition. An eclectic makes his or her own traditions from a myriad of cultures and practices.

- **Name some of today's major Pagan (or Wiccan) traditions. If possible, tell a little bit about them.**

There are now hundreds of these, some large and fairly well-known, others small and secretive. Some books that examine specific traditions are *Ways of the Strega* by Raven Grimassi, my own *Witta: An Irish Pagan Tradition*, and Kisma Stepanich's *Faery Wicca* books. Books that talk about being written from a Gardnerian or Alexandrian tradition are also specific. These are two large and popular traditions that began in England.

- **Give a brief discourse on the attributes of each of the four elements.**

Most books on magick discuss these. (Also see chapter 3.)

- **What is the fifth element? What are its attributes? In a circle, where is it located?**

The fifth element is spirit. See chapter 3 for a discussion.

- **Name at least three tools that correspond to each of the elements.**

These vary greatly by tradition and personal taste. Chapter 3 gives a list of some of these correspondences.

- **What is an initiation? A self-dedication? Are they both valid?**

An initiation is a formal commitment to the Pagan path. A self-dedication is often thought of as something a newcomer does at the commencement of formal studies. Some people also make self-dedications to patron deities. They are valid in general, but will not be accepted within traditions that require you to work through their system if you want to call yourself a part of their tradition.

- **Why is initiation in some form important to functioning as a Pagan/Wiccan?**

Such rituals are important to the psyche, for establishing a break in time, formally letting the mind and the universe know that a commitment to a new way of life has been made. This is another of those questions to which there are many answers— all of them valid.

- **What is the traditional period of study before initiation?**

A year and a day.

- **What is the Wiccan/Pagan Rede?**

"As it harms none, do what you will" is the basic Rede. Longer versions have also been published as have corollaries to the law which focus on issues of self-responsibility.

- **What is the Threefold Law?**

A belief that all the energy we send forth, the good and the bad, will return to us three times over.

- **Does the Threefold Law apply in non-magickal situations?**
- **How does magick work?**

This is a question with many answers. For some it works through self-change, for others it works through changing outside influences. A discussion of magickal physics appears in chapter 1 and in my earlier book *Lady of the Night*; also in Marion Weinstein's *Positive Magic*. Most books on practical magick contain some discussion of the inner workings of magick.

- **What is meant by the term "sympathetic magick"?**

A principle of magick based on the belief that like attracts like.

- **What is the difference between low magick and high magick?**

Low magick is often called folk magick or natural magick, and high magick usually refers to the practices of ceremonial magick (based on the Judeo-Christian mystic teachings).

- **Why do Pagans often place a 'k' at the end of the word "magick"?**

Not all do this, but many do to differentiate between Pagan magick and stage illusion (magic).

- What are the elements of spell construction?
  See chapter 4 for one take on these.

- Give a detailed example of a spell for . . . (fertility, prosperity, health, protection, et cetera).
- When is it permissible to do magick for others?
  See chapter 1 for a discussion of magickal ethics. Also see Marion Weinstein's *Positive Magic*.

- Why is making magick sometimes referred to as spinning, weaving, or crafting a spell? What term do you feel best describes your magick making and why?
- What is meant by charging or empowering?
  This is a method where a magickal catalyst is charged with magickal intent. See chapter 2 for discussion and some methods.

- Is magick a necessary part of Paganism?
- Can magick work outside of Paganism?
- What is meant by "magickal living"?
- Is magick a spiritual pursuit? Why or why not?
- Is magick a religious pursuit? Why or why not?
- Name the prerequisites for successful magick.
  There are some slight variations on this, but most authors and teachers present basically the same ideas. These are, roughly: need, desire, knowledge, and the ability to keep silent. A discussion of this appears in chapter 1.

- How does psychic development relate or not relate to magickal practice?
- Are making magick and working a spell the same thing?
- What Pagan/Wiccan practices are not magickal in nature? Why or why not?
- Is divination magick?
- Give at least one theory for how divination works.
  Divination is believed by most to work by reading potentials already set in motion that have been printed on the collective unconscious, which is accessible to all of us once we are taught to reach it. A brief discussion of this art appears in chapter 1 under the topic of magickal ethics. One book to consult for this is Callia Underhill's *A Witch's Book of Divination*.

- Name some popular methods of divination. Which one attracts you most and why?

- **What is the aura?**

  The aura is the energy field surrounding all living things. Its color and condition can tell a lot about the state of mind and health of an individual. For more, please see Ted Andrews' *How to See And Read the Aura*, or Laneta Gregory and Geoffrey Treissman's *Handbook of the Aura*.

- **Why is it important to do a divination prior to working a spell?**

  To discover if your magick will end as you expect it to and to see if any element of it is harmful to anyone else.

- **Why and how do we use ritual in Pagan religious expression?**

  This is a topic that has been covered in depth by several writers. Chapter 6 addresses it, as does the highly recommended *Reclaiming the Power*.

- **Why and how do we use ritual in magick?**

  See chapter 6 or *Reclaiming the Power*.

- **What are the elements of Pagan ritual construction?**

  See chapter 6 or *Reclaiming the Power.*

- **True or false: One must have a whole collection of tools—at least one for each element—to be a successful Witch.**

  Magickal power comes from within. All tools and other items serve only as catalysts we focus our intent on, but for the most part contain no power in and of themselves. See chapters 2 and 3 for a more detailed discussion.

- **Why do we not touch another Witch's tools without permission?**

  To control the energy they absorb. Personal energies keep tools attuned to the energy pattern of one person and physical contact can unbalance those.

- **What is an . . . (athame, bolleen, scourge, et cetera)?**

  There are many tools used in Pagan/Wiccan practice. Some of these are discussed in chapter 3, others can be found in Doreen Valiente's *An ABC of Witchcraft* or Raymond Buckland's *Buckland's Complete Book of Witchcraft*.

- **Why is a circle cast for magick and ritual?**

  For protection of those inside and for containment of raised energy.

- Is a circle always necessary for magick or divination?
- True or false: There is only one right way to cast a ritual circle.

Though you may find one way that works best for you, there are many ways a circle can be cast. Silver RavenWolf explores several variations in her *To Stir a Magic Cauldron*.

- True or false: The directional attributes of the elements are not changeable.

Many are tempted to say this is true, but the fact is that many traditions have different attributes, and all work equally well.

- Why are timepieces not generally permitted inside the circle?

A circle is a place outside of time in which time should not be a concern. Some Witches also find that their watch's works are upset by the electromagnetic field of the circle.

- Why is it not wise to break the circle once it is cast?

You don't want energy raised to leak out or unwanted energies to find their way inside. (See chapter 6 for discussion.)

- Why do children and animals seem able to break the circle without causing harm?

This question has never been completely answered. In part it may be because children and animals have not learned to compartmentalize their world the way adults have.

- What or who are the Watchtowers? Name the elemental rulers of each quarter (as used in general Wicca or in another tradition you study).

Various discussions of these attributes can be found in most any book on Wiccan/Pagan practice, including here in chapter 3.

- What is deosil? Is it always positive?

Deosil is clockwise or sunwise movement. Whether it is positive or negative depends on intent.

- What is meant by widdershins? Is this something negative?

This is counterclockwise or anti-sunwise movement. Negativity is determined by intent and by whether divinations show whether an action is harmful or not.

- Which direction, deosil or widdershins, would you use for a spell to banish a bad habit? For invoking protection? For gaining a lover?

- **What is a banishing rite? What is psychic self-defense?**

Banishing involves removing an unwanted entity from your presence or your home, psychic self-defense attempts to prevent them from being attracted to you in the first place. A discussion of this art appears in chapter 7. Other books that teach this art are Melita Denning and Osborne Phillips' *Psychic Self-Defense and Well-Being* and Doreen Valiente's *Psychic Self-Defense*.

- **What are the sabbats? Explain in detail the significance of at least one.**

The sabbats are the eight solar festivals of the Wiccan year. These are detailed in my earlier book *The Sabbats* and in Pauline and Dan Campanelli's *Ancient Ways*.

- **Name several modern/mainstream holiday practices with Pagan roots.**

Halloween, Easter, and Christmas all took major parts of the celebrations from Pagan practices.

- **What is an esbat?**

This is a lunar-based festival, usually (but not always) observed at the full moon. I wrote in depth about lunar celebrations and magick in *Lady of the Night,* as did D. J. Conway in *Moon Magick.*

- **Does the Craft have any other holidays and festivals?**

There are hundreds, maybe thousands, of folk festivals and holidays that are still being celebrated or are being reclaimed. Two books detailing some of these are Patricia Telesco's *Seasons of the Sun* and Gerina Dunwich's *The Wicca Book of Days.*

- **Is it permissible to work magick on the sabbats? The esbats? How do you or your tradition view this?**

Some Witches avoid magick on the sabbats because they believe no work that is not absolutely necessary should be performed on these days. The word *sabbat* derives from a Greek word, *sabatu,* meaning "to rest."

- **Which kind of magick would you work on the sabbats or esbats, and for whom can/should it be done?**
- **Who or what is the Triple Goddess?**

The Triple Goddess is a deity comprising three faces, usually maiden, mother, and crone. D. J. Conway wrote *Maiden, Mother, Crone* to discuss this archetype in detail.

- **What is an archetype and how does this term relate to the deities? To divination? To dream interpretation?**

An archetype is a standard pattern that has strong symbolic meanings on an almost universal level. Many people feel deities are archetypes. Archetypes are part of dream language as well.

- **What is meant by "as above, so below"?**

This means that what exists anywhere in the universe—including the astral world—can exist in our world as well. See chapter 1 for a discussion.

- **What is meant by macrocosm and microcosm? How does this relate to Wiccan/Pagan practices and beliefs?**

The macrocosm is the greater universe, the microcosm is the earth. This analogy can be taken down to the lowest level of atomic existence. (See chapter 1.)

- **What do Pagans believe happens to them after death?**

These answers are varied, but reincarnation is a strong component of most of our beliefs. Others base their beliefs on the mythology of a particular culture. My earlier book *Entering the Summerland* discusses some of these beliefs.

- **What are the pros and cons of memorized rituals?**

Memorization can increase smoothness but can also detract from our deeper connection with the meaning of the rite.

- **What is a scourge? Why and how is it used in Pagan practice?**

A scourge is a small whip used in flagellation rites for purification. The scourge is used in many English traditions and even found its ways into some Christian monastic sects. Some use it as a magickal tool.

- **What is the difference, if any, in the symbolism of the cauldron and of the chalice?**

They both represent the cosmic feminine, the womb of the Goddess. There are also some differences as well as other similarities. Please see my earlier *The Bottomless Cauldron* or any book dealing with women's spirituality or Arthurian/Grail legends for more.

- **Why is the study of mythology important to understanding Paganism?**

All religions are based on mythology.

- What is a Book of Shadows and how did it get its name?
- What is a grimoire? A spellbook?

All of these are collections of rituals and spells. See chapters 1 and 2 or other books on basic magick and Wicca.

- What were the Burning Times and why is this label misleading?

The Burning Times is the Pagan name for the years of European Witch hunts and executions (roughly 1100–1800). The term is misleading because the majority of accused Witches were hanged or killed with some method other than fire. Vivianne Crowley discusses this period in her *Wicca: The Old Religion in the New Age*.

- What are differences between monotheism, polytheism, and pantheism? Where does Paganism (or your brand of Paganism/Wicca) fall in this spectrum?

Monotheism means belief in one God, polytheism means belief in many Gods, and pantheism is a belief that the divine is inherent in all living things.

- In general, what is the Pagan/Wiccan concept of the divine? What is your personal concept?
- Talk about one God and one Goddess about whom you have gained insight or knowledge.

This information can be gleaned through reading mythology or by studying several books on the deities. Among these are Patricia Monaghan's *The Book of Goddesses and Heroines*, D.J. Conway's *The Ancient and Shining Ones*, and Janet and Stewart Farrar's *The Witches' Goddess* and *The Witches' God*.

- How do the deities relate to magick?

This is almost a matter of personal practice or tradition. I wrote about one Celtic viewpoint in my *Celtic Myth and Magick*. Some people often petition or invoke deities for magick, others prefer to rely on other catalysts.

- Why do many Pagans have patron deities? Do you have one? Do you want one? Why or why not?
- Why do we choose Craft names? Why are they sometimes kept secret?

One of the reasons we take on new names is to represent our new selves or to call on our new energy patterns. We often keep them secret to protect those energies. Phoenix McFarland's *The Complete Book of Magical Names* and Ted Andrews' *The Sacred Power in Your Name* look at the power of naming.

- **What is a familiar and what does it do?**

A familiar is a living thing, usually an animal, that assists with magick. One book to read on the subject is *The Once Unknown Familiar* by Timothy Roderick.

- **What is handfasting? Wiccaning? Coming of age? Passing over?**

These are the life cycle rites of Paganism. Pauline and Dan Campanelli wrote about all of them in detail in *Rites of Passage: The Pagan Wheel of Life*. Many books on Wiccan/Pagan practice also have some discussion of these.

- **What is the Wiccan Summerland?**

This is one of the many names by which Pagans refer to the afterlife or Land of the Dead.

- **What is the Ceremony of Cakes and Ale?**

This is the forerunner of the Christian communion or Jewish blessing of the bread and wine. Usually done on lunar festivals, this rite celebrates the earth and water manifestations of the Goddess. I give a complete cakes and ale ritual in *Lady of the Night*.

- **What is a libation?**

An offering made to a deity, faery, spirit, or nature during ritual, magick, or when favor is curried.

- **What is meant by skyclad? Why do some Wiccans do this? Name at least one tradition that, as a whole, prefers this option.**

Skyclad is ritual nudity. Some choose this option to represent freedom, equality, or to feel closer to nature and allow for better flow of psychic energy. The Gardnerian and Alexandrian traditions practice this way.

- **What is the significance of each of the three phases of the moon?**

Magickally they represent waxing, waning, and full energies. These energies are detailed in chapter 4 and in *Lady of the Night*, and in D. J. Conway's *Moon Magick*.

- **How is astrology used in Wiccan/Pagan practice?**

See chapter 4 or see Marie K. Simms *The Witches' Circle*.

- **How is astrology used in magick?**

See chapter 4.

- On which day of the week would a fertility spell
  best be worked? A spell for protection? For romance?
  For health? For mental prowess? For protecting
  one's children?
  See chapter 4 for ideas. There are no rights or wrongs here.

- Name the planets associated with each day of the week.
  See chapter 4.

- Should astrology always be consulted before a spell?
- Which astrological aspects are most important to
  magickal efforts?
  See chapter 4.

- What are the planetary hours?
  See chapter 4.

- What is meant by "moon void of course"?
  See chapter 4.

- How would you rework/reword a spell to make it
  more compatible with what at first seems to be an
  inauspicious astrological phase?
  See chapter 4 or *Lady of the Night* for suggestions.

- On which phase of the moon is it best to begin a spell
  for increased prosperity?
- On which day in the phase would it be best? How about
  the right lunar phase and day for a spell for banishing
  harmful influences?
- What kind of spells would you initiate on a full moon?
  A new moon? A lunar eclipse?
- How would you expect a solar eclipse to impact a spell
  for prosperity?
- Do Pagans/Wiccans believe in angels?
  This is an individual decision. Silver RavenWolf wrote about
  one Pagan/Wiccan viewpoint in *Angels: Companions in Magick*.

- How would you banish an unwanted entity?
  See chapter 7 for suggestions.

- How would you deal with an unwanted ghost?
  See chapter 7 or any text on practical parapsychology.

- **Why and how would you contact the dead?**

There are many methods and beliefs about this art. For details and practical instruction please see Raymond Buckland's *Doors to Other Worlds* or Raymond Moody's *Reunions*.

- **Why might you want to do a ritual in a cemetery?**
- **What is meant by the "in between" times and places, and why might they be important to magick?**

In between times and places are those that cannot be easily classified. For example, midnight is neither one day nor another, and the seashore is neither sea nor shore. In the Celtic traditions it is believed that these are gateways to the Otherworld—places of magickal power.

- **How would you deflect negative energy that had been sent your way? How would you protect yourself against reinfestation?**

See chapter 7, Melita Denning and Osborne Phillips' *Psychic Self-Defense and Well-Being*, and Doreen Valiente's *Psychic Self-Defense*.

- **What is "warding"?**

The art of magickal protecting or sealing someone or something from harm or negative influence.

- **What would you do to ward yourself? Your home? Your car? A loved one? A pet?**

See chapter 7 for ideas. Silver RavenWolf also discusses warding in *To Stir a Magic Cauldron*.

- **Explain the magickal significance of at least three colors.**

These are highly individualized. For assistance please see Raymond Buckland's *Practical Color Magic*.

- **What is a catalyst in magick?**

See chapters 1 and 4.

- **How are candles, herbs, stones, and other catalysts used in magick?**

See chapters 1 and 4, also books on herb or stone magick such as those by Scott Cunningham.

- **What is a kitchen Witch? A green Witch?**

A kitchen Witch is someone who uses the culinary arts as a catalyst for magick. See Patricia Telesco's *A Kitchen Witch's Cookbook*. A green Witch is someone who practices close to nature, perhaps focusing on eco-magick. See Kisma Stepanich's *The Gaia Tradition*, Aoumiel Moura's *Green Witchcraft*, or any books on the art of magickal herbalism.

- **What is empowering? How is it done?**

This is the art of projecting magickal energy into an object. See chapter 2 for discussion.

- **What is visualization? Why is it important to magick?**

This is the art of empowering through inner sight. A discussion and instructions appear here in chapter 2. Because this skill is vital to successful magick, most books on the magickal arts discuss it at some length. Books about creative visualization are also good study tools, such as those written by Shakti Gawain and Melita Denning and Osborne Phillips.

- **How would you plan your visualization in relation to spellwork?**
- **Are there any times when magick is best not worked?**
- **What are the chakras? How can these be used in magick or healing?**

The chakras are the energy centers of the human body. See chapter 2, or see *Wheels of Life* by Anodea Judith.

- **What is meant by centering, and how is it done?**

See chapter 2, or Silver RavenWolf's *To Stir a Magic Cauldron*.

- **How would you cleanse and bless an area in which you were about to work a spell or hold a ritual?**

See chapters 4 and 6, or any book on practical magick for suggestions, ideas, and in-depth discussion.

- **What is eco-magick?**

Magick worked for the benefit of the environment.

- **Draw a banishing pentagram. An invoking pentagram.**

Chapter 6 presents two basic models, but these are not the only ones. Some magickal traditions have a different invoking and banishing pentagram for each element.

- **What is grounding and why is it important after magick or ritual?**

  See chapter 2, or Silver RavenWolf's *To Stir a Magic Cauldron*.

- **What is the cone of power?**

  See chapter 2, or look into other books on practical magick such as Doreen Valiente's *Witchcraft for Tomorrow*.

- **Name at least three ways to raise energy.**

  There are hundreds of ways, alone and in combination to achieve this goal. Chapter 2 discusses some of them.

- **Name at least three ways to send raised energy.**

  See Chapter 2, or books on practical magick such as Doreen Valiente's *Witchcraft for Tomorrow* or Silver RavenWolf's *To Stir a Magic Cauldron*.

- **What is the difference, if any, between an amulet and a talisman?**

  Though people often use the term interchangeably, there are two distinctions: one, that amulets are items found in nature and talismans are made by their users, or two, that amulets repel unwanted energies while talismans attract desirable ones.

- **Name at least three people, past or present, who are well-known in Craft circles, and explain why their contribution has been important.**

  Books on general Paganism often go into Craft history. Two I recommend are Vivianne Crowley's *Wicca: The Old Religion in the New Age* and Raymond Buckland's *Witchcraft from the Inside*.

- **What is shamanic Paganism/Wicca?**

  Shamanism is a magickal tradition found in all cultures. It attempts to use journeys into other worlds as a method of reaching the divine and in healing, divination, et cetera. Numerous books have been written on the topic, some very scholarly in nature, and recently several have been issued that look at shamanistic practices in relation to various Pagan/Wiccan traditions. A good overview can be found in Mircea Eliade's *Shamanism: Archaic Techniques of Ecstasy*.

- **What is an animal totem? A plant totem?**

These are living things that share an affinity with the Witch and who agree to share their magickal energies and insights in time of need. Books on shamanistic Paganism often detail these practices.

- **How would one use a bell in ritual? In magick?**

There are many ways bells have been used: to call quarters, to summon spirits, to banish negativity, to chase away faery life, et cetera. Many traditions do not use bells because they feel the noise frightens away beneficial spirits.

- **What is meant by taking one's "measure"?**

This is a coven practice where the length of a person is measured by a cord. See my earlier work *Inside A Witches' Coven,* Raymond Buckland's *Witchcraft From the Inside* or books with a focus on English traditions for history, practical information, and pros and cons.

- **Do Pagans pray?**

Many do. A good discussion and some practical advice is given in Scott Cunningham's *Living Wicca.*

- **What is the meaning of the phrase "so mote it be"? How is it used?**

This is an obsolete term meaning "it must be." It is traditional to use it in Wiccan spellwork to affirm the success of a spell. See chapter 2 for more discussion.

- **What are the traditional words Wiccans use when greeting others at, or when parting from, ritual gatherings? What are the traditional parting words?**

This can vary by tradition and by individual coven, but many use the phrase, "Merry meet, merry part, and merry meet again."

- **What, if any, is the difference between evocation and invocation?**

These terms are often used interchangeably, but when a difference is perceived, evocation is the art of calling something or someone to your presence and invocation draws someone or something into your physical body.

- Name at least one sacred site (more if you can) anywhere in the world and briefly explain why it is significant.

Though the first thing many North Americans think of is Stonehenge in England, many such sites exist all over the world. Several books are now on the market that look at sacred sites, both in depth and in general (Stonehenge has been written about in many books). One of the most recent releases is Bernyce Barlow's *Sacred Sites of the West*. These sites are excellent locations for drawing on magickal energy and for helping to connect with the divine.

- What is the astral/inner-plane? How do you get there and why would you want to?

See Chapters 9 and 10, or try one of the books that discusses nothing but astral projection, such as D.J. Conway's *Flying Without A Broom*, Melita Denning and Osborne Phillips' *Practical Guide to Astral Projection*, J.H. Brennan's *Astral Doorways*, or any of the personal chronicles by Robert Monroe.

- What is meant by astral magick?

One definition is magick worked while in a state of astral projection.

- Can you work magick in the dream state? Why or why not?
- What is a balefire?

A sacred bonfire.

- What is meant by a "Witch's brew"?

This can mean almost anything from a tea to a boiling potpourri. Two good guides to magickal brews are Scott Cunningham's *The Complete Book of Incense, Oils and Brews* and Patricia Telesco's *A Witch's Brew*.

- Explain the Great Rite.

This rite symbolizes the sacred marriage of the God and Goddess. Many books on Pagan/Wiccan practice give some space to discussion of this.

- What are your strengths and weaknesses as a Witch/Pagan?
- What else do you want to learn?
- Where do you go from here?

Glossary

Alchemical Symbols. The four symbols of the elements used by alchemists and by many ceremonial magicians. The glyphs were taken from the six-pointed star figure known today as Solomon's Seal or the Star of David.

Alchemy (AL-kem-ee). A cousin science of ceremonial magick developed in the Middle Ages that sought to magickally and/or chemically turn base metals into gold. Part of its focus was the elevation of the human soul to a more Godlike existence through the role of creation. Alchemists have always referred to their practices as "The Great Work." The word is also used in magick when discussing the transmutation of the self, or of using an intangible medium, such as meditation or music, to effect personal change.

Alignment/Attunement. The art and practice of placing our spiritual and mental selves in sync with the energies of an element, and astronomical event (i.e., full moon) or another being (i.e., a God or Goddess).

Altered State of Consciousness. Synonymous with meditation. For many it is a sustained thought process during which a clear focus for the mind is settled upon to the exclusion of all else. For others, mostly from Asian traditions, it is the complete and controlled absence of thought. In either case, it involves altering one's normal state of consciousness to a slower, more receptive level. In simplest terms it is a deliberate attempt to slow the cycles per second of one's brain waves to generate a consciously controlled sleeping state.

Amulet. From Latin *amolior* meaning "to repel," an amulet is a naturally occurring object reputed to give protection to its bearer.

Archetype. Archetypes are universal symbols defined by Funk and Wagnalls as a "standard pattern" or a "prototype." Archetypal symbols speak to all of us in the ecumenical language of the subconscious. They are the images that cloud our dreams, they are the inherent power of our deities, and they are the machinery that makes all forms of divination possible. Archetypal images are employed because this is the only language our subconscious minds can understand, utilize, and communicate back to our consciousness with.

Aspect. 1) The particular principle or part of the Creative Life Force being worked with or acknowledged at any one time. For example, Brighid is a Mother aspect of the one Goddess, Thor is one aspect of the God, and both are merely single aspects of the divine creative force. 2) The relationship between any two planets as calculated on a conceptualized, earth-centered horoscope drawing of the heavens at any given moment. The number of degrees between the planets determines how they aid or contradict each other's influences.

Astral Plane. A place generally conceptualized as an invisible other world that remains unseen from our own solid world of form.

Astral Projection. The art of "leaving one's body" or "lucid dreaming" whereby someone in a trance state visits other locations, realms, or times. This is often referred to as traveling on the Astral Plane (see above).

Astrology. The study of and belief in the effects the movements and placements of planets and other heavenly bodies have on the lives and behavior of human beings.

Athame (ATH-eh-may). The ritual, double-edged knife often associated with the element of air and the direction of east, though some traditions attribute it to fire and the south.

Aura. The life-energy field surrounding all living things.

Banishing. The act of sending away from ourselves, our ritual areas, or our homes all negative energies and beings.

B.C.E. "Before Common Era." This is a designation scholars often use to denote dates synonymous with B.C., but without the biased religious implications. It is also sometimes abbreviated BCE, without the periods in between.

Balefire. The traditional communal bonfire of the sabbats. The name is derived from the Anglo-Saxon word *boon* meaning a "gift" or "something extra." Even in modern times balefires play a major role in both Pagan and non-Pagan holidays and folk celebrations. The modern word *bonfire* is synonymous with balefire, though it often has no religious significance.

Bealtaine. Also spelled Beltane and Beilltaine. This sabbat, celebrated on May 1, is rife with fertility rituals and symbolism, and is a celebration of the sacred marriage of the Goddess and the God.

Besom (BEE-sum or BESH-um). The Witch's broomstick.

Black Magick. A name applied to any negative magickal working. Persons who regularly indulge in this practice are said to be on the "left hand path."

Book of Shadows. Also called Book of Lights and Shadows. The spell book, diary, and ritual guide used by an individual or coven. Some say the name came from having to hide the workings from church authorities, and others say it means that an unworked spell or ritual is a mere shadow not taking form until performed by a Witch.

The Burning Times. The time from the Spanish Inquisition through the last outbursts of persecution and Witch killings in the mid-nineteenth century (though murderous persecutions began as early as the twelfth century). The last known capital sentence for Witchcraft in the west took place in Scotland in the late 1700s. Figures vary on how many were killed during this hysteria; estimates range anywhere from fifty thousand to as many as nine million. Regardless of the number of lives actually lost, these murders for the sake of religious persecution should never be forgotten. The Jewish Holocaust of this century frighteningly shows us that such atrocities can occur in any age to any of us.

Cauldron. Linked to Witchcraft in the popular mind, this is a primal Goddess image used like a chalice or cup and is sometimes used to represent the element of water.

c.e. "Common Era." This term is often used by scholars to denote time synonymous with A.D. but without a religious bias. It is sometimes abbreviated as CE, without the periods in between.

Ceremonial Magick. A highly codified magickal tradition based on Kaballah, the Jewish-Gnostic mystical teachings. Also known as High Magick.

Chakra. From a Hindustani word loosely translated as "wheel." These are the sacred principal energy centers of the human body, the seven principal centers located at the base of the tail bone, at the navel, the solar plexus, the heart center, the breast bone, the throat, the Third Eye, and just above the crown of the head.

Chalice. The chalice or cup is a ritual tool representing water and the west, and in many western Pagan traditions it is also representative of the feminine principle of creation.

Charging. The act of empowering an herb, stone, or other magickal object with one's own energies directed toward a magickal goal. Charging is synonymous with enchanting or empowering.

Circle. The sacred space wherein magick is to be worked and ritual enacted. The circle both contains raised energy until needed, and provides protection for the Pagan/magician while inside.

Collective Unconsciousness. A term used to describe the sentient connection of all living things, past and present. It is synonymous with the terms *deep mind* and *higher self.* This is believed to be the all-knowing energy source that is tapped during divination.

Cone of Power. The ritual raising of a cone of energy within the circle by an individual or by a coven. When the energy reaches its peak, it is released to do its work. Dancing deosil while chanting or singing is the most common method for raising the cone.

Consecrate. To consecrate something is to dedicate it to a sacred or higher purpose. The word is often used synonymously with the terms *to bless* or *to make holy.*

Conscious Mind. That part of the brain we have access to in the course of a normal waking day. It is the part of the mind that is critical and analytical in nature and that holds retrievable memory.

Coven. A group of Witches who worship and work together. A coven may contain any number of Witches, both male and female, but the traditional number of members is thirteen, which reflects the thirteen moons in the solar year, or three persons for each season plus a priest/ess. Terms synonymous with coven are *circle, sept,* and *grove.*

The Craft. Refers primarily to the religion(s) of Witchcraft, but can also refer to the crafting of magick.

Cross-Quarter Days. A name sometimes given to the Sabbats not falling on the solstices or equinoxes.

Deosil (JES-el). The act of moving, working, or dancing in a clockwise motion. This is the traditional direction one works with for creative magick. Deosil is also called sunwise.

Discarnate. A being in spirit, one that has no corporeal form. A human discarnate might also be called a ghost.

Divination. The act of divining the future by reading potentials currently in motion. Divination can be done through meditation, scrying, astral projection, cards, stones, or any one of a myriad of other means.

Druids. Much speculation still continues on the role of the Druids. They were the priestly class of Celtic society; the magicians and writers, poets, historians, religious leaders, and royal advisors. Their power flourished from the second century B.C.E. to the second century C.E.

Earth Plane. A metaphor for your normal waking consciousness, or for the everyday, solid world we live in.

Eclectic. A Wiccan or Pagan who draws on many different cultures and traditions for his or her magickal/ritual ideas. In general, he or she is said not to be following any one specific Pagan tradition.

Eco-Magick. Also called green magick or environmental magick. These are spells and rituals done to heal and protect Mother Earth and her plants and creatures.

Elementals. Archetypal spirit beings associated with one of the four elements. Elementals are sometimes called faeries and are perceived as inhabiting the faery realms.

The Elements. The four components once thought to make up the entire universe. These are earth, air, fire, and water plus the fifth element of pure spirit in, of, and outside them all. Each Pagan tradition has its own, slightly differing directions, tools, and correspondences for each of these.

Enchanting. The act of empowering an herb, stone, or other magickal object with one's own energies directed toward a magickal goal. Enchanting is synonymous with charging or empowering.

Esbat. A term for a lunar festival or monthly gathering, especially when referring to the full moon. The word comes from the Old French *esbattre* meaning "to frolic." Magick is often performed at esbats, both by individuals and groups.

Exorcism. The art of banishing a discarnate being from your home or ritual area.

Familiar. A Witch's co-worker that is of a non-human existence. Animals are the most common familiars, thus the popularity of the Witch's cat. But familiars can also be discarnate spirits, spirit guides, or elementals. The choice of having a familiar or not is a personal one, and must also be the conscious choice of the other being involved.

Folklore. The traditional sayings, cures, fairy tales, and folk wisdom of a particular locale separate from their mythology.

Gnomes. In many magickal systems these faeries are referred to as elementals, and are thought to be the ruling spirits of the earth element. The name comes from the Greek *gnoma* meaning "knowledge."

Gnostic. Referring to the teachings and practices of Christian mysticism. Gnostic masters were responsible for grafting much of their knowledge onto Kaballistic teachings, and the two systems share similar roots and ideas.

The Great Rite. A ritual that symbolizes the sexual union, or sacred marriage, of the Goddess and the God, from whose union comes all creation. The Rite is performed by one male and one female who are representative of the male and female polarities of deity. This ritual is most often performed by placing a knife (a phallic symbol) into a chalice (primal female image).

Grimoire (Greem-WAHR). A book of magickal spells and rituals. Some claims to their antiquity are highly suspect, and those that are truly ancient contain much apocryphal material. However, this does not invalidate the spells or rituals in the newer ones, it just means they are not old. Any Book of Shadows can also be a grimoire.

Grounding. To disperse excess energy generated during any magickal or occult rite by sending it into the earth. It can also mean the process of centering one's self in the physical world both before and after any ritual or astral experience.

Guided Meditation. A guided, meditative journey into the realm of the unconscious, or astral plane, for the purpose of gaining knowledge and effecting a lasting change on both the conscious and subconscious mind of the one who meditates. The term is synonymous with pathworking.

Herbalism. The art of using herbs to facilitate human needs both magickally and medically. It is also known as "wort cunning." Wort is an obsolete word for herb, and cunning refers to secret knowledge.

Higher Self. That part of us connecting our corporeal minds to the Collective Unconscious and the divine knowledge of the universe. It is often visualized as being connected to the crown chakra, the energy center located just above the head.

Imbolg (EM-bowl/g). Also known as Candlemas, Imbolc or Oimelc. Imbolg, observed on February 2, is a day that honors the Virgin Goddess as the youthful bride of the returning Sun God.

Incense (ritual). The burning of herbs, oils, or other aromatic items to scent the air during acts of magick and ritual and to better help the magician attune to the goal of the working.

Kaballah. The body of mystical teachings from the Jewish-Gnostic tradition upon which both ceremonial magick and the Alexandrian Pagan traditions base their practice. While the principles of Kaballah are ancient, its codification as a system of religious study dates only to the medieval period. Also transliterated from the Hebrew as Qabala and Cabala.

Karma. Hindustani word that reflects the ancient belief that good and evil done will return to a person either in this life or in a succeeding one.

Kerub. The name given to the four creatures that represent the elements in the Biblical story of Ezekial's vision of the wheel. These images are often incorporated in tarot designs for the Wheel of Fortune card.

The Law of Responsibility. This is an often repeated corollary to the other laws of Paganism. It simply means that if you inadvertently violate someone's free will or harm them in any way, you will accept responsibility for your action and seek to make restitution. This, of course, does not apply in cases where you have used magick to protect yourself from someone seeking to harm you.

Lughnasadh (Loo-NAAS-sah). Also known as Lammas or August Eve. This Sabbat celebrates the first harvest. The date is August 1 or 2, depending on your tradition.

Mabon (MAH-bone). Sabbat named for a Welsh God associated with the Arthurian myth cycles. This is the Sabbat observed at the Autumn Equinox and celebrates the second harvest, wine, and balance.

Meditation. A deliberate attempt to slow the cycles per second of one's brain waves to generate a consciously controlled sleeping state.

Mysticism. The art of attempting to raise the human spirit to the place where it reaches and merges with what is known as the Godhead, or source of creation.

Numina. From a Latin word roughly meaning "animate." The spirit or divine essence dwelling in any object, particularly one found in nature. Numina is plural; the singular form is numen.

Occult. The word *occult* literally means "hidden" and is broadly applied to a wide range of metaphysical topics that lie outside of the accepted realm of mainstream theologies. Such topics include, but are not limited to, divination, hauntings, spirit communication, natural magick, ceremonial magick, alternative spirituality, psychic phenomena, alchemy, astrology, demonology, the study of the spiritual practices of ancient civilizations, and the study of any of the above mentioned topics as applied to mainstream religions.

Occultist. One who practices and/or studies a variety of occult subjects.

Old Religion. Another name for Paganism, particularly as practiced in Britain and Ireland.

Ostara (O-STAR-ah). The Sabbat observed at the Vernal Equinox, and often referred to simply as the Spring Equinox. This Sabbat celebrated the sexual union of the Goddess and God in the Norse traditions before the Celts influenced this event to Bealtaine. It is a time to celebrate new life and emerging sexuality. Ostara is symbolized by the egg.

Otherworld. Another name for either the astral/unseen world, or for the Land of the Dead.

Pagan. Generic term for anyone who practices an earth or nature religion.

The Pagan/Wiccan Rede. This is the most basic tenet of Paganism, one nearly universally accepted: "As it harms none, do what you will." The Rede prohibits us from harming any other living thing, or from violating anyone's free will.

Parapsychology. The study of paranormal phenomena. This field has grown tremendously in the past few decades with many highly skilled scientists and psychologists now populating its ranks.

Pentacle. A pentagram surrounded by a circle and carved on a circlet of wood or other natural object. The pentacle is used in some covens to represent the earth element and is also called a disk or shield.

Pentagram. The ancient five-pointed star that has come to symbolize much of western Paganism. It is usually seen with its apex up and can represent the four elements headed by the fifth element of spirit, or it can represent a human with its arms and legs spread to represent mind over matter. When encased in a circle it is properly called a pentacle. *Pentegram* is an alternate spelling.

Power Hand. For purposes of magick, this is the hand that is dominant, usually the one you write with.

Receptive Hand. For purposes of magick, this is the hand that is non-dominant, usually the one you do not use for writing.

Ritual. A systematic, formal or informal, prescribed set of rites whose purpose is to imprint a lasting change on the life and psyche of the participant.

Ritual Tools. A general name for magickal or ritual tools used by a magician. These tools vary by Pagan tradition and usually represent one of the elements. Ritual tools may also be called magickal tools or elemental weapons.

Runes. The ancient writing of the Teutonic people. Today it is considered a magickal alphabet among Pagans and is used for writing in one's Book of Shadows and for divination.

Sabbat. Any of the eight solar festivals or observances of the Wiccan year. The word is derived from the Greek word *sabatu* meaning "to rest." The sabbats are Samhain (October 31), Winter Solstice, Imbolg (February 1 or 2), Spring Equinox, Bealtaine (May 1), Summer Solstice, Lughnasadh (August 1 or 2), and Autumn Equinox.

Salamanders. In many magickal systems these faeries are referred to as elementals, and are thought to be the ruling spirits of the fire element. The name comes from the Greek *salambe* meaning "fireplace."

Samhain (SOW-een, SOW-in, or SAV-awn). This Sabbat is celebrated on the date now called Halloween: October 31. Samhain marked the beginning of winter for the Celts and was also their New Year's Day. It is a day to honor the Crone Goddess and the dying God who will be reborn at Yule. Samhain also marks the end of the harvest season.

Scrying. The divinatory act of gazing at an object or candle until prophetic visions appear.

Shaman (SHAW-men). The word *Shaman* comes from an extinct Ural-Altaic language called Tungus. They are the priests and medicine men of old tribal societies worldwide. Shamans, and also Shamanesses, practice in every known culture, and many are still active today. In many vernaculars the native word for Shaman roughly translates into "walker between the worlds." Shamanism is a religious practice in which one attempts to work in the physical, spiritual and underworld simultaneously. Shamanic practice has been part of all Pagan traditions.

Sigil. A symbol with occult meaning. The term comes from the Latin *sigillum* meaning "a sign." More specifically, a sigil is a drawing used in ceremonial magick to identify a power or being that is captured and controlled through manipulating its sigil.

"So Mote It Be." This is a very old affirmation of an act completed. Mote is an obsolete replacement for the word *must*. When uttered after an invocation, spell, et cetera, it seals the intent by voicing it as a fait accompli, something that is now part of reality rather than an unformed wish. The words are used widely in all traditions of modern Wicca/Paganism.

Solitary. A Pagan who works and worships alone without the aid of a larger coven.

Solitary by Chance. A solitary Pagan who would rather be part of a larger group but has not found one that is compatible. (Be cautious about jumping into a coven just because you want desperately to be a part of one. Be sure your ideologies are in sync first or you could find yourself in a miserable situation.)

Solitary by Choice. A Pagan who practices alone because this is how that person feels most comfortable expressing his or her spirituality. (Being solitary has certain advantages, but can lead to feelings of isolation or loneliness. You might want to consider attending a Pagan festival or gathering once a year or so just to have the support and companionship of like minds.)

Spell. A specific magickal ritual designed for the purpose of obtaining, banishing, or changing one particular thing or condition. Synonyms for making spells are spell weaving, spellcraft, casting, and spinning.

Staff. Ritual tool that corresponds to the wand or athame. A staff is usually used in traditions from mountainous regions because it was a practical device.

Stang. A ritual tool from Pagan Rome that resembles a two-pronged trident. It is sometimes used in place of the wand or staff to represent either fire or air, and is also used in Roman traditions to mark the entry and exit points of the circle. The stang is sacred to the two-faced Roman God Janus.

Subconscious Mind. That part of the mind that functions below the levels we are able to access in the course of a normal waking day. This area stores symbolic knowledge, dreams, and the most minute details of every experience ever had by a person. This is sometimes referred to as the superconscious mind.

Sylphs. In many magickal systems these faeries are referred to as elementals, and are thought to be the ruling spirits of the air element. The name comes from the Greek *silphe* meaning "butterfly."

Sympathetic Magick. A concept of like attracts like. The best example of sympathetic magick was in the hunting dances of Native America. Hunters would dress as the animals they sought and enacted their own slaying. Sympathetic magick is the most common way spells are worked.

Talisman. An object reputed to offer protection or other magickal service to its bearer. It differs from an amulet by being constructed by a human hand (usually) rather than being something found in nature. Talismans are designed to attract specific energies, as opposed to amulets, which are used to drive them away.

Tarot. A set of seventy-two cards containing potent symbols that can be read by the subconscious for divination. The origin of the cards is unknown, but some guess that they originated in the Middle East around three thousand years ago.

Tattwa Symbols (TOT-wah). From a Hindustani word meaning "element." These are the five colored shapes that were discovered to embody the power of the elements and to provide entry points into the elemental realms.

The Threefold Law. The karmic principle of Paganism. It states that any energy released by an individual, either positive or negative, will return to its sender three times over.

Tradition. Referring to the branch of Paganism followed by any individual or coven. There are hundreds of these traditions, most drawn along ethnic or cultural lines, but several are modern amalgamations. The word *tradition* in this case is synonymous with "path."

Traditional. A traditional Wiccan or Pagan is someone who follows a specific path or tradition of Paganism, usually one drawn on cultural or ethnic lines.

Triple Goddess. The one Goddess in all of her three aspects: Maiden, Mother, and Crone. This triple theme of feminine deity has been found in nearly every known culture on the planet.

Undines. In many magickal systems these faeries are referred to as elementals, and are thought to be the ruling spirits of the water element. The name comes from the Latin *unda* meaning "wave."

Vibration. The rate at which molecules move in any given item. Also the rate at which the astral body vibrates, which indicates one's level of spiritual advancement, physical health, or state of mind.

Wand. A ritual tool brought in to the Craft through contact with ceremonial magicians. A wand can symbolize either the element of air and the direction of east, or of south and fire. Or it can be a universal working tool that, like the element of spirit, unifies all the other tools and their attendant elements.

Waning Moon. The name for the phase of the moon from the time it is full until it is new.

Warding. This is a Witch word meaning to guard or protect. It is a term most often heard used in Teutonic (Germanic) Craft traditions, but is becoming more widespread. The word comes from the Anglo-Saxon *weardian* meaning "to keep watch."

Waxing Moon. The name for the phase of the moon from the time it is new until it is full.

Wheel of the Year. The conceptualization of the eternal cycle of time. In Pagan mythology the Goddess turns the Wheel of the Year bringing everything to its season. The Wheel of the Year is symbolized by either a wreath, a ring, a snake holding its tail in its mouth, or an eight-spoked wheel.

Wicca. A tradition of Witchcraft with a huge following among neo-Pagans. Wicca is an Anglo-Saxon word meaning "to bend" or "to have wisdom." Though originally applied to only one English tradition of the Craft, today Wicca has become a term generally used to refer to many of the Pagan traditions from western and northern Europe, and has spawned many sub-traditions.

Widdershins. This word is from the Teutonic Tradition. It means to go backwards and is the act of moving, working, or dancing counter-clockwise in order to banish, diminish, or counter some negative force.

Witch. A name sometimes applied to Pagans of Celtic, Anglo, and/or Saxon Pagan traditions.

Bibliography

Amber, Reuben. *Color Therapy*. Santa Fe, NM: Aurora Press, 1983.

Andrews, Ted. *Dream Alchemy*. St. Paul, MN: Llewellyn, 1987.

———. *How to Meet and Work with Spirit Guides*. St. Paul, MN: Llewellyn, 1996.

———. *The Sacred Power in Your Name*. St. Paul, MN: Llewellyn, 1990.

Barlow, Bernyce. *Sacred Sites of the West*. St. Paul, MN: Llewellyn, 1996.

AMORC. *Behold the Sign*. San Jose: AMORC, 1972.

Beyerl, Paul. *The Master Book of Herbalism*. Custer, WA: Phoenix, 1984.

Bharati, Swami Krishna Tirtha. *Vedic Metaphysics*. Delhi, India: Motilal Barnarsidass, 1988.

Bonewitz, Isaac. *Real Magic*. York Beach, ME: Samuel Weiser, 1989.

Brennan, J. H. *Astral Doorways*. Wellingborough, Northamptonshire: Aquarian Press, 1986.

Bristol, Claude M. *The Magic of Believing*. New York: Simon and Schuster, 1967.

Bronowski, Jacob. *Magic, Science and Civilization*. New York: Columbia University Press, 1978.

Buckland, Raymond. *Advanced Candle Burning*. St. Paul, MN: Llewellyn, 1996.

———. *Buckland's Complete Book of Witchcraft*. St. Paul, MN: Llewellyn, 1986.

———. *Doors to Other Worlds*. St. Paul, MN: Llewellyn, 1993.

———. *Practical Color Magick*. St. Paul, MN: Llewellyn, 1987.

———. *Witchcraft from the Inside* (3rd ed.). St. Paul, MN: Llewellyn, 1995.

Butler, W. E. *Magic: Its Ritual Power and Purpose*. York Beach, ME: Samuel Weiser, 1971.

Campanelli, Pauline and Dan. *Ancient Ways*. St. Paul, MN: Llewellyn, 1991.

———. *Rites of Passage: The Pagan Wheel of Life*. St. Paul, MN: Llewellyn, 1994.

Casteneda, Carlos. *A Separate Reality*. New York: Pocket Books, 1976.

Cabot, Laurie (with Tom Cowan). *Power of the Witch*. New York: Delta Books, 1989.

Conway, D. J. *Ancient and Shining Ones*. St. Paul, MN: Llewellyn, 1993.

———. *Animal Magick: The Art of Recognizing and Working with Familiars*. St. Paul, MN: Llewellyn, 1995.

———. *Astral Love*. St. Paul, MN: Llewellyn, 1996.

———. *Flying Without a Broom*. St. Paul, MN: Llewellyn, 1995.

———. *Maiden, Mother, Crone*. St. Paul, MN: Llewellyn, 1994.

———. *Moon Magick*. St. Paul, MN: Llewellyn, 1995.

Cooper, D. Jason. *Esoteric Rune Magic*. St. Paul, MN: Llewellyn, 1994.

Crowley, Vivianne. *Wicca: The Old Religion in the New Age*. Dorset, UK: Aquarian Press, 1992.

Cunningham, Scott. *The Complete Book of Incense, Oils and Brews.* St. Paul, MN: Llewellyn, 1989.

——. *Cunningham's Encyclopedia of Crystal, Gem and Metal Magic.* St. Paul, MN: Llewellyn, 1987.

——. *Cunningham's Encyclopedia of Magical Herbs.* St. Paul, MN: Llewellyn, 1985.

——. *Earth Power: Techniques of Natural Magic.* St. Paul, MN: Llewellyn, 1987.

——. *Living Wicca.* St. Paul, MN: Llewellyn, 1993.

——. *The Magic of Food.* St. Paul, MN: Llewellyn, 1990.

de Givry, Grillot. *Witchcraft, Magic and Alchemy.* New York: Dover Publications, Inc., 1971 (originally published in French in 1931).

Denning, Melita and Osborne Phillips. *Psychic Self-Defense and Well Being.* St. Paul, MN: Llewellyn, 1980.

——. *The Llewellyn Practical Guide to Creative Visualization* (second edition). St. Paul, MN: Llewellyn, 1983.

Douglas, Nik and Penny Slinger. *Sexual Secrets.* New York: Destiny Books, 1979.

Dunwich, Gerina. *The Wicca Book of Days.* New York: Citadel, 1991.

Eliade, Mircea. *Rites and Symbols of Initiation.* New York: Harper and Row, 1965.

——. *Shamanism: Archaic Techniques of Ecstasy.* Princeton, NJ: Princeton University Press, 1964.

Evola, Julius. *The Metaphysics of Sex.* New York: Inner Traditions International, 1983 (originally published in Italy in 1969).

Farrar, Janet and Stewart. *The Witches' God.* Custer, WA: Phoenix, 1989.

——. *The Witches' Goddess.* Custer, WA: Phoenix, 1987.

Flint, Valerie I. J. *The Rise of Magic in Early Medieval Europe.* Princeton: Princeton University Press, 1991.

Fortune, Dion. *Sane Occultism.* York Beach, ME: Samuel Weiser, 1967.

Gardner, Adelaide. *Meditation: A Practical Study.* Wheaton, IL: Quest Books, 1968.

Gauqueline, Michael. *The Scientific Basis of Astrology.* New York: Stein and Day, 1970.

George, Llewellyn. *The A to Z Horoscope Maker and Delineator* (13th ed.). St. Paul, MN: Llewellyn, 1996.

González-Wippler, Migene. *The Complete Book of Spells, Ceremonies and Magic.* St. Paul, MN: Llewellyn, 1988.

Green, Marian. *Elements of Natural Magic.* Longmeade, Dorset: Element Books, 1989.

Grimassi, Raven. *Ways of the Strega.* St. Paul, MN: Llewellyn, 1995.

Hawking, Stephen. *A Brief History of Time.* New York: Bantam, 1988.

Hitchcock, Ethan Allen. *Alchemy and the Alchemists.* Los Angeles: Philosophical Research Society, 1976 (reprint of work originally published in 1850).

Judith, Anodea. *Wheels of Life.* St. Paul, MN: Llewellyn, 1987.

K, Amber. *True Magick: A Beginner's Guide*. St. Paul, MN: Llewellyn, 1990.

King, Francis and Stephen Skinner. *Techniques of High Magic*. New York: Warner-Destiny Books, 1976.

Knight, Gareth. *Occult Exercises and Practices*. York Beach, ME: Samuel Weiser, 1976.

Kraig, Donald Michael. *Modern Magick: Eleven Lessons in the High Magickal Arts*. St. Paul, MN: Llewellyn, 1988.

Leek, Sybil. *The Complete Art of Witchcraft*. New York: Signet Books, 1971.

Lehner, Ernst. *Symbols, Signs and Signets*. New York: Dover, 1950.

Macvey, John W. *Time Travel: A Guide to Journeys in the Fourth Dimension*. Chelsea, MI: Scarborough House, 1990.

Malbrough, Ray T. *Charms, Spells and Formulas*. St. Paul, MN: Llewellyn, 1986.

McCoy, Edain. *Celtic Myth and Magick*. St. Paul, MN: Llewellyn, 1995.

———. *Entering the Summerland*. St. Paul, MN: Llewellyn, 1996.

———. *Inside a Witches' Coven*. St. Paul, MN: Llewellyn, 1997.

———. *Lady of the Night: A Handbook of Moon Magick and Ritual*. St. Paul, MN: Llewellyn, 1995.

———. *The Sabbats*. St. Paul, MN: Llewellyn, 1994.

———. *A Witch's Guide to Faery Folk*. St. Paul, MN: Llewellyn, 1993.

———. *Witta: An Irish Pagan Tradition*. St. Paul, MN: Llewellyn, 1993.

McFarland, Phoenix. *The Complete Book of Magical Names*. St. Paul, MN: Llewellyn, 1996.

Miller, Richard Alan. *The Magical and Ritual Use of Herbs*. New York: Destiny Books, 1983.

Monahan, Evelyn M. *The Miracle of Metaphysical Healing*. West Nyack, NY: Parker Publishing, 1975.

Monaghan, Patricia. *The Book of Goddesses and Heroines*. St. Paul, MN: Llewellyn, 1990.

Monroe, Douglas. *The 21 Lessons of Merlyn: A Study in Druid Magic and Lore*. St. Paul, MN: Llewellyn, 1992.

Moody, Raymond. *Reunions*. New York: Ivy, 1993.

Mountainwater, Shekinah. *Ariadne's Thread: A Workbook of Goddess Magic*. Freedom, CA: The Crossing Press, 1991.

Moura, Aoumiel. *Green Witchcraft*. St. Paul, MN: Llewellyn, 1996.

Ophiel. *The Art and Practice of Talismanic Magic*. York Beach, ME: Samuel Weiser, 1979.

Pachter, Henry Maximilian. *Paracelsus: Magic Into Science*. New York: Schuman Publishers, 1951.

Perkins, John. *PsychoNavigation: Techniques for Travel Beyond Time*. Rochester, VT: Destiny Books, 1990.

RavenWolf, Silver. *Angels: Companions in Magick*. St. Paul, MN: Llewellyn, 1996.

———. *To Stir a Magic Cauldron*. St. Paul, MN: Llewellyn, 1996.

Regardie, Israel. *The Golden Dawn* (fifth edition). St. Paul, MN: Llewellyn, 1986.

Renee, Janina. *Playful Magic*. St. Paul, MN: Llewellyn, 1994.

Roderick, Timothy. *The Once Unknown Familiar*. St. Paul, MN: Llewellyn, 1996.

Sabrina, Lady. *Reclaiming the Power*. St. Paul, MN: Llewellyn, 1992.

Sheba, Lady. *The Grimoire of Lady Sheba*. St. Paul, MN: Llewellyn, 1971.

Simms, Marie K. *The Witches' Circle*. St. Paul, MN: Llewellyn, 1994.

Skelton, Robin. *Talismanic Magic*. York Beach, ME: Samuel Weiser, 1985.

Starhawk. *The Spiral Dance*. San Francisco: Harper and Row, 1979.

Stepanich, Kisma. *Faery Wicca* (books I and II). St. Paul, MN: Llewellyn, 1994, 1995.

——. *The Gaia Tradition*. St. Paul, MN: Llewellyn, 1991.

Stevens, Jose and Lena. *The Secrets of Shamanism*. New York: Avon, 1988.

Stutley, Margaret. *Ancient Indian Magic and Folklore*. London: Routledge and Kegan Paul, 1980.

Telesco, Patricia. *Folkways*. St. Paul, MN: Llewellyn, 1995.

——. *A Kitchen Witch's Cookbook*. St. Paul, MN: Llewellyn, 1995.

——. *Seasons of the Sun*. York Beach, ME: Samuel Weiser, 1996.

——. *A Witch's Brew*. St. Paul, MN: Llewellyn, 1995.

Thompson, Janet. *Magical Hearth: Home for the Modern Pagan*. York Beach, ME: Samuel Weiser, 1995.

Thorsson, Edred. *Futhark: A Handbook of Rune Magick*. York Beach, ME: Samuel Weiser, 1984.

Tyson, Donald, ed. *Three Books of Occult Philosophy*. St. Paul, MN: Llewellyn, 1995. (These collected writings of occultist Henry Cornelius Agrippa, originally published in 1531, include the helpful annotations and commentary of Tyson, a practicing ceremonial magician.)

Underhill, Callia. *A Witch's Book of Divination*. St. Paul, MN: Llewellyn, 1996.

Valiente, Doreen. *An ABC of Witchcraft*. Custer, WA: Phoenix, 1988.

——. *Natural Magic*. Custer, WA: Phoenix, 1980.

——. *Psychic Self-Defense*. Custer, WA: Phoenix, 1977.

——. *Witchcraft for Tomorrow*. Custer, WA: Phoenix, 1978.

Weinstein, Marion. *Earth Magic: A Dianic Book of Shadows*. Custer, WA: Phoenix, 1986.

——. *Positive Magic*. Custer, WA: Phoenix, 1980.

Woolfold, Joanna Martine. *The Only Astrology Book You'll Ever Need*. New York: Stein and Day, 1982.

Wright, Elbee. *The Book of Legendary Spells*. Minneapolis, MN: Marlar Publishing Co, 1974.

Index

🌙 LLEWELLYN ORDERING INFORMATION

 ### Order Online:
Visit our website at www.llewellyn.com, select your books, and order them
on our secure server.

 ### Order by Phone:
- Call toll-free within the U.S. at 1-877-NEW-WRLD
  (1-877-639-9753). Call toll-free within Canada at
  1-866-NEW-WRLD (1-866-639-9753)
- We accept VISA, MasterCard, and American Express

Order by Mail:
Send the full price of your order (MN residents add 7% sales tax) in U.S.
funds, plus postage & handling to:
Llewellyn Worldwide
P.O. Box 64383, Dept. 1-56718-670-x
St. Paul, MN 55164-0383, U.S.A.

Postage & Handling:
Standard (U.S., Mexico, & Canada). If your order is:
    Up to $25.00, add $3.50
    $25.01 - $48.99, add $4.00
    $49.00 and over, FREE STANDARD SHIPPING
(Continental U.S. orders ship UPS. AK, HI, PR, & P.O. Boxes ship
USPS 1st class. Mex. & Can. ship PMB.)

International Orders:
    Surface Mail: For orders of $20.00 or less, add $5 plus $1 per
    item ordered. For orders of $20.01 and over, add $6 plus $1
    per item ordered.

    Air Mail:
    Books: Postage & Handling is equal to the total retail price of
    all books in the order.
    Non-book items: Add $5 for each item.

Orders are processed within 2 business days.
Please allow for normal shipping time. Postage and handling rates subject to change.

Advanced Witchcraft

Go Deeper, Reach Further, Fly Higher

EDAIN McCOY

Cross the well-guarded threshold into advanced practice with *Advanced Witchcraft*.

The numbers of intermediate practitioners of the Craft are growing. As they stand at the gateway to advanced practice, they need a teacher to guide them on a new and advanced path that will bring them closer to the deities.

Fast-paced, no-nonsense, and thorough, *Advanced Witchcraft* is that teacher. It leaps into the soul of Witchcraft by presuming you've already gone through the beginning and intermediate levels. It challenges your thinking and forces you to gain wisdom through experience. Practical applications include moving into the true realm of shapeshifting, practicing shamanism to heal the shattered soul, pathworking to the source of creation, employing dark witchery without negativity, and much more.

0-7387-0513-6
336 pp., 7½ x 9⅛, illus. $17.95

To order, call 1-877-NEW-WRLD
Prices subject to change without notice

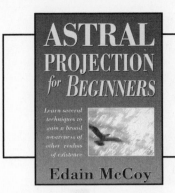

Astral Projection for Beginners

EDAIN MCCOY

Enter a world in which time and space have no meaning or influence. This is the world of the astral plane, an ethereal, unseen realm often perceived as parallel to and interpenetrating our physical world. *Astral Projection for Beginners* shows you how to send your consciousness at will to these other places, then bring it back with full knowledge of what you have experienced.

Explore the misconceptions and half-truths that often impede the beginner, and create a mental atmosphere in which you become free to explore the universe both inside and outside your consciousness. This book offers six different methods for you to try: general transfer of consciousness, projecting through the chakras, meditating towards astral separation, guided meditation, using symbolic gateways, and stepping out of your dreams. Ultimately you will be able to condition your mind to allow you to project at will.

1-56718-625-4
256 pp., 5³⁄₁₆ x 8 $9.95

The Witch's Coven
Finding or Forming Your Own Circle

EDAIN McCOY

(Formerly *Inside a Witches' Coven*)

As a practicing solitary witch, do you ever wonder what it's like to be a member of a coven . . . what happens at an initiation . . . how covens perform magick and healing?

Edain McCoy has been involved in Witchcraft for two decades. She wrote this book to answer all of these questions and more. Learn how a real Witch's coven operates, from initiation and secret vows to parting rituals. You'll get step-by-step guidance for joining or forming a coven, plus sage advice and exclusive insights to help you decide which group is the right one for you.

- Helps make the novice's entry into any coven easy and safe
- Explains the many different types of covens so you can find the one that's right for you
- Shows established covens how to screen potential members and avoid common problems that hurt covens
- Provides ideas for organizing a teaching circle or mediating conflicts

0-7387-0388-5
5¼ x 8, 224 pp., appendix, bibliog, index $12.95

Magick & Rituals
of the Moon

EDAIN McCOY

(Formerly *Lady of the Night*)

Moon-centered ritual, a deeply woven thread in Pagan culture, is often confined to celebration of the full moon. Edain McCoy revitalizes the full potential of the lunar mysteries in this exclusive guide for Pagans.

    Magick & Rituals of the Moon explores the lore, rituals, and unique magickal potential associated with all phases of the moon: full, waxing, waning, moonrise/moonset and dark/new. Combined with an in-depth look at moon magick and rituals, this book offers a complete system for riding the tides of lunar magick.

    Written for both solitary and group practice, *Magick & Rituals of the Moon* breaks new ground by showing how both men and women can Draw Down the Moon for enhanced spirituality. Pagans will find fun and spirited suggestions on how to make the mystery of the moon accessible to non-Pagans through creative party planning and popular folklore.

0-7387-0092-4
256 pp., 7 x 10 $14.95

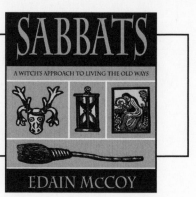

Sabbats

A Witch's Guide to
Living the Old Ways

EDAIN McCoy

Sabbats offers many fresh, exciting ways to deepen your connection to the turning of the Wheel of the Year. This tremendously practical guide to Pagan solar festivals does more than teach you about the "old ways"—you will learn workable ideas for combining old customs with new expressions of those beliefs that will be congruent with your lifestyle and tradition.

Sabbats begins with background on Paganism (tenets, teachings, and tools) and origins of the eight Sabbats, followed by comprehensive chapters on each Sabbat. These pages are full of ideas for inexpensive seasonal parties in which Pagans and non-Pagans alike can participate, as well as numerous craft ideas and recipes to enrich your celebrations. The last section provides sixteen complete texts of Sabbat rituals—for both covens and solitaries—with detailed guidelines for adapting rituals to specific traditions or individual tastes. Includes an extensive reference section with a resources guide, bibliography, musical scores for rituals, and more.

This book may contain the most practical advice ever for incorporating the old ways into your Pagan lifestyle!

1-56718-663-7
320 pp., 7 x 10, illus., photos   **$17.95**